A Cabinet of
Philosophical
Curiosities

D1464181

ROY SORENSEN never told you that he is the son of Ted Sorensen,
President Kennedy's speech writer and confidant. For it is not
true. Roy Sorensen is a professor of philosophy at Washington
University in St Louis. He is the author of *Seeing Dark Things*,
A Brief History of the Paradox, *Thought Experiments* and
Blindspots.

A Cabinet of Philosophical Curiosities

A Collection of Puzzles, Oddities, Riddles and Dilemmas

Roy Sorensen

P

PROFILE BOOKS

This paperback edition published in 2017

First published in Great Britain in 2016 by
PROFILE BOOKS LTD
3 Holford Yard
Bevin Way
London WC1X 9HD
www.profilebooks.com

10 9 8 7 6 5 4 3 2 1

Typeset in ITC Charter by MacGuru Ltd

Printed and bound in Great Britain by
Clays Ltd, Elcograf S.p.A.

A CIP catalogue record for this book is available from the British Library.

ISBN 978 1 84668 522 4
eISBN 978 1 84765 925 5

Contents

Dedication

To
My Broken Arm

I am a better starter than finisher. For wont of endings, this book became late, Late, LATE!

After my right arm broke, I could type s-l -o-w-l -y with my left hand.[1] This forced me to spend the summer completing what was nearly done rather than darting to other projects.[2]

The lessons taught by my broken arm began with the Emergency Room poster 'No head injury is too trivial to be ignored'. The sentence is intended to be read as: *However trivial a head injury is, it should not be ignored*. But what the sentence really means is the opposite: *However trivial a head injury is, it should be ignored*. After all, the warning has the same syntax as: *No missile is too small to be banned.*[3]

If you only have a broken arm, do not bring this reversal to the attention of the nurses. They will take the wrong kind of interest. Soon you will be holding your head very still in a computerised tomography scanner.

After surgery, my arm was paralysed for a day. This gave me a phantom limb – and an eerie appreciation of Horatio Nelson's argument for immortality. In 1797, the British admiral was wounded in his right arm. After amputation, he vividly

---

[1] Editorial note: we had nothing to do with the breaking of Professor Sorensen's arm.

[2] And I became more interested in left-handed riddles such as 'Which of the United States can be typed with only the left hand?'

[3] Linguists characterise 'No head injury is too trivial to be ignored' as a depth charge sentence. After the initial splash on the surface of consciousness, the sentence penetrates to a deeper level of analysis at which its real meaning detonates in contradiction to the surface meaning.

experienced the presence of his arm, a limb that he could feel but could no longer see. Lord Nelson reasoned that if an arm can persist after being annihilated, so can the whole person.

My broken limb outlived my phantom limb. It taught me how to be a lefty in a world that is subtly right-handed – and less subtly two-handed. Like a good teacher, my broken arm made the novel familiar and the familiar novel.[4]

---

[4] Experiment revealed that TEXAS is the only the state that can be typed lefty. Thought experiment revealed that OHIO is the only state that can be typed righty.

Introduction

I build up castles.
I tear down mountains.
I make some men blind,
I help others to see.
♀ What am I?

A great quantity is said to be 'without number'. An offended mathematician, Archimedes, believed this confused our inability to number the objects with an objective absence of number. The Roman numerals of his day abetted this confusion. In the *The Sand Reckoner* Archimedes developed another notation that enabled him to estimate the number of grains of sand in the universe. Now suppose another sand reckoner claims to have learned the exact number of grains. ♀ Could you perform an experiment to test his claim? (Questions which are answered at the rear of this book are preceded with ♀.)

Suppose everything is made up of atoms[5] and that any combination of atoms is an object. ♀ Given that there are only finitely many atoms, prove that you are in an odd universe. Side question: Could you be in an even universe?

Lewis Carroll subliminated his philosophical interests in whimsical dialogues and silly syllogisms:

Men over 5 feet high are numerous.
Men over 10 feet high are not numerous.
Therefore men over 10 feet high are not over 5 feet high.
♀ What lesson is to be drawn about numerosity?

---

[5] Atoms are indivisible in mereology, the logic of parts and wholes. The elements in the periodic table qualify as atoms for chemical purposes but not for the physical processes discovered by Marie and Pierre Curie. Physicists do not know whether anything qualifies as an atom for all physical purposes. Reality might be bottomless.

This book has numerous riddles such as the above. They reflect a philosopher's interest in logic and language, history and mathematics. The puzzles evolved from a habit I copied from Charles Darwin. He was impressed by how quickly he forgot objections to his theories. Darwin took to writing them down promptly in notebooks.

Psychologists support Darwin's policy by asking you to continue the sequence 2, 4, 6, ... You guess 8, 10, 12. They congratulate you, 'Right! But what is the rule for continuing the sequence?' You announce the sequence is just the ascending even numbers. 'Sorry, that is not the rule generating the numbers. Would you like try again?'

You try a more complicated hypothesis. You test by asking whether another triplet of numbers is in the sequence. The good news is that, yes those particular numbers are part of the sequence. The bad news is that, once again, your hypothesised rule is mistaken. The good news/bad news cycle continues until you reverse your strategy of seeking to verify your hypotheses. You must instead try to falsify your hypotheses.

The rule intended by the psychologist is: 2, 4, 6, then the numbers after 6. This floods the search space with confirming instances. The rule is difficult to discover because we test our hypotheses by seeking confirmations rather than refutations. One motive for this confirmation bias is that we are fond of our hypotheses. We do not look for bad news. Even when we get counterevidence, we protect our pet theories by forgetting failures and exaggerating successes.

Confirmation bias is highly confirmed! When I asked one lecturer whether there were any counterexamples, she could not think of any. But then again, she sheepishly admitted, this could be because she never tried to refute the principle that we are biased towards confirming hypotheses. Then the psychologist brightened up, 'Hey, that proves my point!'

Nevertheless, the anomaly collector should include anomalous anomalies. The 'paradoxes of confirmation theory' show how a theory can be disconfirmed by combining data that is separately confirming. In 'Conform to Confound' I discuss examples that conform to a generalisation and yet disconfirm it. There is even hope for the inheritor in the Charles Dana Gibson cartoon:

Cousin Kate: Now that you are well off, Charles, you mustn't let them say of you, a fool and his money are soon parted.
Charles: No, you bet I won't; I'll show them that I'm an exception to the rule.

Philosophers of science and historians of science have disconcerting ironies that do not make it into the pious methodology sections of science textbooks.

Psychologists focus on the confirmation bias we harbour towards our own hypotheses. We are not invested in the theories of others. Indeed, children go through a counter-suggestible phase. Told 'Nobody is perfect', one little girl in Sunday School silently pointed up.

Lawyers make a living generating counterexamples. In response to the retaliatory principle 'an eye for an eye and a tooth for tooth', William Blackstone (1723–1780) queried, 'What if a two-eyed man knocks out the eye of a one-eyed man?'

Since we enjoy counterexampling our adversaries, we

can counter confirmation bias by imagining someone else has come up with the principle. This is the method of 'auto-sadism', a term I picked up from a rental car agent.

Even with my nurturing, most of the anomalies that made it into storage perished from neglect. However, a minority took on a life of their own.

Their paths of development proliferated under the influence of a 'letter' I received, as a graduate student, from the logician Bas van Fraassen. He was in a hurry and mailed me notes for a letter instead of the letter. The notes showed a different style of thinking than his polished correspondence and articles. Instead of marching through a proof, Professor van Fraassen engaged in a lively inner debate.

I was impressed by how his dialogue grew alternatives, how it inhibited premature fixation of one's opinions, how it encouraged synthesis. In addition to writing dialogues, I tried other stylistic variations.

My files grew into a cabinet. Then a bank of cabinets. The cabinets were then transmuted into virtual cabinets on my computer.

The anomalies cross-fertilised into advertisements, contests and poems. Some of these were published in professional journals and anthologies, others appeared in newspapers and magazines, and many reappear in this volume. But many needed a different environment.

A promising niche was revealed by Ian Stewart's *Cabinet of Mathematical Curiosities*. As a 14-year-old, he began to fill notebooks with interesting 'maths' he found outside the classroom. After the notes migrated into filing cabinets, he assembled them into a miscellany of marvels. They could be enjoyed independently but gained mutual support when read in Stewart's clusters and mini-series.

That is the format I borrow for this book. Just as Professor Stewart exhibits the interesting mathematics that can be found outside the classroom, I exhibit the interesting logic that can be found outside the classroom.

Logic is everywhere there is a motive to imply rather than say.

One does not need to step far outside the classroom to feel the bite of an enthymeme (an argument with a suppressed premise or conclusion). Consider the Oxford undergraduate who spotted Sir John Pentland Mahaffy (1839–1919) chatting with a colleague in a corridor of Trinity College. The desperate student interrupted the professors to ask the location of a lavatory. 'At the end of the corridor,' Mahaffy grandly gestured, 'you will find a door marked GENTLEMEN: but don't let that stop you.'

Some of the logic in this book might have started in the classroom – and got expelled! As a cadet at West Point, George Derby (1823–1861) enrolled in a class on military strategy: 'A thousand men are besieging a fortress that contains these quantities of equipment and provisions,' said the instructor, displaying a chart. 'It is a military axiom that at the end of 45 days the fort will surrender. If you were in command of this fortress, what would you do?' Derby raised his hand, 'I would march out, let the enemy in, and at the end of 45 days I would change places with him.'

Derby went on to a distinguished career as an officer – and humorist. The pairing is less incongruous when you reflect on the reciprocal relationship between humour and rules. A joke requires building expectation. Nothing grounds expectations as efficiently as a rule. Ludwig Wittgenstein suggested that a serious philosophical book might contain nothing but jokes:

> The problems arising through a misinterpretation of our forms of language have the character of depth. They are deep disquietudes; their roots are as deep in us as the forms of our language and their significance is as great as the importance of our language. – Let us ask ourselves: why do we feel a grammatical joke to be deep? (And that is what the depth of philosophy is.)
>
> – Wittgenstein, *Philosophical Investigations*, 1958, §111

In the Spanish proverb '*Mañana* is the busiest day of the week', *mañana* is treated as a day of the week such as Monday, Tuesday, and Wednesday. '*Mañana*' is actually an indexical term in the same category as 'yesterday' and 'today', 'now', 'before', 'past'. An indexical takes a feature of its own utterance, such as when or where or who uttered it, as an input to determine its output meaning. This recursion makes indexicals popular in calculative riddles: ♀ José will patch the roof three days after two days before the day before tomorrow. When will the roof be patched? There is a whole logic of time that systematises this dynamic manner of orienting to the world (which contrasts with the static coordinate system of physics). Wittgenstein believed that our tendency to model all words on names is a fertile source of philosophical perplexities: 'When is it now now?, What does "I" refer to?, and 'How can we know that the future will resemble the past?'

Or consider the problem of evaluating counterfactuals such as 'If the numeral for three was "2", then 2 + 2 would equal 6.' To protect the necessary truth of 2 + 2 = 4, logicians invoke a riddle Abraham Lincoln formulated to rebut legislation that euphemised slavery as 'protection'. 'If you call the tail of a calf a leg, how many legs would a calf have?' Lincoln's answer: 'Four, calling a tail a leg does not make it one.' When evaluating a counterfactual, we must hold the language constant. If the language is, say, present-day English then we stick with present-day English even when imagining situations in which a slight variation of English is spoken. The evaluating language can be any language but once you choose this unit of measurement, you must stick with it *exactly*.

On 23 September 1999, the $125 million Mars Climate Orbiter failed to manoeuvre into a stable orbit. One engineering team had used the imperial measurement system for the aerobraking sequence while another team used the metric system.

Metaphysicians studying other possible worlds have never made such a costly error. Usually, nothing is damaged. To illustrate the safety, I shall eventually lure you into a painless metaphysical error with the help of a mysterious footnote.[6] Relax! You will feel nothing.

---

[6] EQC OBA ERO BOH QRG

Conform to Confound

Whereas a 51-foot-tall woman is a counterexample to 'All women are less than a fifty-one feet tall' a 50-foot tall woman is a conform-example to it. A conform-example conforms to 'All *F*s are *G*s' by being both *F* and *G* but *dis*confirms the generalisation. Once you learn there is a 50-foot-tall woman, you lose confidence in 'All women are less than fifty-one feet tall.'

There is a tradition of conform-examples in biology. In 1938 'All coelacanths are dead' became *less* probable to the ichthyologist J. L. B. Smith when he examined a freshly dead coelacanth. The fish had been netted by a South African trawler. Smith was astounded because the species had been thought to be extinct for 40 million years. Although the dead specimen conformed to the generalisation that there are no living coelacanths, it was strong evidence for the incompatible hypothesis that there were some live coelacanths. When a live specimen was finally caught in 1952, the South African prime minister, D. F. Malan, was aghast, 'Why, it's ugly! Is this where we come from?'

Conform-examples have been historically momentous. Consider the generalisation that nuclear weapons never detonate accidentally because they are equipped with many safety devices. In 1961, a B-52 bomber carrying two hydrogen bombs disintegrated in flight over North Carolina. Five out of its six safety devices failed. But just as the generalisation implies, the sixth safety device succeeded.

Yet the Secretary of Defense, Robert McNamara, was not heartened by this successful prediction. Instead he cited this incident to justify a new policy of nuclear disarmament.

To sum up, a conform-example is a non-exception that disproves the rule.

Razing Hopes

> Undergraduate: When may we hope to see
> your Harvard lectures published sir?
> Professor J. L. Austin: You may hope to
> see them published any time.

Are two reasons for hope always better than one reason for hope? Sorry, reasons that separately raise hope can jointly dash that hope.

Suppose Nick and Nora bet another couple that all three drunks leaving a party have mixed up each other's hats. Nick learns that the first drunk took the second drunk's hat. This raises Nick's hope that all of the drunks mixed up each other's hats.

Nora learns that second drunk took the first drunk's hat. This raises Nora's hope that all of the drunks mixed up each other's hats. But when the couple's reasons are pooled together, they collectively dash hope of winning the bet. For, together, the two reasons guarantee that the third man is wearing his own hat. The conjunction of good news can be bad news.

The winning couple draws the optimistic lesson. Conjoining a reason to fear with a reason to fear can yield a conjunction that is welcome. Two facts, considered in isolation can each be bad news. Considered together, as a conjunction, they are good news.

Put neutrally, the moral is that what is individually confirming can be collectively disconfirming.

Hidden Messages in Songs

Some songs, such as 'Don't Advertise Your Man', have frank lyrics. Others have hidden messages.

Listeners say that the subtle messages are put there with literary techniques. Peter, Paul and Mary's 'Where Have All the Flowers Gone?' is an allegorical anti-war song. The flowers are soldiers. The singers' association with the counterculture of the 1960s led their rendition of 'Puff the Magic Dragon' to be interpreted as a veiled exhortation to smoke marijuana. This led to rebuttals by the singers. Such controversies were grist for English teachers who could display the contemporary relevance of rhetorical devices such as irony, allusion, and so on.

Not wishing to be left out of the hermeneutical melee, some logic professors claimed to glean hidden messages by deduction. The long-distance interpreters reasoned from many lines of lyrics. The sprinters competed for how quickly they could extract the consequence. One claimed to obtain the hidden message of 'Everybody Loves a Lover' from its opening two lines:

Everybody loves a lover
I'm a lover, everybody loves me.

The singer explicitly deduces the lemma, 'Everybody loves me'.[7] This helps us reach the ultimate consequence that we are all lovers. (The logician was assuming that loving one person sufficed for being a lover, just as having one child suffices for being a parent.) Since we are all lovers, everybody loves everybody – including themselves!

---

[7] A lemma is a valid inference made on the way to a conclusion. A corollary is a valid inference made from a conclusion. A lemma helps you reach the conclusion. A corollary extends the reach of the conclusion.

The logician did not believe this consequence. He was just showing that it followed from the premises 'Everybody loves a lover' and 'I'm a lover'. The job of the logician is to figure out what entails what. He has no expertise in telling whether the premises are true.

A second logician was even quicker, getting a hidden message from just the title of 'Everybody Loves My Baby, but My Baby Don't Love Nobody but Me'. ♡ What is the surprising consequence?

A Blessed Book Curse

SOR	SUP	NO	SCRIP	LI	POTI
TE	ER	RUM	TOR	BRI	ATUR
MOR	INF	NO	RAP	LI	MORI

	WROTE	PROCURE	JOYS	LIFE SUPERNAL
MAY HE WHO	THIS BOOK		THE	OF
	STEALS	ENDURE	PANGS	DEATH INFERNAL

The above inscription is borrowed from a collection of English court transcripts made by William Easingwold around 1491. Before the printing press, books were so valuable that they needed every protection. But as we now know from the anti-piracy messages on rented movies, it is off-putting to greet your audience with a threat.

William Easingwold compromises with an inscription that can be read two ways. The Latin lines form a code ingeniously translated by Carl S. Partum III in his blog *Got Medieval*. When the top two lines are read together, a pleasant message results. When the bottom two are read, the message is unpleasant.

During a tour of the old Bodleian library at Oxford University, I learned of a surprising drawback to physical means of protecting books. The guide drew our attention to the backward orientation of the books. Their spines faced the wall like those of prisoners on a row of toilets. This was to accommodate a book chain. Since each book had its own chain, the library must have clanged like a galley ship rowed by captives.

The Bodleian gift shop had mugs – with just the right inscription!

silence
please

In 1598 the Bodleian library had more books than words in its longest book. ♀ Prove that there were at least two books of the same word length.

Consider a unique library that forbids books from having the same number of words. This library also has more books than words in its longest book. ♀What is one of its books about?

Listen for a Counterexample

In the course of demarcating the senses, Aristotle defined sound as the proper object of hearing: 'sight has colour, hearing sound, and taste flavour' (*De anima*, II.6, 418b13). Sound cannot be seen, tasted, smelled, or felt. And nothing other than sound can be directly heard. (Objects are heard indirectly by virtue of the sounds they produce.) All subsequent commentators agree, often characterising 'Only sound can be heard' as true by virtue of its meaning. For instance, Geoffrey Warnock says 'sound' is the tautological accusative of the verb 'hear'.

There is exactly one counterexample to Aristotle's generalisation. ♀ Have you heard it?

Hint 1: You can listen to it if everything is _____ (fill the blank with an anagram of LISTEN).

Hint 2: The counterexample is so fragile that being mentioned destroys it.

Schopenhauer's Intelligence Test

> What comes with a cart, and goes with a cart; is of no use
> to a cart, and yet the cart cannot move without it?

Noise! Arthur Schopenhauer (1788–1860) contends that there is no point in arguing about whether noise is annoying. If noise bothers you, then you do not need convincing. If you are not bothered by noise, then that shows you cannot concentrate and therefore cannot combine premises into a syllogism.

Still with me?

Despite the futility of *arguing* about noise, there is a point in *explaining* why the intelligent are so averse to shouts, bangs, barks, and whistles. In 'On Noise', Schopenhauer focuses on focus:

> If you cut up a large diamond into little bits, it will entirely
> lose the value it had as a whole; and an army divided up
> into small bodies of soldiers, loses all its strength. So a
> great intellect sinks to the level of an ordinary one, as soon
> as it is interrupted and disturbed, its attention distracted
> and drawn off from the matter in hand; for its superiority
> depends upon its power of concentration – of bringing all
> its strength to bear upon one theme, in the same way as a
> concave mirror collects into one point all the rays of light
> that strike upon it. Noisy interruption is a hindrance to this
> concentration. That is why distinguished minds have always
> shown such an extreme dislike to disturbance in any form, as
> something that breaks in upon and distracts their thoughts.

Tolerance of noise is inversely proportional to mental capacity. Therefore, Schopenhauer takes intolerance of noise to be a fair measure of intelligence.

Charles Babbage passes the test. The inventor of the first programmable computer was a systematic enemy of organ grinders. He would chase them and their monkeys around town. Professor Babbage would dragoon police officers into arresting his quarry. He kept records, wrote essays, and lobbied. Babbage converted MP Michael Thomas Bass to the cause.

The bulk of Schopenhauer's essay 'On Noise' is devoted to 'the most inexcusable and disgraceful of all noises'. It isn't street music. ♀ What is it?

A Knucklehead on My Premises

Crack. CRACK! **C R A C K**!!
Therefore, there is a knucklehead on my premises.

My ears led me to the finger joints of my son Zachary. I channelled the wisdom of my father: 'Knuckle cracking leads to arthritis.'

Instead of deferring to Dr Dad, Zachary opened his laptop computer. In a couple of minutes, he cited Donald Unger's 'Does Knuckle Cracking Lead to Arthritis of the Fingers?' (*Arthritis & Rheumatology*, 1998, 41(5): 949–50). Dr Unger reports a '50-year controlled study by one participant'. After Unger's mother told him what I told my son, Unger the Younger applied the scientific method. He cracked the knuckles of his left hand, but not his right, at least twice a day. That is more than 36,500 cracks. He reports no arthritis in either hand: 'This result calls into question whether other parental beliefs, e.g., the importance of eating spinach, are also flawed.'

I consulted the oracle myself. There were plenty of references to the very warning I had handed down from my father. If knuckle cracking did cause arthritis, then some of the anti-crackers would have found some evidence. The medical websites agreed that there was no evidence for me to find.

Chastened, I thought aloud: 'Much advice is cast as being in the interest of the hearer when it is actually in the interest of the speaker. Perhaps fathers are not as selflessly concerned about their sons as they think!'

Zachary concurred. Instead of relying on my pseudo-altruism we decided to rely on his genuine altruism. Given my acoustic aversion, he would refrain from cracking his knuckles – when I am in earshot.

My argument was unsound.[8] But my conclusion was correct. There was a knucklehead on my premises!

The Tversky Intelligence Test

How are you going to teach logic in a world where everybody talks about the sun setting, when it's really the horizon rising?

Cal Craig

Awe of Amos Tversky led psychologists to formulate an intelligence test: 'The faster you realise Tversky is smarter than you, the smarter you are.'

This is a severe test. Amos Tversky could never realise that he is smarter than himself. So Tversky could never rank high on the Tversky intelligence test. The implication is even more humbling for the rest of us!

Amos Tversky collaborated with Daniel Kahneman in the discovery of systematic human cognitive bias and handling of risk. The duo would construct puzzles, like those in this book, and use their intuitive reactions to discover deviations from probability theory and economic principles.

For instance, is it more likely that a word randomly sampled from an English text begins with r or has r as its third letter? Most readers answer by recalling words that begin with r (rod) and recalling words that have r in the third position (tar). Since it is easier to search for words by their first letter than by their third letter, most people infer that more words start with r in the first position than in the third position. This is an example of the availability heuristic: Judge the probability

---

[8] An argument is sound exactly if its premises are true and it is valid. An argument is valid if and only if it is impossible for the premises to be true and the conclusion false. All sound arguments have true conclusions but not vice versa.

of an event or the frequency of a class by the ease with which occurrences or instances can be brought to mind.

Heuristics are rules of thumb that allow us to reach a quick conclusion, though at some cost to reliability and accuracy. These mental shortcuts account for systematic error in intuitive judgements. When asked to make a sequence of choices, we diversify – even when this is no longer related to risk reduction.

We also use prior investments in a project as a guide to assessing how much more we should invest. Since prudence is a matter of maximising good consequences, I should ignore the past. But to avoid counting past effort as a loss, I stick with the project. After an expensive transmission repair I ruefully asked the mechanic how much more he could earn keeping my old car running. Wasn't he worried that I would just replace it? He serenely folded the cheque into his pocket, 'No, sir, I ain't concerned. Now you are married to it.'

Little children are immune to the sunk-cost fallacy. Once full, they do not finish the food on their plate. They abandon a toy, for which they just howled, in favour of a slightly more amusing toy. They live in the here and now. This short time horizon prevents them from worrying about waste. Only after they mature do they become vulnerable to the sunk-cost fallacy.

The least reliable heuristic is anchoring. When children are asked to estimate how many jellybeans are in a jar, they pick a number close to a recently mentioned number. This effect can arise even when the subject knows that the base number is irrelevant (say, the winning number on a roulette wheel).

When Tversky and Kahneman had the same intuitive but irrational reaction to a puzzle, they would try it out on more people. The plural of 'anecdote' is data!

Actually, Tversky and Kahneman would bring the result up to scientific standards with a controlled experiment.

These experiments were the only official justification for their theory that we are systematically irrational.

But Tversky and Kahneman's own theory of irrationality made them receptive to another explanation of why their work became so influential. Readers could instantly test their own reactions to the puzzles.

At age 58 Tversky discovered he had terminal cancer. Tversky declined to endure the side effects of therapy that would extend his life a few weeks. Pressed by his oncologist, Tversky explained that he and his cancer were not playing a zero-sum game.[9] Not everything that was bad for the tumour was good for him.

A Matter of Life and Death

You are a physician. You are to recommend either surgery or radiation for lung cancer patients. The one-month survival rate for surgery is 90%. Should your patients get surgery?

Whoops! What I meant to say is that there is a 10% mortality rate in the first month. ♀ What do you recommend in light of this correction?

The Identity of Indiscernibles

Almost all philosophers accept the principle that identicals are indiscernible: For any property F, if $x = y$ and x has F, then y has F. If Gottfried Leibniz is identical to Georgius Ulicovius Lithuanus and Leibniz has the property of being German, then Lithuanus has the property of being German. And so on for every property. There can be no discernible difference between Leibniz and Lithuanus.

Gottfried Leibniz also accepted the converse, that indiscernible things are identical: If x and y share all their properties, then $x = y$. Astronomers may have used this principle to

---

[9] In a zero-sum game, the gains and losses of the participants balance. Cutting a cake is a zero-sum game because whatever I gain, you lose. The tendency to misperceive situations as zero-sum games is epitomised by the joke about a peasant who is offered a wish by a genie. The catch is that the peasant's neighbour will get double. The peasant replies, 'Poke out one of my eyes.'

discover that the morning star is the evening star. The heavenly body that is first visible in the morning has all the same properties as the body first visible in the evening. So they must be the same heavenly body – Venus.

Since Leibniz accepted the identity of indiscernibles, he denied that there are can be two perfectly indiscernible objects. Although *you* may be unable to tell the difference between two lookalikes, there will be some difference. ♀ Are there any counterexamples to the identity of indiscernibles?

Indiscernible Pills

Each day you must take an A pill and a B pill. After you tap an A pill into your palm you inadvertently tap two B pills into your hand. The A and B pills are indistinguishable. The pills are expensive and you must not overdose. ♀ Can you still use the pills you have mixed up?

Telling a Clover from a Plover

♀ How can you tell a clover from a plover?

The Emotional Range of Logicians

According to stereotype, the logician 'runs the whole gamut of emotions, from A to B'. I think the range must be wider, at least from A to E. For when a logician's proof is shown to be fallacious, he goes through five stages of grief: denial, anger, bargaining, depression, and acceptance.

Elisabeth Kübler-Ross, the psychiatrist best known for developing the 'Five Stages of Grief', focused on dying. But she also had a remarkable birth. Elisabeth was born fifteen minutes before her sister Erika. The two were identical and had the same mother. Yet Elisabeth and Erika were not twins. ♀ How may the logician calmly explain this?

A Pebble from the Baths of Caracalla

In the course of his long career as Nero's teacher, the Stoic philosopher Seneca (*c.* 4 BC–AD 65) became one of the wealthiest men in the Roman Empire. Despite his high-mindedness, Seneca had always been willing to make moral compromises. As a young man, he gave up his vegetarianism to avoid the appearance of sympathising with Judaism. When he entered law, he was not above rhetorical subterfuge and sophistry. Politics is the art of the possible. Ethics is about limits. Seneca accepted the friction. After all, *someone* would be advising the emperor; it was better that the adviser be a moral man rather than an opportunist.

To win respect from coarse compatriots, Seneca had to become rich. To prevent unscrupulous men from gaining favour by performing services no one else would, Seneca had to pre-empt them by doing a little dirty work himself.

While a tourist in Rome, I visited the magnificent bath complex built by Emperor Caracalla (188–217). My imagination for what transpired was guided by Seneca's letters to Lucilius. In letter 56, 'On Quiet and Study', Seneca suggests immersion in noise as a method of overcoming the scholar's dependency on silence:

> I have lodgings right over a bathing establishment. So
> picture to yourself the assortment of sounds, which
> are strong enough to make me hate my very powers of
> hearing! When your strenuous gentleman, for example, is
> exercising himself by flourishing leaden weights; when he
> is working hard, or else pretends to be working hard, I can
> hear him grunt; and whenever he releases his imprisoned
> breath, I can hear him panting in wheezy and high-pitched
> tones. Or perhaps I notice some lazy fellow, content with
> a cheap rubdown, and hear the crack of the pummelling
> hand on his shoulder, varying in sound according as the
> hand is laid on flat or hollow. Then, perhaps, a professional
> comes along, shouting out the score; that is the finishing
> touch.

Seneca goes on to chronicle the shouts of vendors, the scuffles of captured pickpockets, the splash of belly-floppers, and the cries of the hair-pluckers.

Being in the boisterous baths brought its own tests of the Stoic ideal of impassiveness. Seneca advocated several techniques for remaining tranquil in face of insult: interpret the provocation as a joke, accept the remark as an accurate criticism and basis of reform, dwell on the credentials of the source of the insult. Seneca also endorses a tactic applied by Cato the Younger: lying. While bathing, Cato was struck but could not tell by whom. His assailant, after realising that he had struck *Cato,* apologised. Cato responded, 'I don't remember being struck.' According to Seneca, this refusal to acknowledge the blow was more magnanimous than pardoning the assault.

The 'Cathedrals of Flesh' fell into ruins after the Christians took control. The empty shells I visited were silent in the hot, still summer air. The guards had retreated into the air-conditioned mobile home that served as the ticket office. The absence of supervision enhanced the mute poignancy of the deserted complex.

My attention alighted on a hole in the ancient mosaic floor. The outer edge of the antique hole looked surprisingly fresh. I crouched for a closer look. When I put a finger on a pebble at the edge, the pebble toppled. I picked it up and realised why the ancient hole looked fresh: Tourists would see the fresh ring of dirt at the edge of the hole, come over to investigate, crouch, and then topple a pebble. They would then pocket the pebble as a souvenir, thereby widening the hole.

I lamented this cycle of ant-like destruction. Ancient Rome was being carried away pebble by pebble!

That still left the issue of what should be done with the pebble between my fingers. If I put it back, a less scrupulous tourist would steal the pebble. Surely, it was better for the pebble to be in the pocket of a moral man rather than an immoral one ...

Assassination Proof

As Nero became more powerful there appeared to be no limit on who he could eliminate – even his mother. His philosophy teacher, Seneca, warned Nero that there was someone he could not kill? ♀ Who was it?

How to Succeed Your Successor

Grover Cleveland was inaugurated as the 22nd and 24th US president, succeeding Benjamin Harrison, who was the 23rd president. ♀ Who was the other president who succeeded his successor?

Hint: You do not need any historical hints.

Not All Logicians Are Saints

Peter Abelard (1079–1142) was the greatest logician since antiquity. He developed a purely truth-functional propositional logic. He drew the distinction between force and content that was later refined by the German logician Gottlob Frege some eight centuries later. And Peter Abelard developed a complete theory of entailment as it functions in argument.

Abelard tutoring Heloise.

But Abelard was no saint. He tricked Heloise's uncle into giving him room and board. In exchange, Abelard would tutor Heloise. But his real aim was seduction. Heloise resisted. Abelard persisted. She wound up pregnant and disgraced.

You cannot always trust a logician!

A few logicians have been saints. Alcuin of York (735–804) is the earliest.

After the fall of Rome, the educational system withered. Charlemagne (742–814) countered by recruiting scholars. Alcuin left Britain to become headmaster of the Palace School.

Alcuin's textbook *Propositiones ad Acuendos Juvenes* (Problems to Sharpen the Young), contains the earliest presentation of transport riddles. Problem 18 requires you ferry a wolf, a goat, and a cabbage across a river without the wolf eating the goat or the goat eating the cabbage. You can transport only one item on each trip. ♡ How do you get them safely across?

Problem 17 is a more complicated transport problem involving three pairs of brothers and sisters. The three couples must cross a river using a boat which can hold at most two people. No woman can be in the presence of another man unless her brother is also present.

In later versions, from the thirteenth to the fifteenth century, the couples become husbands and wives. The husbands are so jealous that they will not trust their wives in the presence of another man even if the man's wife is also present!

Some tried to vary the problem by increasing the number of couples to four. But then there is no solution. This led to the postulation of an island. Further variations subtract arms so that certain parties cannot serve as rowers.

In the nineteenth century, husbands and wives become missionaries and cannibals. This is the incarnation most familiar to researchers in artificial intelligence.

My favourite missionaries and cannibals problem features three cannibals and three missionaries. The cannibals agree to help the missionaries across the river. But the boat can only accommodate two people at a time and missionaries cannot let the cannibals outnumber them. ♀ How can the missionaries safely cross?

Some of Alcuin's problems stress efficiency rather than mere correctness. Problem 42 features a 100-step staircase. The first step has one pigeon, the second two pigeons, and so on up to the hundredth step. What is the total number of pigeons?

Instead of laboriously adding the pigeons in step order, Alcuin observes that there are a hundred pigeons on steps 1 and 99, a hundred more on steps 2 and 98, and so on for all the pairs of steps – with the exception of the 50th and 100th.

Yet more efficient is the solution to an equivalent problem that was posed to the 10-year-old Carl Friedrich Gauss (1777–1855). As an exercise, a schoolmaster ordered his charges to add the first hundred numbers. Young Gauss astonished the teacher by quickly answering 5,050. Unlike Alcuin, Gauss regarded 0 as a number. This allowed Gauss to reorganise the sequence as 50 pairs:

$$100 + 0, 99 + 1, 98 + 2, \text{ and so on.}$$

Each pair totals 100. So the 50 pairs sum to 5,000. When 5,000 is added to the unpaired central number, 50, the final sum is reached: 5,050. (I hope this is a true story about Gauss but no historian endorses it.)

In addition to promoting basic literacy, Alcuin recruited other scholars. He pleaded to have some of the books he collected at York sent across the English Channel, 'I say this that you may agree to send some of our boys to get everything we need from there and bring the flowers of Britain back to France that as well as the walled garden in York there may be off-shoots of paradise bearing fruit in Tours.' Near the end of his life, Alcuin summed up his career, 'In the morning, at the height of my powers, I sowed the seed in Britain, now in the evening when my blood is growing cold I am still sowing in France, hoping both will grow, by the grace of God, giving some the honey of the holy scriptures, making others drunk on the old wine of ancient learning.'

In his textbook, solutions are provided for all the problems. Well, not quite all. No solution is provided to Problem 43:

> A certain man has 300 pigs. He ordered all of them slaughtered in three days, but with an uneven number killed each day. What number were to be killed each day?

The problem is impossible because three odd numbers cannot sum to 300. Why was it posed? Reportedly, to frustrate difficult students.

You cannot always trust a saint!

Lewis Carroll's Peek at Meno's Slave Boy

Classicists have detected glancing references to Plato's dialogues in the works of Lewis Carroll. They specifically cite the *Hippias Major*, *Euthyphro*, and the *Republic*.

Although Carroll preferred (prepubescent) girls, I conjecture that the following riddle is written with a view to the boy in Meno's large entourage of slaves:

> I don't know if you are fond of puzzles, or not. If you are, try this … A gentleman (a nobleman let us say, to make it more interesting) had a sitting-room with only one window in it – a square window, 3 feet high and 3 feet wide. Now he had weak eyes, and the window gave too much light, *so* (don't you like '*so*' in a story?) he sent for the builder, and told him to alter it, so as only to give half the light. Only, he was to keep it square – he was to keep it 3 feet high – and he was to keep it 3 feet wide. How did he do it? Remember, he wasn't allowed to use curtains, or shutters, or coloured glass, or anything of that sort.

– *The Lewis Carroll Picture Book*, 1899, p. 214

Readers of Plato's *Meno* may recall the solution. ♀ Can you draw it?

The Elderly Scientist

'If an elderly but distinguished scientist says that something is possible he is almost certainly right, but if he says that it is impossible he is very probably wrong,' declared Arthur C. Clarke (*New Yorker*, 9 August 1969).

An elderly but distinguished scientist replies, 'It is impossible for Mr Clarke to be correct.' ♀ How likely is the elderly scientist's claim?

More Proof!

The Tale of the Mexican Intuitionist

Once upon a time, an American student travelled to Mexico City to attend a logic conference. His parents objected because a British philosopher, Gareth Evans, had been shot in the leg there a couple of years earlier.

The student explained that the professor was collateral damage. 'Who was the target?' asked his parents. 'Oh, that was his student – a son of the Mexican ambassador to the United States.' Aspiring kidnappers tried to subdue the student and professor by shooting their legs. The student bled to death. Professor Evans was abandoned to his fate (which was to drive in a taxi to hospitals reluctant to treat gunshot wounds). The professor survived. Sadly, Evans died shortly after returning to Oxford from aggressive lung cancer.

The parents of the American student forbade their son from travelling to Mexico. But the son felt that he had outgrown parental hysteria about Mexican kidnapping. He discreetly went anyway.

At the conference the American student heard a Mexican logician object to a proof that relied on the principle of double negation: $\sim \sim p$, therefore p. The student had heard that this challenge was popular at Oxford University. He asked the logician to explain his objection over lunch.

The objection, the Mexican mathematician revealed, goes

back to Immanuel Kant, who viewed mathematics as a mental construction. Whenever the mathematician makes an assertion, he is claiming to have a positive proof. Negation just reports an absence of proof (as in a jury verdict of 'Not Guilty'). The absence of a proof that there is an absence of proof that p is not a proof that p.

The mathematician L. E. J. Brouwer made the Kantian objection rigorous. The exclusion of indirect methods led to intuitionist logic. Although the system is widely regarded as overly severe, it yields proofs that are more explanatory than classical proofs. So mathematicians prefer intuitionistic proofs.

Mathematics seems more central than philosophy. So it is surprising that when Brouwer noticed a conflict he chose to resolve it in favour of philosophy. Although only a small minority of mathematicians followed him, a much larger group was influenced.

The American student was impressed with the strictness of the intuitionist. But he was also distracted by the Mexican's left hand. His index finger was missing. The Mexican explained that kidnappers had removed the finger. Aghast, the American blurted out, 'Too bad they did not take a pinky!'

The Mexican mathematician assumed a professorial air and lectured: 'No, for a right-handed man, the left index finger is the least crippling finger to remove. The pinky is needed for grip strength. My kidnappers were experts, not the amateurs responsible for the incident with the British professor. My hosts had once kidnapped a surgeon. Out of respect for his medical erudition, they let *him* choose which finger to remove. The surgeon thought aloud, mentioning the above facts. He also explained that the other fingers compensate well when the index finger is removed. The index finger yields the best ransom while also doing the least harm to the victim. Everybody wins.'

Looking down at the Mexican's sandals, the queasy American then noticed that the Mexican was also missing his second, long toe. 'Why did the kidnappers also take a toe?' 'Ah,' replied the Mexican, 'that takes us back to logic. My father was also an intuitionist; he wanted more proof.'

Emily Dickinson's Hummingbird

The last two stanzas of Emily Dickinson's 'Within My Garden, Rides a Bird' refer to a puzzle posed by a hummingbird.

> And He and I, perplex us,
> If positive, 'twere we—
> Or bore the Garden in the Brain
> This Curiosity—
>
> But He, the best Logician,
> Refers my clumsy eye—
> To just vibrating Blossoms!
> An Exquisite Reply!

I reconstruct the puzzle as follows. A bowling ball will be rolled into an empty square room. A hummingbird must leave its egg on the floor. 💡 Is there a safe spot?

Plato's Packing Problem

The atomists are famous for saying that there is nothing but atoms and the void. But why the void? Why not have just the atoms?

Well, it has been tried. In the *Timaeus* Plato presents a version of atomism designed to preclude the void. He says his universe is completely packed with five types of atoms. Their shapes are based on the five regular polyhedra. Johannes Kepler portrays these 'Platonic solids' in his *Mysterium Cosmographicum*:

| Cube | Tetrahedron | Dodecahedron | Icosahedron | Octahedron |
| Earth | Fire | the Universe | Water | Air |

Kepler's portrayal of the Platonic solids.

Plato associates four Platonic solids with the four classical elements. The fifth Platonic solid, the dodecahedron, composes the heavens. Plato modestly calls his plenist atomism a likely story, not a certainty.

Aristotle protests that Plato's story is worse than uncertain: it is impossible. A mixture of all five Platonic solids cannot be snugly packed like cubes. There must be interstitial vacua such as the gaps that would inevitably form if all the atoms were balls.

Not leaving well enough alone, Aristotle goes on to claim that tetrahedra can complete space. This commits an even simpler version of the fallacy. For there is only one shape to test.

It is a testament to Aristotle's authority that philosophers and mathematicians alike accepted this claim for seventeen hundred years. For it is easily refuted by simply taking tetrahedra and trying to fit them together. These experiments always yield gaps. The tetrahedra do not even fit around a single point.

Recently, a consolation prize has been discovered. Tetrahedra do fill a larger percentage of a volume than any other shape when the packing is by random pouring and shaking (76% compared with 64% for spheres).

Atomism does not entail the void. However, geometry creates considerable pressure on the atomist to acknowledge microvoids. And once you allow little voids, there is no motive to exclude bigger voids. Since the atomists were stuck with the void, they learned to make good use of it.

Telepathy for the Absent-Minded

Pick a triplet of letters from the following list:

EQG   OBH   EBO   BQH   EBQ   QRC

Now look at the list of triplets in footnote 6. Your triplet is not there. 💡 How did I manage to remove your triplet?

Order of Absence versus Absence of Order

People do attend to absences of bad stuff: dirt, war, coercion. They prefer to use positive terms: cleanliness, peace, freedom. But they measure progress by the *amount* of absence.

Is progress always a matter of reducing bad things? Suppose you will play a single round of Russian roulette. The gun is a standard six-chamber revolver. Natasha puts two bullets in adjacent chambers. She spins, points the gun at her own head, and pulls the trigger. Click. She hands the gun to you. In a sporting mood, she gives you the option of spinning the chamber. ♡ Should you spin?

Neglect of the Absent

♡ What remains after removing twenty letters from

TNWOENTYTLHEITNTEGRS?

Who are the most neglected? The elderly, the poor, the sick, each have their spokesmen. One group you do not hear from are the absent.

Francis Bacon noted the neglect of the absent in 1620. In the *Novum Organum*, he writes:

> It was a good answer that was made by one who when they showed him hanging in a temple a picture of those who had paid their vows as having escaped shipwreck, and would have him say whether he did not now acknowledge the power of the gods, – 'Aye,' asked he again, 'but where are they painted that were drowned after their vows?' And such is the way of all superstition, whether in astrology, dreams, omens, divine judgments, or the like; wherein men, having a delight in such vanities, mark the events where they are fulfilled, but where they fail, though this happens much oftener, neglect and pass them by.

You hear from swimmers who were pulled towards shore by dolphins. You do not hear from swimmers pulled out to sea by dolphins.

In World War II, German anti-aircraft guns shot down many planes. The Royal Air Force decided to add armour. But where? They presented the mathematician Abraham Wald with composite maps of bullet holes from returning planes. There were holes almost everywhere. The Royal Air Force expected Wald to allocate the armour to where the plane attracted the most fire. Wald recommended that armour go to those areas in which there were no holes. His explanation was that the sample failed to include the planes that had been shot down. The absence of holes near the engine, cockpit, and tail control suggested that these are the areas least able to withstand bullets.

If you ask students to estimate the average number of children couples have, they are apt to engage in an impromptu survey. Students report how many children their parents had. Averaging these amounts overlooks the couples who had no children.

A sister fallacy occurs when you ask 'Do brothers have more sisters than sisters?' The males in the class tend to report more sisters than the females. To check the survey, widen the poll to hypothetical combinations: A family comprising a boy and a girl has one brother's sister and no sister's sister. In a family comprising one boy and two girls, the boy has two sisters and his sisters only have one sister. Thus the hypothetical survey tends to corroborate the empirical survey. But both techniques neglect the absent males. If a couple has only two daughters, then the number of sisters of sons is zero and number of sisters of daughters is two.

Once we agree that the absent are neglected, you may wonder how large this group is. In 1990, Amartya Sen deduced: 'More Than 100 Million Women Are Missing' (*New York Review of Books*, 20 December 1990). Sen makes sense: Given equal treatment, girls have a slightly higher survival than boys. But the actual sex ratio for the world is skewed in favour of boys.

Girls have been reduced through selective abortion, infanticide, and inadequate nutrition during infancy.

But has Sen gone far enough?

When you were conceived, millions of other sperm–egg fusions were precluded. The average man releases 250 million sperm. That is many missing babies. Amartya Sen does not speak up for them! A 100 million missing people is a tragedy. A 100 nonillion missing people is a statistic.

Child Proof

I child-proofed my house – but they keep getting in!

Children are born empiricists. A little boy demonstrated that Styrofoam weighs nothing by placing some in my hand. A little girl showed me that I could hear the ocean by having me listen to her seashell.

Sigmund Freud recalls one of these powerful empirical demonstrations:

> When I was six years old, and receiving my first lessons
> from my mother, I was expected to believe that we are
> made of dust, and must, therefore, return to dust. But
> this did not please me, and I questioned the doctrine.
> Thereupon my mother rubbed the palms of her hands
> together – just as in making dumplings, except that
> there was no dough between them – and showed me the
> blackish scales of epidermis which were thus rubbed off,
> as a proof that it is of dust that we are made. Great was
> my astonishment at this demonstration *ad oculos*, and I
> acquiesced in the idea which I was later to hear expressed
> in the words: 'Thou owest nature a death.' [The Hamlet
> quotation is actually 'Thou owest God a death' said to
> someone who faked death in battle to survive.]
>
> – Freud, *Interpretation of Dreams*, 1997 (Wadsworth), p. 105

Subsequent psychologists studied the reasoning of children. One important finding is that children younger than 10 exhibit 'empiricist bias'. If they cannot find empirical support for a statement, they lapse into agnosticism.[10] Eight-year-olds were asked about a single-coloured poker chip hidden in the experimenter's hand: *Is it true that 'Either the chip in my hand is yellow or it's not yellow?'*. Since they could not *see* the concealed chip, the children answered, 'I don't know.'

Psychologists expose empiricist bias with problems that have a slow *a posteriori* solution and a quick *a priori* solution.[11] Children are blind to the *a priori* solution. For instance, 5-year-olds are presented with a picture of boys and girls and asked, 'Are there more boys than children?' They laboriously count the boys and girls and then answer. Children over the age of 10 do not bother to count. They exploit the fact that any boy is a child and quickly reach the same answer.

With coaching, a large percentage of the 5-year-olds will suddenly improve – matching the performance of 10-year-olds. The 5-year-olds are thrilled by the shortcut.

Adults relive the thrill in puzzles that at first seem to require *a posteriori* labour but can actually be solved *a priori*. A spherical loaf of bread is cut into parallel slices of equal width. Each child values the crust, not the volume of the bread. ♀ How can you guarantee that each child has the same amount of crust?

Problems that have an illusion of indeterminacy generate

---

[10] Thomas Huxley coined 'Agnostic' in 1869 to denote those who believed that there was no way to know whether God exists. Philosophers generalised so that an agnostic about X is someone who thinks there is no way to know about X. In 1918, when Bertrand Russell surrendered to Brixton prison to serve his sentence for anti-war agitation, he was asked for his particulars. 'Religion?' inquired the warder of the gate, 'Agnostic,' answered Russell.' The warder of the gate sighed, entered Russell's answer into his log, and waxed philosophical 'Well, there are many religions, but I suppose they all worship the same God.'

[11] A proposition is *a priori* if and only if it is knowable without experience. It is *a posteriori* just in case experience is required. Most *a priori* propositions are actually learned through experience. Testimony, calculators, and computers are usually more efficient and reliable than pure thought.

a similar thrill. Agnosticism seems required because there is not enough information. Then you see there is enough for a decisive answer. Here is a nostalgic example for those who enjoy the history of geometry. A blind carp is released at the edge of a circular pool. First, the fish swims 80 metres in a straight line. Bump! Having reached an edge, the carp turns 90 degrees and swims another 60 metres in a straight line. Bump! ♡ Given these two contacts with the circular wall, how wide is the pool? First hint: The pool is in Miletus. Second hint: Water. Third Hint: More water.

The *a priori* thrill is also produced by puzzles that require a stage of *a posteriori* reasoning and then an *a priori* finish. This accounts for the charm of the nine-coin problem: You have nine coins and a balance scale. One of the coins is counterfeit and so lighter than the others. ♡ Is it possible to identify the counterfeit in only two weighings?

Anthropologists discovered the same empiricist bias in adults who lack formal schooling. This emerged from studies in deductive reasoning. Psychologists were surprised by how poorly students performed on syllogism tests if they had never studied syllogisms. They were even more surprised when they asked non-students. The very attempt to measure reasoning was frustrated by people who had never learned how to be tested for reasoning.

To get large groups of naive subjects, ethnologists went to uncollectivised farms in Soviet Georgia and rural areas of Africa. These people had never been inside a schoolroom. The interviewers posed questions intended to elicit syllogistic reasoning:

All people who live in Monrovia are married.
Kemu is not married.
Does she live in Monrovia?

Many interviewees answered by simply contradicting what was stipulated: 'Yes. Monrovia is not for any one kind of people, so Kemu came to live there.' Others tried to override the stipulated constraint by adding evidence. In response to:

All people who own houses pay house tax.
Boima does not pay house tax.
Does he own a house?

One interviewee added his own instalment to the saga: 'Boima has a house but he is exempted from paying house tax. The government appointed Boima to collect house tax, so they exempted him from paying house tax.' Other syllogisms elicited principles of unschooled epistemology (theory of knowledge):

In the far north, all bears are white.
Novaya Zemlya is in the far north.
What colour are the bears there?

The interviewer gets a little scolding: 'You should ask the people who have been there and seen them, we always speak of only what we see.'

In the terminology of epistemologists, 'empiricist bias' amounts to defeatism about purely *a priori* issues. If a problem is posed in a way that does not permit the application of perception, memory, or testimony, then it is dismissed as insoluble.

Admittedly, this characterisation oversophisticates unschooled epistemology. For the terminology implies a grasp of the distinction between the *a priori* and the *a posteriori*. The distinction does not even occur to people who lack formal education.

The term 'empiricist bias' suffers from the same tendency to oversophisticate. In the historic debate between empiricists and rationalists, both sides were fluent in the vocabulary of the other. They could switch sides and argue well for the opposition's thesis.

Unschooled people lack this versatility. When they encounter this conversational role switching, they condemn the fast-talkers as liars. In 155 BC the Athenians sent a delegation of three philosophers on an embassy to Rome. The sceptic Carneades addressed a crowd of thousands. On the first day, he argued that you should be just for the sake of justice itself. The audience marvelled at the cogency of his reasoning. On the second day Carneades argued, with equal force, that you should be just only because justice is in your self-interest. Scandalised, Marcus Porcius Cato (the Censor) led a conservative backlash that expelled the philosophers.

Ignorance impairs metacognition. The more ignorant people are, the worse their self-knowledge of their ignorance. As people become less ignorant, their estimates of their ignorance increase. So they are better able to make use of feedback from their performance. This leads to the irony that the people who rank themselves the most ignorant know more than those who rank themselves less ignorant.

'Ignorance breeds meta-ignorance' has practical implications. A university student realises he is ignorant about syllogisms and so may choose to study them. An unschooled person thinks that the interviewer is the one who needs to be taught. For the unschooled, there is no problem to solve.

Schooled people will regress to unschooled responses when stressed. Jonathan Haidt studied university students' reactions to uncomfortable, off-putting hypothetical situations that prompted their disgust. One example he used concerned a family that was going hungry, and when their dog was run over by a car, the family ate it. Yuck! The notion of eating a beloved pet was repulsive to Haidt's subjects. (Another scenario involves incest between a brother and sister who double up on birth control. Double yuck! I am sticking with Haidt's dog food for fear of freaking you out.) The students wanted to rationally explain their disapproval of pet consumption. But Haidt had crafted the scenario to defeat these explanations. Subjects started behaving like the unschooled. They selectively attended to only some of the stipulated conditions. They added other assumptions such as the dog being ill and so dangerous to consume.

Since Jonathan Haidt's subjects were competent at reasoning from suppositions these were performance errors. The disgusted subjects were like drivers who know how to parallel park but cannot perform the manoeuvre when being honked at.

Wittgenstein's Parallelograms

💡 Can a rectangle be made of two parallelograms and two triangles? Would a child agree with you?

Knowing the Area of a Parallelogram

Do you *know* how to calculate the area of a parallelogram?

You will have to answer for yourself after checking below. Bear in mind that the question is whether you *know* the area of a parallelogram, not the equation itself.

When asked for the area of a parallelogram, many people start with the limit case of a rectangle. They know the area of a rectangle is the product of its base and height.

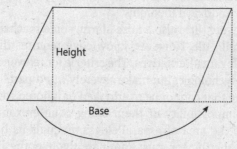

Area of a parallelogram.

They then tilt the rectangle into a parallelogram, amputate one protruding side, and attach it to other side – yielding the original parallelogram. The mental constructor concludes that the area of a parallelogram is the product of its base and height.

This argument rests on the paralemma that *all* parallelograms can be reduced to rectangles by a two-step cut and paste operation.[12] This oversimplification is refuted by severely tilted parallelograms.

---

[12] A paralemma is an invalid intermediate step. A paralemma can be true. It might entail a conclusion that is entailed by the premises.

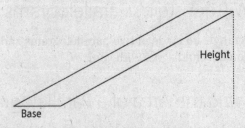

Base

Severely tilted parallelogram.

The angle can sharpen indefinitely. As the angle becomes more acute, the *perimeter* of the parallelogram grows without limit. Many worry that the *area* of the parallelogram will eventually exceed base × height. To their relief, the area of the parallelogram is conserved regardless of the length of the sides. Proclus characterises this robust constancy of area as one of Euclid's 'paradoxical theorems'.

Since severe tilts raise a false alarm, some teachers present only the mild tilt. However, knowledge requires the elimination of relevant alternatives. The criteria for relevance are sufficiently psychological to make severely tilted parallelograms a challenge that cannot be overlooked or ignored (despite the objective impossibility of them being counterexamples). To know that the area of a parallelogram equals its base times its height, the thinker must eliminate the hypothesis that the equation breaks down for severely tilted parallelograms.

Consequently, rigorous teachers complain that the incomplete demonstration is an intellectual fraud. The aim of demonstration is to produce knowledge of the conclusion – not the *feeling* of knowledge.

Freud versus the Dreaming Logicians

If you negate, must you be awake? According to Sigmund Freud, 'There is no negation in dreams.' He regards dreams as the royal road to the unconscious, a realm of ideas that involves:

> No negation, no doubt, no degree of certainty ... To sum up: *exemption from mutual contradiction, primary process* (mobility of cathexes) *timelessness*, and *replacement of external by psychical reality* – these are the characteristics which we may expect to find in processes belonging to the system Ucs.

> – Freud, *The Unconscious*, 1984 (Penguin), pp. 190–91

If negationless experience seems difficult to imagine, consider purely instrumental music (bereft of lyrics). Although music resembles language, music lacks negation. Nor does it have other logical constants such as conjunction and disjunction. There are no ifs, ands, or buts. Consequently, one cannot reason in music.

Considerable calculation goes into the composition of music. But the music itself is incapable of expressing $7 + 5 = 12$. Analogously, considerable calculation goes into the construction of a dream. But the calculation cannot occur within the dream itself. The presence of numerals must be explained in the same terms as mathematical puns: $2n + 2n$ is $4n$ to dreams. The poor arithmetic of the dream is not arithmetic at all.

Freud allows that the words for the logical constants (*and, or, if* and *only if*) may be *mentioned* in dreams. But they are not being used in inference. This explains the apparent illogicality in dreams. According to Freud, dreams are alogical rather than illogical. Any logical notation in a dream has the same inert status as the logical notation left on the blackboard after class. When I apologised to an English professor for my frequent failure to erase the blackboard, he urged me never to erase the proofs. The proofs were lovely wallpaper, a fitting backdrop for his postmodernist ironies.

The lack of *functioning* logical words would neatly explain the dearth of metacognition in dreams. When awake, people worry about whether they are misremembering or misperceiving or reasoning fallaciously. The dreamer does not try recalling his sources of information. He does not double-check his calculations. Maybe the dreamer does not metacognise because he is operating in a medium that lacks the equipment for inference.

Dreamers have ample evidence that they are dreaming. They just cannot marshal the evidence.

Freud's elegant explanation has not won over logicians. Emotions are relevant here. Logicians are embarrassed by their poor reasoning in dreams. Poor reasoning is reasoning. So they must be reasoning in their dreams, perhaps in a delirium.

Lewis Carroll dates the following dream to 15 May 1879:

Last night I had a dream which I record as a curiosity, so far as I know, in the literature of dreams. I was staying, with my sisters, in some suburb of London, and had heard that the Terrys were staying near us, so went to call, and found Mrs. Terry at home, who told us that Marion [nicknamed 'Polly'] and Florence were at the theatre, 'the Walter House,' where they had a good engagement.

'In that case,' I said, 'I'll go on there at once, and see the performance – and may I take Polly with me?'

'Certainly,' said Mrs. Terry. And there was Polly, the child, seated in the room, and looking about nine or ten years old: and I was distinctly conscious of the fact, yet without any feeling of surprise at its incongruity, that I was going to take the child Polly with me to the theatre, to see the grown-up Polly act!

Both pictures, Polly as a child, and Polly as a woman, are, I suppose, equally clear in my ordinary waking memory: and it seems that in sleep I had contrived to give the two pictures separate individualities.

– From: S. D. Collingwood's *The Life and Letters of Lewis Carroll*, 1899

In Carroll's dream there is a juxtaposition of inferences that are reasonable but not co-reasonable: 'Polly has a good role in a play so I should attend' and 'Polly is good company at plays, so I should take her along to see the play'. For Carroll, the problem is not a simple dearth of inference. The insanity of dreams is a combination of inferential overactivity at the base level and inferential underactivity at the meta-level. The dreamer fails to take a step back and check lower-level reasoning.

Strong emotion also chokes metacognition. In dreams, one is often angry or fearful. The source of these emotions is often as mysterious as the emotion stimulated by music. The emotion seems directly implanted instead of arising from outer circumstances.

Perhaps the reasoning is not always bad. Timothy Williamson, Wykeham Professor of Logic at Oxford, reports working out that he was dreaming in a dream. In the dream he looked at his bedside clock and it displayed 6:66. Since that is not a possible time, Williamson concluded that he had not yet awoken from the dream but was still asleep.

There are also logicians who implicitly take credit for the reasoning of characters in a dream. In his 1847 *Formal Logic* Augustus De Morgan writes: 'It is not impossible that in a real dream of sleep, some one may have created an antagonist who beat him in an argument.'

Do Butterflies Dream?

If people never dreamed, would it make a difference to how they picture reality? Or themselves?

Philosophers would certainly lose the most natural way of introducing scepticism. The Chinese Taoist Chuang Tzu (*fl.* fourth century BC) dreamt he was a butterfly. When he awoke he wondered whether he was a man who had dreamt he was a butterfly or a butterfly now dreaming he was a man. Any experience can be explained as either a faithful representation of the world or as a mere figment of a sleeper's imagination.

René Descartes (1596–1650) tried to put science on a foundation of absolute certainty by devising a test for whether he was dreaming. In his last of the *Meditations on First Philosophy* Descartes suggests that he cannot be dreaming if he has a 'clear and distinct idea' of being awake. Descartes's reasoning was that he had earlier proved in his third meditation that God exists (without the premise that he was awake) and that God would not have created the world in which even responsible thinkers were doomed to err. For if God created a world in which logically innocent people made mistakes, then their errors would be God's fault. Since God's goodness precludes Him from being a deceiver, the methodologically scrupulous are infallible. Ironically, Descartes's 'clear and distinct idea' test was inspired by a dream (while in military service on 10 November 1619 in Ulm, Germany) in which God revealed the treasure chest of knowledge.

I have never had a dream directly about God. My dreams are generally nightmares about lecturing mishaps. For instance, in one dream a perceptive student asks, 'Professor Sorensen, why are you dressed in pyjamas?'

Sometimes these anxiety dreams are more erudite. When I first lectured on my hero, David Hume (1711–1776), I was nervous about whether I correctly interpreted his subtle objection to the following argument:

1. If there are miracles, then God exists.
2. There are miracles.
3. Therefore, God exists.

Hume baulked at premise 2 but not on the grounds that it is false.[13] His complaint was that no one can rationally believe premise 2. Miracles are intrinsically incredible. A breach of a

---

[13] In the reign of Louis the fourteenth, miracles were said to be wrought in France at the tomb of a Frenchman, called Abbe Paris. But the king commanded the burying ground to be shut up, and all the miracles ceased; so that of one of the French wits inscribed on the gates of the burying ground, 'By order of His Majesty the King; the Almighty is forbidden to work any more miracles here.' James Bennett, *An Antidote to Infidelity*, 1831, p 8.

natural law is as improbable as the law is probable. Consequently, we should always bet on the lesser miracle that the evidence for the miracle is misleading.

Ever the over-preparer, I summarised Hume's reasoning in a detailed handout. After distributing it to the class, I discovered a typo. Instead of saying 'You CANNOT know that there are miracles' the handout read 'You CAN know that there are miracles.' I told everybody to correct the error by writing NOT after CAN. We all did so.

Ten seconds later, the NOT disappeared from each person's page! The class let out a collective gasp. Resolving not to panic, I announced in a businesslike tone: 'That correction did not take. Please write NOT again.'

I mentally counted down: '10, 9, 8, 7, 6, 5, 4, 3, 2, 1. Aha, still there! I wonder what the scientific ... explanation was for, er, ...' I had counted too fast: the NOT made another majestic exit.

There were now thirty pairs of eyes focused on me. The brains behind those eyes were not impressed with David Hume. Nor were they impressed with me. Could my hero have led me into a worse pedagogical debacle?

I attempted a cheerful face and squeaked, 'Gee whiz, isn't that strange! I wonder what would happen if we wrote in NOT again?' The students mercilessly complied.

Yes, the NOT again evaporated. As did my composure. The students began to laugh at me. Softly at first, then louder and louder. My voice cracking, I once again asked them to insert the NOT. This merely amplified their swirling derision. I could hardly hear myself think! Blood rushed to my cheeks. My mouth ran dry. I racked my brains for the most probable hypothesis. Finally, I stammered, 'I must be dreaming!'

And I was.

Descartes's Disappearance

There was a young student called Fred
Who was questioned on Descartes and said:
'It's perfectly clear
That I'm not really here,
For I haven't a thought in my head.'

V. R. Ormerod

The following joke should have a warning label: 'Hazardous to Logicians'. The joke lures them into misclassifying a valid inference as invalid.

Scene of the joke. René Descartes is in a tavern. The bartender cautions, 'Monsieur, I think you have had enough.' Descartes slurs back, 'I think not!' and vanishes.

Those who are in the habit of correcting fallacious reasoning, such as mathematics teachers, will reflexively object:

> Unfortunately, this joke is not correct. If thinking implies existence, then it does follow that not thinking implies non-existence.
>
> – Michael Stueben and Diane Sandford, *Twenty Years before the Blackboard*, p. 98 fn. 8

But Descartes chooses 'I think, therefore I exist' rather than 'I drink, therefore I exist' because of an essential connection between thinking and existence.[14] For a mind, to be is to think. So necessarily, if I exist, I think.

> I am; I exist – this is certain. But for how long? For as long as I am thinking; for perhaps it could also come to pass that if I were to cease all thinking I would then utterly cease to exist. At this time I admit nothing that is not necessarily true.
>
> Descartes, *Meditations on First Philosophy*, Second Meditation, p. 27

---

[14] In 1984, John Davey recalls, Oxford University Press Christmas show, *Rick Whittington* (music Bob Elliot, lyrics Ron Heapy), featured Shireen Nathoo as a memorable-looking woman leaning against a bar with a cocktail glass and a long cigarette-holder singing in a husky voice a melancholy song entitled, 'I Think, Therefore I Drink'.

Compare Descartes's principle connecting thinking and human existence with another Cartesian principle connecting being extended in three dimensions with physical existence: Necessarily if a body exists, it is extended in space. If a physical thing ceases to be extended, then it ceases to exist. Similarly, if a mind exists, it thinks. And if the mind ceases to think, then it ceases to exist.

The wit who composed the joke was probably ignorant of Descartes's principle that he is essentially a thinking being. If so, the joke composer committed the fallacy of denying the antecedent.

But one can reason invalidly about an argument that is itself valid. Consider this argument about the lily pond that the impressionist Claude Monet so frequently painted:

A lily patch in the Giverny Pond doubles in size each day.
It takes 48 days for the patch to cover the entire pond.
Therefore, Giverny Pond will have less than half of its
   surface covered in 23 days.

Most reason through the paralemma that Giverny Pond will be half filled in $48/2 = 24$ days. They mistakenly treat the growth as arithmetic rather than exponential. The conclusion's choice of 23 days panders to this fallacious calculation. The genuine lemma is that Giverny Pond will be half full after 47 days. Since this paralemma also entails the conclusion, the misstep cannot be detected by any defect in the conclusion. As long as the reasoning is unarticulated, the invalid step will pass unnoticed. The argument is valid even though it might have been constructed through an invalid thought process. Arguments take on a life of their own.

Conclusion: The jokester reasoned incorrectly but his joke is correct. Logicians beware!

The Most Fairly Distributed Good

♀ According to René Descartes, what resource is the most fairly distributed?

Fairness Framed

In 1995, the *US News & World Report* conducted a poll. Half of their readers were asked: 'If someone sues you and you win the case, should he pay your legal costs?' A total of 85% of respondents said yes. The other half were asked a differently phrased question: 'If you sue someone and lose the case, should you pay his costs?' This time only 44% said yes.

'Philosophy,' wrote Oscar Wilde in *The Picture of Dorian Gray*, 'teaches us to bear with equanimity the misfortunes of others.'

Towards a Fairer Share of Dishwashing

One of my university housemates, Greg, refused to divide anything by lot. He objected that this procedure discriminates against the unlucky people. Steadfast randomisers replied that 'unlucky' fails to select a natural class of people. The fact that someone is Indian today is a good reason to believe he will be Indian tomorrow. But being unlucky today provides no grounds for predicting being unlucky tomorrow.

I began to see less of my housemates as I began to see more of my future wife. She and I moved to a cheap flat. We agreed to transcend gender-based division of labour.

This made dishwashing a delicate issue. We tried team dishwashing. But two people cannot wash much quicker than one. We tried rotating the chore. But that raised suspicions of 'insensitive dish-dirtying' on one's days off. Dismissing Greg's reservations, we changed to a policy of determining the night's dishwasher by flipping a coin after dinner.

At first, our chancy arrangement created an exciting

casino-night atmosphere. But then I lost five times in a row. I kept thinking about the coin in the opening scene of Tom Stoppard's play *Rosencrantz and Guildenstern Are Dead*. It lands heads on 179 consecutive tosses.

For a while I had the consoling thought that the law of averages would ensure that everything would even out in the long run. But then I realised this was an instance of the gambler's fallacy. If a coin lands heads on five consecutive tosses, devotees of the gambler's fallacy bet on tails. They think that the law of averages works by compensation. But the law of averages actually works by brute force. A lop-sided run of five heads disturbs the ratio of heads to tails over the short run. But the five-toss streak has steadily less impact on the 1 : 1 ratio over the long run. This does not mean the five-head surplus disappears; it is merely dwarfed into statistical insignificance by the growing number of coin tosses.

Luck has no memory. The law of averages does not try to make up for past imbalances. Bottom line: My five nights' worth of dishes were a dead loss! Just processes do not guarantee just outcomes.

Here is a dishwashing scheme that does guarantee a just outcome because it does work by compensation. Instead of flipping a coin, choose from a deck of cards. If the card is red, my wife washes. If the card is black, I wash. Since the card does not return to the deck, the washer has a lower chance of being selected on the next round. And both parties are guaranteed to wash an equal number of times. Cards are fairer than coins. Coins provide a fair process but fail to ensure a fair result.

The belief that just processes ensure just results is important to political philosophers who reject the principle that the end justifies the means. For instance, in *Anarchy, State, and Utopia*, Robert Nozick uses the principle to defend the unfettered accumulation of wealth by capitalists. As long as each small transaction is fair, then the cumulative redistribution of wealth is fair, that is, the transfer of money from the many poor to the few rich.

Perhaps Nozick would try to smooth troubled waters with the observation that people do tend to acquiesce to the results of processes they perceive to be fair. Agreed, but there are other explanations. For the sake of domestic tranquillity, I might agree to abide by the outcome of some process – regardless of whether it is fair. But then it is my consent that obliges me to accept the outcome, not the justice of the procedure.

The means do not justify the end.

What the Dishwasher Missed

A colleague, Frances Kamm, pointed out a hitch to my card solution to the dishwashing problem. The scheme fails for people who remember how many times they have done the dishes. They will be able to predict the colour of the last card.

Such foreknowledge would raise the spectre of insensitive dish-dirtying. Knowing that I would not be washing the dishes on day 52 (corresponding to the last card in the deck), my dish use would not be disciplined by the fear that I might have to wash the dishes I dirtied.

There is a good chance it could be worse. Thanks to my bad luck earlier in the sequence, I might store up enough dishwashing karma to finish my 26 dishwashings early. Foreseeing that my wife owed the last five dishwashings I could dirty dishes with impunity (which cannot be removed with detergent).

◊ How might I amend my card scheme to avoid this predictability?

Kamm was surprised that I overlooked this backwards reasoning. For I had written many articles on backwards mathematical inductions.[15]

---

[15] A mathematical induction is a slippery-slope argument compactly expressed as a numeric progression. Base step: A billion is a large number. Induction step: If n is a large number, then $n + 1$ is a large number. Conclusion: Two billion is a large number. Voilà! A billion-step argument shoehorned into a footnote!

I was less surprised. My expertise had not been cued into operation. I was in the same class of bumblers as the academics Tversky and Kahneman would interview at psychology conventions. Despite training in statistics, the professionals would commit the same fallacies as untrained people when a question was posed in an unfamiliar fashion.

But Kamm was still incredulous. For one of the oldest backward inductions involves a deck of cards: Your task is to place the ace of spades in a surprising position in the deck. I will turn over the cards one by one. If I am ever in a position to foresee that the ace of spades is next, then I win. If you place the card in a position I cannot foresee, then you win.

This game is easy for you to win. Indeed, you seem to *know* you will win. It also seems that I know you know this, you know I know that, and so on. It is common knowledge that you can win.

But if it really is common knowledge, then I can argue as follows. You cannot have put the ace of spades at the bottom of the deck. For then I could predict its position after the penultimate card, card 51, had been revealed. Knowing this, I can also exclude the possibility that the card is at position 51. For when card 50 is revealed, I will know that the card is at either 51 or 52. By the previous reasoning I will know that the card cannot be at position 52. So I will foresee it as being at position 51. By mathematical induction I can reverse-eliminate all the alternatives in the deck.

Economists accept the argument as a *reductio ad absurdum* of the supposition that it is common knowledge that I will lose. They stress that common knowledge is a very strong condition that is rarely, if ever, satisfied in practice.

Philosophers disagree. If common knowledge were so rare, they would not be able to use it to analyse phenomena such as convention and meaning.

Part of the disagreement may arise from the fact that philosophers focus on a more naturalistic version of the puzzle. In the surprise-test paradox, a teacher informs her student of a disjunction:

Either

(i)　the test is on Monday and the student does not know it before Monday, or

(ii)　the test is on Wednesday and the student does not know it before Wednesday, or

(iii)　the test is on Friday and the student does not know it before Friday.

The student protests that the surprise test is impossible. He knows that the test cannot be held on Friday. For on Thursday he would be able to deduce that the test is on Friday. This reasoning would be available to the student on Sunday, the first day of the week. Thus, if no test is given Monday, the student would know on Tuesday that the test must be on Wednesday. The preceding reasoning is also available to the student on Sunday. So even back then, the student could know that a Wednesday test is also impossible. Consequently, back on Sunday he will know the test is on Monday. Therefore, there is no day on which the surprise test can take place.

The teacher gives the test on Monday. The student did not know it beforehand. Reality has spat in the eye of logic!

My diagnosis is that the student will start out knowing the announcement but will lose that knowledge if the test is not given by Thursday. For the only uneliminated alternative in the announcement will be (iii). And it is impossible for the student on Thursday to know (iii).

For (iii) entails that the student on Thursday does not know (iii). The teacher can know (iii) because the ignorance is not being ascribed to her. The self-defeat of the teacher's announcement is contingent and developmental.

The same goes for larger-scale versions of the puzzle. If the ace of spades is among the last few cards, I will lose knowledge that 'the ace of spades has been placed in a position that you can never foresee'. For at that stage I have gained evidence that undermines my original knowledge that you have placed the card in an unknowable position. The details are in *Blindspots* – which Kamm emphasised, I had just published!

Developmental Self-Defeat

In 1998 the Bureau for At-Risk Youth, based in Plainview, New York, distributed pencils to schoolchildren with the slogan TOO COOL TO DO DRUGS. A 10-year-old student at Ticonderoga Elementary School, Kodi Mosier, eventually made a discovery. As a result, the pencils were recalled. ♀ What did Kodi discover?

Random Quiz

Professor Statistics announces she will give random quizzes: 'Class meets every day of the week. Each day I will open by rolling a die. When the roll yields a six, I will immediately give a quiz.' Today, Monday, a six came up. So you are taking a quiz. The last question of her quiz is: ♀ 'Which of the subsequent days is most likely to be the day of the next random test?'

Enforcing Gresham's Law[16]

April 1, 1965. Someone has played a trick on you!

You have been collecting American silver quarters. Prior to 1965 they were made of 90% silver. You hoped that their value would increase. (And you were right, thanks to the rise in the price of silver, each quarter is now worth more than three dollars.)

After 1964, quarters are made of nickel and copper. You can tell the difference by looking at the edge – which is all silver for silver quarters.

---

[16] Queen Elizabeth asked Sir Thomas Gresham why the old English shilling was disappearing after a debased shilling was substituted. In a letter written on occasion of her accession in 1558, her financial agent explained that bad money drives out good. When coins have the same value as legal tender but differ in other respects of value (say as a useful metal), the inferior coins will be used for payment. The better coins will be hoarded.

Your collection method employed three buckets. One bucket was filled with quarters and labelled Mixed. The other two buckets, labelled Silver and Non-silver, were for sorting.

Silver		Mixed		Non-silver

But your little bother, I mean brother, thought it would be an amusing April Fool's prank to switch all the labels on the buckets. You wish to return the labels to their appropriate buckets. ♀ How many quarters do you need to reinspect?

Gresham's Law of Numbers

Single-digit numbers are easier to use and represent the more fundamental numbers. There are endlessly many big numbers. Our stock of small numbers is limited. Sadly, the small numbers tend to get hoarded.

Baseball players were initially numbered 1 through 9 to match their batting order. But instead of building on this order, there has been growing entropy.

Sentimentality ruined the system. The numbers became associated with beloved players. When those players retired, they were honoured by also retiring their numbers.

1	2	3
Billy Martin	Derek Jeter	Babe Ruth
4	5	5
Lou Gehrig	Joe DiMaggio	Stan Musial
7	8	9
Mickey Mantle	Yogi Berra	Ted Williams

Yankee numeral retirements.

Official retirement is not the only factor. Current baseball players avoid all single-digit numbers. They do not want to put themselves in the same class as the great players of the past. What remains is double-digit chaos.

If you want a game that makes exemplary use of 1 through 9, consider Ronald Graham's addition game. Two players in turn say a number between 1 and 9. A particular number may not be repeated. Victory goes to the first player who has exactly three numbers that add up to 15.

This is a challenging game. The number of combinations is enormous.

Nevertheless, you can quickly become invincible. Your perfect play will make onlookers speculate about what would happen if you were matched against another perfect player.

Would the player who chose the first number always win the game?

The answer follows as an elegant corollary to a reduction of Graham's addition game to noughts-and-crosses (tic-tac-toe). Plot the numbers 1 through 9 below ten on a 3 × 3 magic square. The rows, columns, and diagonal of the magic square sum to 15. This game exactly corresponds to noughts-and-crosses. Three numbers will be arranged in a straight line exactly when they total 15.

2	7	6
9	5	1
4	3	8

This magic square can become the basis for a computer program to play noughts-and-crosses. This raises an interesting question of which game is being played by the computer. You might ask whether the computer is playing any game at all.

But let us return to the question of who would win if ideal thinkers played the game. Well, you already know that noughts-and-crosses is a draw. Since Graham's challenging game reduces to noughts-and-crosses, you know both games are draws under perfect play.

Laziest *Reductio*

In 'First-check chess' victory goes to the first player to check their adversary. Martin Gardner trivialised this game by showing that White had a forced mate from the opening position (*Mathematical Circus*, p. 183). The knights suffice.

Now consider two-move chess in which each side makes two moves each turn. ♀ Is two-move chess at least a draw for White?

Imaginary Travel Companions

Travelling alone is less scary when you bring along an imaginary friend. He is a good listener. He can also help you solve problems by participating in thought experiments.

I am walking towards the Pentagon in Arlington, Virginia, from a random direction. ♀ What is the probability that I will see three sides of the building?

At sunrise I hike up to the Kežmarské Hut on the icy tundra of the High Tatra Mountains in Slovakia. This cubical hostel was built by the Czech architectural firm Atelier 8000. Set with one corner of the cube in the ground, the building looks like a die that might roll off the mountain. Inside, the windows are oriented oddly. An advantage is that I can sleep facing the stars. At sunrise, I descend the mountain down the same path. I travel more quickly because the walk is downhill. ♀ What is the chance that there is a point on the path that I will pass at the same time on both the ascent and the descent?

In addition to answering questions, an imaginary friend can also ask some questions. At Stonehenge, I am awestruck by how the structure aligns with the midsummer sunrise and the midwinter sunset. I wonder what significance the planners attached to this seasonal regularity.

Returning to New York on 11 July, my imaginary friend is awestruck by how the setting sun aligns perfectly with the east–west streets in Manhattan's main grid. He wonders what significance the planners attached to this seasonal regularity.

The Twin Cities Race

Twin sisters must travel together, from Minneapolis to Saint Paul, the Twin Cities. They have only one unicycle and decide to rotate. One twin will ride a kilometre, leave the unicycle for her sister to ride, and continue on foot. The newly mounted twin will then ride a kilometre beyond her sister and leave it for her. The rotation will continue until they reach Saint Paul.

There is a man, Solo, walking the same route, setting out at the same time. He can walk faster than either twin. However, Solo is only half as fast as a unicycling twin.

Nevertheless, Solo reasons that he will reach Saint Paul before both twins arrive. For whenever one twin is walking, she is walking slower than Solo. Since Solo always maintains his lead, he must finish first.

The twins reason that they will finish first because whenever Solo is walking, a unicycling twin is outpacing him.

♡ Who will finish first, Solo or the twins?

Fugu for Two

The Japanese puffer fish, fugu, is a delicacy that must be eaten with careful abstention from the creature's neurotoxic gonads, liver, and skin. At a light dose, fugu neurotoxin creates an interesting numbing sensation much prized by gourmets (perhaps also enjoyed by adolescent dolphins who have been filmed chewing on a puffer fish and passing it around to the next dolphin).

Fugu was banned in some areas during the Tokugawa shogunate period (1603–1868) and again during the Meiji Era (1867–1912). Traditionally, the Emperor is forbidden from partaking. However, the contemporary Japanese attitude is summed up in their proverb: 'Those who eat fugu soup are stupid. But those who don't eat fugu soup are also stupid.'

Fugu bones are present in 2,300-year-old shell middens from the Jōmon period. Fears of poisoning are enshrined in culinary lore:

Two gourmands prepare fugu stew. Each invites the other to eat first. Politeness puts the gentlemen at an impasse.

Through a window, they spot a beggar in the street. They offer a generous portion to the hungry man. After an hour, they check on the beggar. He displays no paralysis. The gourmands are delighted by the beggar's health. They heartily indulge in their fugu stew.

Later that evening, the sated diners re-encounter the beggar, now with his daughter: 'Mendicant! Have you ever tasted such delicious stew?' The ragged man shrugs in ignorance. Insulted, the gourmands stride away.

The beggar, delighted by the sure-footedness of the gourmands, confides to his daughter that he will soon know the answer to the gourmands' question. He takes out the stew from a hiding place and shares the delicacy.

Deducing Names

The author of the *Iliad* is either Homer or, if not
Homer, somebody else of the same name.
Aldous Huxley

What belongs to you but others use it more than you do?

Your name. Indeed, others find your name so useful that you may wish to keep your name secret. When I know your name but you do not know mine, I can easily identify you but you are liable to lose track of me.

Your name is part of a causal chain extending from your baptism to present uses. By learning your name, I can trace your identity through a social network. Once police learn a criminal's name, they can locate him through records and through his contacts in the underworld. What might appear to be a useless label is actually a powerful investigatory tool.

To restore parity, you may point this out: 'Sir, you have the advantage over me,' hoping that I will volunteer my name. Or you might say, 'What did you say your name was?' to which I may coyly reply, 'I did not say.'

Secrecy about names exasperates anthropologists. E. E. Evans-Pritchard (*The Nuer*, p. 12) ranks the Nuer people of South Sudan as 'expert at sabotaging an inquiry'. He recommends their techniques to all natives 'who are inconvenienced by the curiosity of ethnologists'. A Nuer informant shows up to be treated to some tobacco. But once the discussion goes beyond generalities, conversation slows to a crawl: *Who are you?* A man. *What is your name?* Do you want to know my name? *Yes.* You want to know my name?

Evans-Pritchard does not consider the hypothesis that his informants had doubts about *his* candour. English names do not sound like the names with which the natives are familiar. They suspect they are being hoodwinked into exchanging their genuine name for a counterfeit name. In *The Malay Archipelago* (1869) Alfred Russel Wallace recalls the suspicions of the natives in his chapter on the Aru Islands:

> Two or three of them got round me and begged me for the twentieth time to tell them the name of my country. Then, as they could not pronounce it satisfactorily, they insisted that I was deceiving them, and that it was a name of my own invention. One funny old man, who bore a ludicrous resemblance to a friend of mine at home, was almost indignant. 'Ung-lung!' said he, 'who ever heard of such a name? – ang lang – anger-lung – that can't be the name of your country; you are playing with us.' Then he tried to give a convincing illustration. 'My country is Wanumbai – anybody can say Wanumbai. I'm an orang-Wanumbai; but, N-glung! who ever heard of such a name? Do tell us the real name of your country, and then when you are gone we shall know how to talk about you.'

The worry about revealing names and receiving false names is found in Homer's epics. The one-eyed giant Polyphemus tries to trick Odysseus into revealing his name. The Cyclops says he needs the name to bestow a favour. The wily Odysseus answers, 'Nobody'. The favour? To be eaten last!

When Odysseus' crew blinds Polyphemus at night,

Polyphemus' neighbours hear his scream. The concerned giants ask whether he is under assault. Polyphemus answers, 'Nobody is attacking me.' His neighbours return to their beds.

While fleeing in a boat, Nobody impetuously shouts his real name, taking credit for blinding Polyphemus. Odysseus pays later for this indiscretion.

Such is the anthropology, history, and mythology of the name riddle. When you tell one, or solve one, you add another chapter to an ancient book.

Practise your wiles:

1. Theognis' father had five children Argeia, Artemisia, Menexene, and Pantacleia. All were daughters who became logicians in the third century BC. ♀ What is the fifth daughter's name?
2. Operation Pied Piper commenced on 1 September 1939 to evacuate children from areas at risk of Nazi bombing raids.

LEAVE THIS TO US SONNY — <u>YOU</u> OUGHT TO BE OUT OF LONDON

MINISTRY OF HEALTH EVACUATION SCHEME

One of the organisers, a retired nursing instructor, spotted a former student at Paddington Station. They had not spoken in twenty years. The former student had married a surgeon twelve years ago. They had a son, now rather intimidated by the commotion on the train platform. 'Sonny, what is your name?' she asked. 'Jake,' whispered the lad. The old nurse then inquired, 'Which train will Jake Junior be taking?' The instructor had never met the surgeon. ♀ How did she know the boy was Jake *Junior*?

3. I Met A Man And Drew His Name. He Tipped His Hat And Played My Game. ♀ What is his name?

4. The name of the husband of the logician Ruth Barcan Marcus was Jules Alexander Marcus. ♀ What was the name of the husband of Kurt Gödel's wife?

5. Suppose you fly a small shuttle plane in Siberia. Your passenger list at take-off comprises 5 men, 1 woman, and her twin girls. At the second stop, 3 men get off and one couple gets on with their son. At the third stop, the twins and their mother get off. ♀ What is the pilot's name?

Richard Feynman is Inconsistent

Nothing can be inferred from words I smiled to myself, because my father had already taught me that [the name] doesn't tell me anything about the bird. He taught me: 'See that bird? It's a brown-throated thrush, but in Germany it's called a *halsenflügel*, and in Chinese they call it a *chung ling*, and even if you know all those names for it, you still know nothing about the bird – you only know something about people; what they call that bird. Now that thrush sings, and teaches its young to fly, and flies so many miles away during the summer across the country, and nobody knows how it finds its way ... ,' and so forth. There is a difference between the name of the thing and what goes on.

– Richard Feynman, 'What is Science?', *The Physics Teacher*, 1969, 7(6): 313–20.

'Look at this,' remarked Richard. 'The capital [of Tuva] is spelled K-Y-Z-Y-L.'
'That's crazy,' I said. 'There's not a legitimate vowel anywhere!'

'We must go there,' said Gweneth [Feynman's wife].

'Yeah!' exclaimed Richard. 'A place that's spelled K-Y-Z-Y-L has just got to be interesting!'

Richard and I grinned at each other and shook hands.

– Ralph Leighton, *Tuva or Bust! Richard Feynman's Last Journey*, 2000 (Norton), p. 3.

One might defend Feynman's consistency. In the first passage, he concedes that a name might teach you something about the people who use the name. A tourist could send an informative postcard: Grtngs frm Kyzyl! Tvns r hppy flks. Bt thy 8 vwlls. Bst wshs, Rchrd.

This defence overlooks the fact that people are part of nature. When you learn the Germans denote that a bird species with *halsenflügel* you have a trace of the species. This tracking device enables you to learn more about those birds. There is linguistic division of labour among the Germans. Once they can identify what you are curious about, they can redirect your inquiry to birdwatchers and ornithologists. These experts connect to the species itself.

As we age, our ability to access names declines. We can still refer indirectly through the medium of definite descriptions such as 'the famous physicist investigating the *Challenger* disaster'. But the sufferer cannot connect directly.

Happily, there are other people who can come up with the name in response to our description. But suppose we all became name-blind. This would prevent us from referring to objects until we could accurately single them out by description. Names let us tag the item and figure it out later.

Galbraith's Cow

The referent of 'that' seems supremely direct and straightforward. There is something right in front of you. You harpoon it with this convenient demonstrative term.

You can be quite ignorant about the nature of the referent. In their 'What the Hell Is That?' sketch (*Saturday Night Live*, season 5 number 1), Steve Martin and Bill Murray play a couple of inquisitive American tourists. Martin wanders on stage, squints into the camera, and asks, 'What the hell is that?' Bill Murray joins him to double-team the enigma. They ask how that got there, warn their children not to go near that, ... or at least not to put their lips on it!

Murray has a flash of insight: 'I know what that is!' Martin chimes in with a knowing chuckle, 'Oh yeah, of course.' But their confidence fades. Martin shrugs his shoulders and decides he should at least get a picture of himself with that. Martin hands his camera to Murray, scurries out of visibility, and asks Murray to snap the photograph. Their inquiry unrewarded, the pair sourly declare that they do not care what that is. They swagger off exuding indifference. But Martin darts back into view. 'What is that?' ...

Despite their ignorance, the crude tourists are talking about the same thing. Just as a photograph does not need to know what it is a photograph of, speakers do not need to know what they are pointing to. 'That' tolerates stupidity.

Names inherit their stupidity tolerance from 'that'. For we attach the name N to its bearer by pointing and declaring: 'Call that N.'

'The' is more cognitively demanding than 'that'. Definite descriptions require you to *net* your referent with a list of features that uniquely applies to the referent. Items that do not match the properties are filtered out. Often your definite description will fail to net anything: the fountain of youth, the moon of Mars, the effect of radiation, and so on. With 'that' it is difficult to miss.

The point of 'that' is to first secure the referent and then later learn about its nature. We haul in whatever we harpooned and examine the beast at our leisure.

But there is a twist in the tale of 'that'.

The economist John Kenneth Galbraith grew up on a farm in Canada. One spring, young Galbraith and a girl he fancied were sitting on a fence observing a bull service a cow. Galbraith turned to the girl with a suggestive look and said, 'That looks like it would be fun.' She replied, 'Well ... she's your cow.'

The girl's joke shows how abstract 'that' can be. What Galbraith and the girl were witnessing was a graphic instance of the relation: x copulates with y. But what Galbraith intended was copulation in general. He was abstracting away from the particular bull and the particular cow. He was hoping that his coy allusion to copulation might yield a fresh instance of x copulates with y.

The girl's rejoinder meets Galbraith halfway. She abstracts away from the bull but not the cow. She pretends he was referring to the partially abstracted relation: x copulates with Galbraith's cow.

There is an echo of the girl's joke in Professor Galbraith's theorising about speculative bubbles: 'Wisdom is often an abstraction associated not with fact or reality but with the man who asserts it and the manner of its assertion' (*The Great Crash of 1929*).

Logical Names for Babies

The logician Diodorus Cronus gave one of his daughters a male name, 'Theognis', to prove that names are conventional. ('Theognis' was also the name of a famous sixth-century BC lyric poet.) This may have spurred Theognis to follow her father's profession. Indeed, all five of his daughters became noted dialecticians.

Other philosophers are more interested in practice than theory. Buddhists prefer *useful* names.

When still Prince Siddhartha, Buddha had resolved to leave the palace. Since his wife Yashodhara was pregnant, there was a looming temptation to scale back his quest for Enlightenment. When told of his son's birth, Siddhartha replied, 'A rāhu is born, a fetter has arisen.' This made a suitable warning label: Rāhula, means 'fetter' or 'impediment'.

In addition to warning Siddhartha, the name may have helped Rāhula himself. Rāhula was raised by his mother and grandfather, King Suddhodana. At the age of 7, Rāhula requested to see his father. His mother agreed. She wanted her son to secure the succession.

On the seventh day of the Buddha's return, she took her son to meet his father. As instructed, Rāhula said to the Buddha, 'Give me my inheritance.' The Buddha said nothing. He let the boy follow him. Rāhula was happy, saying 'Lord, even your shadow is pleasing to me.'

When father and son reached the Park of Nigrodha, Buddha reflected on the boy's future. Rāhula wants his father's inheritance. But that earthly inheritance is wrought with troubles. Better that he receive the benefit of Enlightenment. So Rāhula received a transcendental inheritance. Buddha ordained Rāhula, making the 7-year-old boy the first Sāmanera (novice monk).

When my wife ruminated about having children, I tried nominal birth control: come up with a name that no woman would tolerate for her child.

An excellent candidate was found in a 1948 issue of *Analysis*. In 'Mr Ill-named' Peter Geach begins by noting that some people are well-named because they serve as accurate descriptions. The baker, Mr Baker, is well-named. However, the lawyer, Mr Cook, is ill-named because his name yields an inaccurate description. Now consider a man named 'Ill-named'. Is Mr Ill-named well-named or ill-named? If he is ill-named, then his name describes him accurately. So if he is ill-named, then he is well-named. But if Ill-named is well-named, then his name cannot accurately describe him.

Professor Geach was presenting a novel variation of the liar paradox:

L: This statement is not true.

If L is true, then since it says that it is not true, it must be not true. But if statement L is not true, then things are just as L says – in which case L is true after all. The liar paradox goes back to the ancient Greek philosopher Eubulides. It is the father of many variant paradoxes: the Grelling 'heterological' paradox, the Berry paradox, Richard's paradox. Important new variations are still being discovered!

Excited by all of this history and ongoing research, I proposed to name my child 'Ill-named'. Other children are slowly introduced to philosophical issues. Our child would have a head start.

Many people would at first conclude that the child is ill-named. But this conclusion would occasion second thoughts. And those second thoughts are grounds for third thoughts. Pretty soon, there is a whole lot of thinking going on. And I like to make people think!

In addition to being the object of these cogitations, the contemplated child could not help but participate in the ruminations himself. Whereas other children would have been given meaningless labels as names, ours would have been given an intellectual *nom de guerre*.

My wife did a little research on her own. She discovered that mothers in New York have complete legal control over the names of their newborns. Sadly, I cannot recommend nominal birth control to my fellow New Yorkers.

Being Relatively Ill-Named

Great Wymondley, in Hertfordshire, is smaller than Little Wymondley. The two are ill-named *as a pair*, not as individuals.

A name need not have any descriptive content to be infelicitous. Evelyn Waugh's first wife was named Evelyn. The problem here is that each has a name that fails to distinguish husband from wife.

Episode 22 of *Monty Python's Flying Circus* television show had a sketch featuring the Australian philosophy department at the University of Woolamaloo. Each of the faculty is named

Bruce. When a new instructor is introduced to the staff, Michael Baldwin, they ask whether he minds being called Bruce to avoid confusion.

Roman Resemblance Humour

Ancient jokes are made more humorous by their resemblance to contemporary jokes. Across a millennium, we hear of the young intellectual who is told his beard is coming in. He waits at the rear entrance. A second intellectual laughs at him, 'No wonder we intellectuals are mocked for our lack of common sense! How do you know it is not coming in through the *front* entrance?'

According to the *Augustan History*, a series of imperial biographies, Emperor Elagabalus 'had the custom of asking to dinner eight bald men, or else eight one-eyed men or eight men who suffered from gout, or eight deaf men, or eight men of dark complexion, or eight tall men or eight fat men – his purpose being in the case of these last, since they could not be accommodated on one couch, to call forth general laughter.'

Why should suprising resemblances be risible? According to Henri Bergson, the nineteenth-century philosopher, we laugh at living things that appear mechanical. When you slip on a banana peel, you behave as any falling object. When you absent-mindedly pet your wife and kiss your dog, you slip into the rigid behaviour of an automaton. A third way to resemble a machine is through homogeneity. The wheelright makes wheels by the cartload. If you look mass produced, you are brought down to the level of a product.

The deflating effect of resemblance is greatest when we are striving to be creative – as when we show up in the same costume at a Halloween party.

I once had an inspiration about how to continue an essay on imagination that had been stalled for six months. I opened the file and typed excitedly for an hour. Then I noticed that I had begun the composition higher than some previous material left over from six months ago. Scrolling down I could see an old paragraph that had an uncanny resemblance to what I had just written. Scrolling further down, I rediscovered the objection that had stumped me six months previously. I was stuck again.

The Prison-House of Language

You are in a room without doors or windows. ♀ How do you get out?

Bilingual Humour

Linguists love language. But they bravely renounce the most popular justification for studying other languages; a second language allows you to think thoughts that are not available in your native language. This is forced upon them by their egalitarian doctrine that each natural language is expressively complete. No natural language can provide more access to truth than any other language. It is always a tie.

Noam Chomsky goes further. He claims that a Martian who visited Earth would conclude that everyone speaks the same language. The Martian would regard the differences between languages as trivial. And this would not be because the Martian is naive. The Martian would be perceiving a deep commonality in *Homo sapiens*. Through gritted teeth, I heard one prominent linguist concede: In principle, a monolingual could be a competent linguist.

I do not know any monolingual linguists. In addition to speaking several languages, most linguists poke fun at monolinguals. Here are some of their jokes:

A person who speaks two languages is bilingual.
A person who speaks three languages is trilingual.
A person who speaks four or more languages is
    multilingual.
♀ What is a person who speaks one language?

A Texas sheriff has arrested a Mexican for robbing a bank. The interrogation has been through a translator.

Sheriff: I am asking you one last time. Where did you hide the money?

Mexican: Yo no robé el banco.

Translator: He says he did not rob the bank.

Sheriff [putting a pistol to the Mexican's temple]: If you do not tell me where the money is, I will blow your head to Tijuana!

Mexican: Por favor, no disparen! Tengo una familia! El dinero está en el hueco del árbol de roble grande en la parte posterior del banco.

Translator: He says you are too cowardly to shoot.

This joke can be understood without understanding Spanish. (The length of the answer does the trick.) But one needs a little French for some bilingual gags. Eldon Dedini has a *New Yorker* cartoon featuring an American traffic cop on a motorcycle. He has just pulled over a man in a beret at the wheel of a French convertible. The officer leans over with his ticket pad, 'Où est le feu?'

And a little phonology is required for bilingual puns: ♡ Why do the French only have one egg for breakfast?

In my final example, the butt of the joke might be contested: A Swiss driver is lost in New Jersey. Hoping for directions, he asks two natives waiting at a bus stop:

'Entschuldigung, sprechen Sie Deutsch?' says the driver. The two Americans just look at him like a pair of unaddressed envelopes.

'Excusez-moi, parlez-vous français?' The Americans remain blank.

'Parlate italiano?' The pair continue to vacantly stare.

'¿Hablan ustedes español?' No response.

Shaking his head, the Swiss motorist speeds away in disgust.

Stung by the contempt, one citizen of the Garden State is embarrassed: 'Maybe we should learn a second language.'

The second American is unruffled: 'Why? That guy knew *four* languages, and it did not help him!'

The Pierre Puzzle and Implicit Racism

Saul Kripke has a puzzle about belief. Pierre is a monolingual Frenchman who reads about a beautiful city, Londres. He moves to a British city, London, and learns English by immersion. Since Pierre happens to be in an ugly section, he sincerely says, 'London is not pretty.' He does not realize that London is Londres. So when Pierre is asked in French, he sincerely answers, 'Londres est jolie', which translates as 'London is pretty.' Does Pierre believe London is pretty? That is a difficult question.

Here is another difficult question. Bilingual Israelis have unconscious aversion to Palestinians when questioned in Hebrew but not when questioned in Arabic (as measured by word associations and physiological indicators of anxiety). These negative associations occur independently of conscious beliefs. Many conscious opponents of racism have reaction times suggesting unconscious hostility and fear towards the race. These anti-racists are disturbed by their 'implicit racism'. Are the bilingual Israelis implicit racists in Hebrew but not Arabic?

Capital Pronunciation

Languages differ in how they are written as well as in how they spoken. ♀ In which language is pronunciation altered by capitalization?

Logically Perfect Language

Bertrand Russell viewed *Principia Mathematica* as one instalment of a logically perfect language. In this perfect notation, you would be safe from pseudo-questions.

There would be no temptation to answer them because the language would prevent you from asking them. To a limited extent, written English silences pseudo-questions. In oral lectures, I illustrate this prophylactic punctuation with a puzzle sentence devised by Richard Lederer and Gary Hallock. Read it aloud: what is a four-letter word for a three-letter word which has five letters yet is still spelled with three letters, while it has only two and rarely has six and never is spelled with five.

💡 Why must the riddle be spoken instead of written?

Eyebrow Punctuation

Quotation marks have leapt off the page and into spoken English. Finger quotes became popular in the 1990s, perhaps because of Steve Martin's exaggerated use of them in his comedy routines. Martin Gary's 'Air Quotes' traces them back to 1927. In this era, other punctuation signs attempted migration:

> Mr Beach was too well bred to be inquisitive, but his eyebrows were not.
>> 'Ah!' he said.
>> '?', cried the eyebrows. '? ? ?'
>> Ashe ignored the eyebrows.
>
>> ...
>
> Mr Beach's eyebrows were still mutely urging him to reveal all, but Ashe directed his gaze at that portion of the room which Mr Beach did not fill. He was hanged if he was going to let himself be hypnotised by a pair of eyebrows into incriminating himself.
>
> – P. G. Wodehouse, *Something Fresh*

Kierkegaard's 1 AU Dash

> I have just now come from a party where I was its life and soul; witticisms streamed from my lips, everyone laughed and admired me, but I went away – yes, the dash should be as long as the radius of the earth's orbit ————————— ——————————— and wanted to shoot myself.
>
> *The Journals of Kierkegaard*, March 1836

Putting Out Your Second Eye

And if thine eye offend thee, pluck it out, and cast it from thee.

Matthew 18:9

When asked when he was born, Augustus De Morgan answered that he was x years old in the year x^2. ♀ From that formula you can work out his birth year. De Morgan was pointing out an unusual fact about himself. ♀ Will any reader of this book be x years old in the year x^2?

In a review of a geometry book, Augustus De Morgan chides those who voluntarily adopt the perspective of a Cyclops:

> We know that mathematicians care no more for logic than logicians for mathematics. The two eyes of science are mathematics and logic; the mathematical set puts out the logical eye, the logical set puts out the mathematical eye; each believing that it sees better with one eye than with two.
>
> – De Morgan, *Athenaeum*, 1868, Vol. 2: 71–73

Commentators note that Augustus De Morgan had only one functional eye. He lost use of his right eye a month after birth.

The withered eye gave De Morgan the appearance of Cyclops.

In the same speculative spirit, I note that Augustus De Morgan was familiar with a critic of logic who, in his later years, did try to pluck his own eye out.

This aspiring Cyclops was the satirist Jonathan Swift (1667–1745), author of *Gulliver's Travels*. Swift is well known to philosophers. He invited the young Idealist George Berkeley to dinner. Berkeley was famous for his principle 'To be is to be perceived'. When Berkeley appeared at the door, Swift told the young man that, given his philosophy, the following should prove no obstacle to his entry – and shut the door in Berkeley's face.

Swift poked fun at the pretensions of reason. He enjoyed paradoxes as instructive embarrassments to logic. With legal conundrums, practical reason gets its comeuppance. In *Memoirs of Martinus Scriblerus* (1741), Swift and Alexander Pope describe a will in which Sir John Swale bequeaths to Matthew Stradling 'all my black and white Horses'. There are 18 horses: six black, six white, and six pied horses. Should Matthew get the horses that have white and black patches?

We are plunged into an antinomy: Proof of the affirmative: 'Whatever is Black and White is Pyed, and whatever is Pyed is Black and White; ergo, Black and White is Pyed, and, vice versa, Pyed is Black and White.'

Proof of the negative: 'A pyed Horse is not a white Horse, neither is a pyed a black Horse; how then can pyed Horses come under the Words of black and white Horses?'

Swift believed that reason needs to be humbled because reason is dangerous. Fanatics are all too comprehensible when they reason through to logical conclusions.

In 'A Modest Proposal', Jonathan Swift campaigned for destitute Irish children by arguing with dispassionate utilitarian logic that they be eaten. To be effective, Swift had to argue impeccably. If he reasoned sloppily, the friends of reason would just trace the horrible conclusion to *insufficient* reason. To show the need for instinct, the satirical irrationalist must reason superbly.

Swift composed conceptually interesting poetry:

So nat'ralists observe, a flea
Hath smaller fleas that on him prey,
And these have smaller fleas that bite 'em,
And so proceed *ad infinitum*.

This verse, from 'On Poetry: A Rhapsody', alludes to a part–whole relationship in which each part has a part.[17] So there is infinite divisibility without any bottom layer to reality. Matter that has this structure is now called 'gunk'.

Gunk is bad news for reductionists who believe that parts are more basic than wholes they compose. For instance, reductionists believe that the handle and blade of an axe are prior to the object they compose. They are happy to lengthen the chain of dependence. Iron atoms are prior to the blade. Their idea is that explanations scale *up*. They start from the littlest things and explain the whole in terms of these parts. If there is gunk, this bottom–up explanatory strategy has no bottom and so cannot get started.

Gunk is good news for those who hold the reverse view that wholes are prior to their parts. Their explanations dangle downwards from the One to the many. The Cosmos stands to its constituents as a circle stands to its semicircles. The halves are derived from whole circle, not vice versa. Reality has a top–down direction. That's why the valves and muscles that compose the heart must be understood in terms of the whole organ. This top–down direction also explains why the organs must in turn be understood in terms of the whole organism. And so on up to the level of species and beyond. Each thing belongs to a system of nested parts and wholes. The only thing that is not dependent on anything higher is the Cosmos.

The logical structure of this debate caught the eye of Augustus De Morgan. In *A Budget of Paradoxes* (1872), he continues Swift's verse to show how Reality might be *both* bottomless and topless:

---

[17] By 'part' I mean 'proper part', a part that is not equivalent to the whole. You are an improper part of yourself just as the set {a, b} is an improper subset of itself.

> Great fleas have little fleas upon their backs to bite 'em,
> And little fleas have lesser fleas, and so *ad infinitum*.
> And the great fleas themselves, in turn, have greater fleas
>   to go on,
> While these again have greater still, and greater still, and
>   so on.

De Morgan is envisaging both gunk and its reversal knug (the backwards spelling of 'gunk') . Knug is matter in which each whole is part of some bigger whole. Suppose our world is a particle in a larger world that is itself a particle in a yet larger world. That is knug. Suppose each particle of your body is composed of a miniature world – and that each particle in that miniature world is composed of still smaller worlds, *ad infinitum*. That is gunk.

Swift's thought: Crush a flea and you crush a Russian doll sequence of littler and littler worlds. De Morgan's thought: Our world may also be in a Russian doll sequence – crushed with as little thought as we crush a flea. Swift believed men overestimate the power of reason and underestimate the sagacity of animal instinct. His symbol of this hubris about reason is Smiglesius (1564–1618). Although now obscure, Smiglesius was a Polish Jesuit philosopher, known in Swift's day for his 1618 textbook *Logica*. Smiglesius is now remembered chiefly for being targeted by Swift in 'The Logicians Refuted':

> Logicians have but ill defined
> As rational, the human kind;
> Reason, they say, belongs to man,
> But let them prove it if they can.
> Wise Aristotle and Smiglesius,
> By ratiocinations specious,
> Have strove to prove, with great precision,
> With definition and division,
> *Homo est ratione praeditum*;
> But for my soul I cannot credit 'em,
> And must, in spite of them, maintain,

That man and all his ways are vain;
And that this boasted lord of nature
Is both a weak and erring creature;
That instinct is a surer guide
Than reason, boasting mortals' pride;
And that brute beasts are far before 'em.

Despite exalting instinct, Swift had a great fear of losing his reason. He detected signs of his mental decline. Pointing to a dying tree, he bitterly remarked, 'I shall be like that tree, I shall die at the top.'

And he did so horribly. One of Swift's eyes swelled to the size of an egg. The eye bothered him so much that two minders had to be employed to prevent Swift from plucking it out. Swift's swollen eye may have been just as much an influence in August De Morgan's metaphor as his own withered eye. (De Morgan has detailed discussion of Swift's satires of scientists in a *Budget of Paradoxes*.)

Why did the Cyclops quit teaching? Because he only had one pupil. Why did De Morgan quit teaching? On principle, twice! De Morgan insisted on religious neutrality. When he believed the university violated the policy, he resigned. De Morgan died a few years after his resignation in 1871 of nervous prostration.

A Pyramid Schema

When I taught logic, a mathematics student pointed to ∴ and asked 'What is that?' How could he be ignorant of this common abbreviation? Retaining my professionalism, I gently answered 'Therefore'. 'Thank you, Professor, but don't you mean there are *three*?'

Well, I had not heard all the maths jokes yet! In *A History of Mathematical Notations*, Florian Cajori traces the pyramid of dots ∴ to Johann Rahn's German edition of *Teutsche Algebra* (1659). Inverting the dots from ∴ to ∵ yields the because sign.

In addition to brevity, ∴ has the aesthetic advantage of

symmetry. ∴ provides a general schema for palindromic arguments. Just fill in the blank with a palindrome:

_____ ∴ _____

Macbeth's witches are ugly, but they may reason beautifully:

FAIR IS FOUL ∴ FOUL IS FAIR.

As a *memento mori*, the hags can answer 'Shall we all die?' with

We shall die all ∴ All die shall we.

Or we might answer directly with a palindrome of 'Shall we all die?': 'Die all we shall.' The witches traffic in word-level palindromes. Are there letter-level palindromic arguments? Here is a Japanese import:

A Toyota's a Toyota ∴ A Toyota's a Toyota

The argument is circular but it still compels assent. The conclusion is a *tautological* echo of the premise.

A mathematician can construct palindromic arguments without leaving mathematical notation:

$$111111111 \times 111111111 = 12345678987654321 \therefore 12345678987654321 = 111111111 \times 111111111$$

while his North American[18] colleague in botany can compose palindromic arguments to commemorate the close of another fall semester:

...
    leaves
       fall

        ∴

          fall
            leaves
              ...

---

[18] 'Fall' may originate from the Middle English 'fall of the leaf'. However, the British adopted 'autumn'. In the United States and Canada, 'autumn' sounds archaic and poetic. Our lyrical botanist can hope that 'fall' sounds that way to British readers.

The Eighteenth Camel

The life of the law has not been logic; it has been experience...
The law embodies the story of a nation's development through
many centuries, and it cannot be dealt with as if it contained
only the axioms and corollaries of a book of mathematics.

Oliver Wendell Holmes, Jr

There is an old Arab inheritance puzzle that illustrates the difference between two kinds of judges. A man has died leaving
his camels to his three sons. 'I bequeath my eldest son half
of my camels, my middle son a third, and my youngest son a
ninth.' The sons discover there are seventeen camels. Seventeen is a prime number. Two, three, or nine cannot divide it.
The sons squabble.

Hearing the dispute, a butcher offers his services. The
oldest son is tempted. But the middle son objects that sixteen
live camels is not divisible by three. The butcher suggests he
reduce the herd to fifteen. But the youngest son objects that
fifteen is not divisible by nine.

The sons dismiss the butcher and resume their debate. Their
wives, hands over their ears, send for a judge who has recently
retired to their formerly quiet neighbourhood. The old man
studies the will. The judge announces that he values peace
among neighbours so much that he will donate his own camel.
That will change the number to eighteen. The sons calculate
their shares: $18/2 = 9$ camels to the eldest, $18/3 = 6$ camels
to the middle son, and $18/9 = 2$ camels to the youngest. That
leaves one camel as a remainder, so the judge takes back the
camel he donated. All the parties to the dispute are satisfied.
Tranquillity returns to the neighbourhood.

In the nearby town there is a younger judge. He strives for
clearly reasoned verdicts.

♀ How would the second kind of judge handle the problem?

The Negation Test for Nonsense

One *quick* test for nonsense is to inject a negation into the text. If this does not disturb the meaning, then there was no meaning to disturb. 'All mimsy were the borogoves' is nonsense because 'Not all mimsy were the borogoves' fails to reverse the meaning.

To test for bullshit,[19] Gerald Cohen applies a new-fangled version of the test framed in terms of plausibility rather than meaning. Following Arthur Brown, Cohen classifies a statement as bullshit if adding or subtracting 'a negation sign from a text makes no difference to its level of plausibility: no force in a statement has been grasped if its putative grasper would react no differently to its negation from how he reacts to the original statement' (Cohen, *Finding Oneself in the Other*, 2012, pp. 105–6).

Cohen applies his plausibility test against the following statement from the Marxist Étienne Balibar: 'This is precisely the first meaning we can give the idea of dialectic: a logic or form of explanation specifically adapted to the determinant intervention of class struggle in the very fabric of history.' (Cohen, 2012, p. 108 fn. 29). Cohen declares the statement to be bullshit.

This plausibility condition inflicts collateral damage for statements that are equiprobable with their negations. Adding a negation sign to 'The number of stars is even' does not yield a statement that differs in plausibility.

The old semantic criterion correctly classifies the above cases as meaningful. But it must be used carefully when 'not' is used to strengthen the act of denying rather than negating content. It is well known that extra negations are sometimes used to intensify denial rather than to reverse the content: 'I didn't go nowhere today.'

---

[19] I apologise for lumbering the reader with another technical term. In *On Bullshit*, Harry Frankfurt argues that the bullshitter promotes a reputation by means of assertions that are indifferent to the truth. Cohen switches the focus from the speaker's motives to what he says. For instance, Cohen characterises Étienne Balibar's writings as bullshit but denies that Barber is a bullshitter.

Less well known is Paul Postal's remarkable discovery that there are English constructions in which 'not' can be added or removed without a change of meaning:

(1) Eddie knows squat about phrenology.
(2) Eddie doesn't know squat about phrenology.

Sentences (1) and (2) mean that Eddie knows nothing about phrenology. But Cohen's test misclassifies this equivalence as an absence of meaning.

Postal notes that other 'vulgar minimisers' depolarise negation: *jack, beans, diddly,* and more relevantly for Professor Cohen, *shit.* As I heard one gardener complain of an apprentice, 'He knows shit about shit.' Smelling fresh manure mixed in with year-old manure, I had to agree, 'Yup, he doesn't know shit about shit.' In addition to vulgar minimisers, Postal notes other forms of negation indifference:

(3) a. That'll teach you not to tease the alligators.
    b. That'll teach you to tease the alligators.
(4) a. I wonder whether we can't find some time to shoot pool this evening.
    b. I wonder whether we can find some time to shoot pool this evening.
(5) a. You shouldn't play with the alligators, I don't think.
    b. You shouldn't play with the alligators, I think.
(6) a. I couldn't care less about monster trucks.
    b. I could care less about monster trucks.

There might be a way to apply the logician's model of negation – after heavy syntactical computation. These complications prevent the negation test from always being a *quick* test.

UN intervention can backfire: 'President Ford's shoelaces were loosened' is confirmed rather than contradicted by 'President Ford's shoelaces were unloosened'. The negation test trips over words that are ambiguous between contrary meanings: oversight (attention/inattention), buckle (secure/collapse), and sanction (permit/restrict).

The potential for misunderstanding is exploited in the

Amelia Bedelia children's books. She is a literal-minded maid who follows figures of speech to their logical conclusion. When told to dust the furniture, Amelia adds dust instead of removing dust. Readers can just as well say either

(7) a. Amelia Bedelia is dusting the furniture.
    b. Amelia Bedelia is not dusting the furniture.

Thank goodness Amelia can always win everybody back by baking a delicious pie!

And let us not forget pragmatics – the way people use language. You do not hear 'Now you see it and now you don't' as a contradiction. You find a consistent interpretation by indexing the first 'now' to an earlier time than the second 'now'. We manipulate the background so that the foreground makes sense. Viewing the losing boxer, a physician says, 'The champ gave him a good beating.' Onlookers would have also agreed if the physician had said, 'The champ gave him a bad beating.' For the audience will just switch the terms of evaluation to make the speaker's utterance sensible.

Standards also shift for rough attributions of shapes. If a tourist says Slovenia is shaped like a chicken, then you will agree:

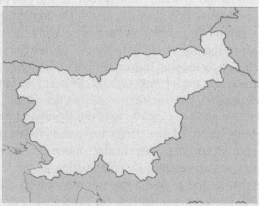

This comparison will help you remember the shape of the country and identify it on a map. But if another speaker says

'Slovenia is not shaped like a chicken', then you will notice differences. You raise the standards so that the new speaker prevails.

Final exhibit: the *Daily News* once ran a story saying that half of the Members of Parliament were crooks. The government demanded a retraction. The editors were contrite, assuring their readers the very next day that half of the Members of Parliament were not crooks.

Shifty O's

I was interested in numbers from a very early age. When I was five, I said to my mother on a walk one day, 'Isn't it strange that if a zero comes at the end of a number it means a lot but if it is at the beginning, it doesn't mean anything?'

Hans Bethe, quoted in Jeremy Bernstein's *A Child's Garden of Science*

'A circle is a round straight line with a hole in the middle.'

Mark Twain, quoting a schoolchild in 'English as She Is Taught', *Century Magazine*, May 1887

In 1773 there was born a thoroughbred racehorse: Potooooooooo. ♀ How was 'Potooooooooo' pronounced?

In an Abbott and Costello comedy routine, the pair conspire against a performer in a guessing game. The performer picks a number behind Lou Costello's back, displaying the number on a poster to the audience. Bud Abbott can see the number and signals Lou by tapping him on the back with a newspaper. The scheme works for 3 (three taps on the back) and they win the bet. Surprised, the performer asks to bet again, double or nothing. He picks 7. Costello gets the signal and picks the number. Very surprised, the performer pleads to bet one last time, double or nothing. The cheaters agree. The performer then selects a card reading 0, emphasising to his laughing audience that he has picked a fine number indeed. Abbott is flummoxed. Costello is impatient for his signal. ♀ How does Abbott finally get Costello to utter the correct answer?

A Plenum of Palindromes
for Lewis Carroll

'When I make a word do a lot of extra work like that,'
said Humpty Dumpty, 'I always pay it extra.'

Lewis Carroll, *Through the Looking Glass*

Imagine old British ten-shilling notes serenely floating in water. Now make those bob bob by tossing in another ten bob. The new bob bob bob. Bob that bob bob, may themselves bob bob. In that case, bob bob bob bob bob. In other words, ten-shilling notes [that] ten-shilling notes bob [also] bob ten-shilling notes. By throwing bob after bob into the water, we can make bob bob *ad infinitum*.

Transitive verbs that are also plural nouns often form grammatical sentences by repetition: fish, perch, seal. Mathematical linguists call these star words. S* denotes the set of sentences of the form SSS ... S. Officially then, a word S is a star (*) word if any sequence SSS ... S is a grammatical sentence. BOB is a star word.

BOB is also a palindrome. Palindromes, such as 'radar', read the same backwards and forwards. Hence the sentences formed by repeating BOB are themselves palindromes. Linguists characterise palindromic sentences, such as 'Step on no pets', as among the most difficult sentences to construct. Georges Perec won acclaim for constructing a palindrome (about palindromes!) of over 5,000 letters. In contrast, BOB palindromes are easy. You just write one BOB after another.[20]

The composition of long palindromes is eased by BOB being an ambigram. An ambigram is a word that looks the same in a mirror or when rotated. In particular, BOB is a horizontal ambigram. If you hold a mirror beneath the word, the reflection looks the same as the word. Just picture BOB sitting at the edge of a tranquil pond:

---

[20] Watch your step in this footnote. POOP is another unlimited palindrome.

BOB

BOB's horizontal reflection is BOB. This holds even if BOBs are stacked on top of each other. Consequently, holding a mirror beneath several lines of BOB text doubles the amount of BOB text.

I became interested in BOB because of an ambition to write the longest palindromic poem in honour of Lewis Carroll. Before BOB, palindrome construction was a cottage industry. Now the door is open to mass production. To top Georges Perec's record, I programmed my computer to assemble a 50 × 50 matrix of BOBs. The resulting square palindrome, BIG BOB, is also the longest ambigrammatic poem. I underscore this feature by inviting inquirers to place a mirror beneath the poem.

Although my ambigrammatic palindrome was easy to write, it is a hard poem to understand. Noam Chomsky's colleagues at MIT could interpret BIG BOB with the help of pencil and paper. But the meaning is too complex to work out in your head. Transformational grammarians make no concession to convenience or style when distinguishing between grammatical and ungrammatical sentences. The mind-numbingly repetitive 'Darwin's father's father's father's father's father's father was a human being' is grammatical solely because it satisfies the rules that constitute competence in English. These linguists sharply distinguish between competence and performance.

In *Through the Looking Glass*, Alice is given an oral examination. The White Queen asks 'What's one and one and one and one and one and one and one and one and one and one?' Alice confesses she does not know. She lost count. The Red Queen concludes Alice can't add. Alice's ignorance is better explained as an effect of limited short-term memory. Knowing arithmetic is a matter of knowing the general rules rather than knowing the particular cases. Similarly, a speaker's inability to understand a sentence may be due to shortcomings of retention and patience. Most people who have mastered English are fooled into dismissing 'garden path' sentences as ungrammatical. For instance, 'The prime number few' looks ill formed until one sees how it behaves in 'The mediocre are many but the prime number few.' So although long BOB sentences are 'unacceptable', they are grammatical sentences of English.

Acrostic verse was a favourite among Lewis Carroll's fellow Victorians. In this genre, parts of each line spell out something meaningful when read horizontally. *Through the Looking Glass* closes with an acrostic poem that reveals Alice's identity: The initial letters of each verse collectively spell ALICE PLEAS-ANCE LIDDELL. In double-acrostics, the endings of the line also form a message. Lewis Carroll appears to have generalised the idea of an acrostic in the following poem:

I	often	wondered	when	I	Cursed
Often	feared	where	I	would	Be
Wondered	where	she'd	yield	her	love
When	I	yield,	so	will	she
I	would	her	will	be	pitied
Cursed	be	love!	She	pitied	me

I have used a 6 × 6 matrix to show that the verses read the same column by column as they do row by row. The poem was first published by Trevor Wakefield in his *Lewis Carroll Circular* No. 2 (November 1974). His attribution to Lewis Carroll is not certain. The poem was quoted in a letter written to the *Daily Express* (1 January 1974) by someone who alludes to a privately printed book entitled *Memoirs of Lady Ure*. Wakefield says that no one has located a copy of this book.

Acrostic verse can be further generalised to the idea of a no-nonsense poetry. 'Jabberwocky' is a nonsense poem because it makes no sense even when read as Carroll intended. Normal poems fall into an intermediate case; they make sense when read as the poet intended but not when read out of order. No-nonsense poetry makes sense every which way:

BOB	BOB	BOB	BOB	BOB	BOB
BOB	BOB	BOB	BOB	BOB	BOB
BOB	BOB	BOB	BOB	BOB	BOB
BOB	BOB	BOB	BOB	BOB	BOB
BOB	BOB	BOB	BOB	BOB	BOB
BOB	BOB	BOB	BOB	BOB	BOB

Like Carroll's generalised acrostic, this poem makes sense when read vertically or horizontally. But LITTLE BOB also makes sense given any combination of any number of cells. It is impossible to form an ungrammatical verse.

The longest nonsense poem in the English language is *The Hunting of the Snark*. In 1874, a solitary verse occurred to Lewis Carroll: 'For the Snark *was* a Boojum, you see.' Carroll attached no meaning to the line. But it inspired him to work forward, or rather, backward, until he had an epic poem that ended with exactly that verse. As a logician, Carroll was used to working backward. Proofs are commonly constructed by starting with the conclusion and then reasoning backward to the premises.

BIG BOB is the longest no-nonsense poem. It is much easier to memorise. Members of the BOB family are readily abbreviated. For instance, LITTLE BOB condenses to $BOB^{6,6}$ (a two-dimensional matrix, basically a 6×6 square of BOBs). This notation addresses any concern that the BOB poems are too long to recite. Poetry readings in this genre could be super-scripted into five-second presentations. People on the go will also appreciate the theoretical possibilities suggested by matrix notation. Poetry can go three-dimensional with $BOB^{6,6,6}$. (Biblical scholars will readily distinguish this cubic poem from BEAST BOB whose designation is BOB^{666}.) Mathematicians do not shy away from the fourth dimension, and so will quickly reach for the hypercube, $BOB^{6,6,6,6}$. The BOB poems are esoteric. Normally a poem is esoteric because it involves arcane knowledge. The BOB genre owe their difficulty to our trouble in deploying our linguistic competence. There are no hidden facts but plenty of hidden meanings.

Enough! As my literary friends have advised me, we should not become preoccupied with the literal meaning of a poem. A poem opens many dimensions of aesthetic appreciation. I have already dwelt on how symmetrical BIG BOB looks – especially in the mirror. And BIG BOB sounds good too. Nowadays you are lucky to just get the last words of a poem to harmonise. BIG BOB and his kin really deliver on the rhymes.

An epic poem ought to have a moral. What BIG BOB teaches us is that there are palindromes of every finite length. Therefore, there are infinitely many palindromes. Yet no palindrome is infinitely long. After all, a palindrome must read the same way backwards. If the sentence went on for ever, where would one begin the reversal? The end?

Pining for the Impossible

In his 1947 article 'The Claims of Philosophy', A. J. Ayer argues that the question 'What is the meaning of life?' falsely presupposes that it is possible for there to be an ultimate purpose of our existence.

> Consequently, the fact that they are disappointed is not, as some romanticists would make it, an occasion for cynicism or despair. It is not an occasion for any emotional attitude at all. And the reason why it is not is just that it could not conceivably have been otherwise. If it were logically possible for our existence to have a purpose, in the sense required, then it might be sensible to lament the fact that it had none. But it is not sensible to cry for what is logically impossible. If a question is so framed as to be unanswerable, then it is not a matter for regret that it remains unanswered.

After Sadi Carnot proved that perpetual motion machines are impossible, engineers stopped longing for them.

The same goes for impossibilities imposed by physical *constants*. Edward Teller was reluctant to abandon his initial recipe for a hydrogen bomb, 'the classical Super', despite growing evidence that his pet idea was infeasible. Eventually, his subordinate Stanislaw Ulam recruited Enrico Fermi to help demonstrate its physical impossibility:

> In the final report that the two men wrote Fermi puckishly defined the difficulty as one that would vanish if only the basic physical constants would be changed: 'If the cross sections for the nuclear reactions could somehow be two or three times larger than what was measured and assumed, the reaction could behave more successfully.'
>
> – Richard Rhodes, *The Making of the Atomic Bomb*, p. 456

Fermi was teasing Teller. After Teller relented, Ulam was freed to develop another idea that succeeded. Teller's sluggish recognition of the impossibility resulted in much wasted time and effort. At least for practical projects, the personal and social pressure to align hopes and fears with objective possibilities is strong.

Hans Bethe opposed the development of the hydrogen bomb. He hoped it was impossible. Once the development programme was adopted, he joined the team for two reasons. He had a motive to prove the impossibility of the hydrogen bomb and so might discover the proof in time to prevent much wasted effort. Second, if the bomb were developed, his contribution would give him enough standing to restrain its use. This is what actually happened. By his own description, Bethe played a Socratic role:

> After the H-bomb was made, reporters started to call Teller the father of the H-bomb. For the sake of history, I think it is more precise to say that Ulam is the father, because he provided the seed, and Teller is the mother, because he remained with the child. As for me, I guess I am the midwife.

Bethe campaigned with the Emergency Committee of Atomic Scientists against nuclear testing and the nuclear arms race. He helped the passage of the 1963 Partial Nuclear Test Ban Treaty. Bethe showed that decoys would easily overwhelm an intercontinental anti-missile system. This helped the passage of 1972 Anti-Ballistic Missile Treaty (SALT I). In 1995, Bethe called for all scientists to stop working on any aspect of nuclear weapons development and manufacture.

Wishing can be dispositional or occurrent (an actual mental act of wishing). Bethe's occurrent wishing for impossibility of the hydrogen bomb may have ended on 1 November 1952 with the successful testing on Eniwetok, an atoll in the Pacific Ocean.

Occurrent wishes generally require triggering of the disposition. Annoying sounds are effective triggers because human beings have trouble adapting to them. This includes sounds that other people find pleasant:

> Dr Johnson was observed by a musical friend of his to
> be extremely inattentive at a concert, whilst a celebrated
> solo player was running up the divisions and subdivisions
> of notes upon his violin. His friend, to induce him to
> take greater notice of what was going on, told him how
> extremely difficult it was. 'Difficult do you call it, Sir?'
> replied the Doctor; 'I wish it were impossible.'

Johnson wishes something to be impossible. Can we get to the positive case of recognising something is impossible but still wishing it?

Yes! Anything that is possible is necessarily possible. So Samuel Johnson was lamenting something that he had always known to be a necessary truth, that is, that violin playing is possible. After all, what is actual is possible and whatever is possible is necessarily possible.

Johnson's regret is stable. He is not suffering a temporary disappointment that could be expected to pass with time. For he cannot adapt to unwanted sound.

Johnson was not being eccentric. A desire for the impossible can be kindled by someone who has always believed the proposition to be possible. For they may have instead been ignorant that the proposition is nearly impossible. News that a bad event would have been impossible had conditions been slightly different makes us wish that the bad thing was impossible.

This trigger for desire may have evolved from our interest in preventing bad events. Although we cannot stop the original bad event we may be able to exploit the information to prevent similar bad events.

This line of reasoning is a resource for the pessimist David Benatar, author of *Better to Have Never Been: The Harm of Coming into Existence*. What should his attitude be to news from astronomers that life is a near miss of a physical impossibility? Had the physical constants been only slightly different, molecules necessary for life could not have formed. If the physicist were to go on emphasising how difficult it is for life to begin, Benatar could echo Johnson, 'Difficult, do you call it, sir? I wish it were impossible.'

Anything Is Possible?

There seems to be a consensus:

> There is nothing impossible to him who will try.
>
> Alexander the Great

The Greek classicists I have consulted missed this remark by Aristotle's student. Fortunately, early motivational thinkers have been more observant. Orison Swett Marden reports Alexander said this when taking charge of an attack on a fortress, in *Pushing to the Front, or, Success under Difficulties: A Book of Inspiration* (1896, p. 55).

> The word impossible is not in my dictionary.
>
> Napoleon Bonaparte

Napoleon wrote something at least close to this in a letter to General Lemarois on 9 July 1813. But Napoleon casts his point generally, that 'impossible' is not in the French language. That is why 'impossible' is not in the general's dictionary. This lexical gap must have been highly motivating to those French patriots who spoke a language with more expressive power than French.

Every noble work is at first impossible.

Thomas Carlyle, *Past and Present*, Chap. 11

The best scientist is open to experience and begins with romance – the idea that anything is possible.

Ray Bradbury, *Los Angeles Times*, 9 August 1976

When you're surrounded by people who share a passionate commitment around a common purpose, anything is possible.

Howard Schultz, founder of Starbucks, supplier of caffeinated beverages that put the exclamation mark in 'Anything is possible!'

It's kind of fun to do the impossible.

Walt Disney (attributed by Derek Walker in *Animated Architecture*, 1982, p. 10)

If people take anything from my music, it should be motivation to know that anything is possible, as long as you keep workin' at it and don't back down.

Marshall Bruce Mathers III, rapper performing under the stage name 'Eminem', *The Dark Story of Eminem* by Nick Hasted, p. 32

♀ Question: But really, is anything possible?

Half Full or Half Empty?

A 400-millilitre cup contains 200 millilitres of water. Is the cup half full or half empty?

Both. The cup is both half full *and* half empty because the three remaining alternatives are false:

1. The glass is half full but not half empty.
2. The glass is not half full but is half empty.
3. The glass is neither half full nor half empty.

Answering 'Half full' is more *helpful* than answering 'Half empty' when describing a process of filling. That conveys the existence of an end state. But the helpfulness of the remark involves more than its truth.

This book is radioactive. Even you are a little radioactive. But it was not helpful of me to bring that up. Just mentioning the book's radioactivity suggests the fact is relevant, as it would be if the book was dangerously radioactive. Marie Curie's century-old notebook is helpfully described as radioactive; it is kept in a lead-lined box at France's Bibliothèque nationale.

Debates about whether a glass is half full or half empty are proxy conflicts over the appropriateness of descriptions. People are debating the metalinguistic question: Is it more appropriate to answer 'Half full' or 'Half empty'? If a husband is halfway through filling his glass and his wife is halfway through emptying her glass, then his glass is half full while her glass is half empty. Or more carefully, his glass is more helpfully described as 'half full' while her glass is more helpfully described as 'half empty'.

The quotation marks show we have shifted from the material mode (talking about things) to the formal mode (talking about representations of things). The strategy of semantic ascent is to switch from a controversy about objects to the less controversial topic of how the relevant words work. If a neuroscientist says that there are auras, you are prudent to check how the term 'aura' is used.

Choices between logically equivalent descriptions can convey empirical information. 'Some chimps are vicious animals' conveys more about chimps than 'Some vicious animals are chimps.' But the extra information is coming from how the speaker has chosen to express the fact, not the fact itself.

Here is a related but much less discussed question. A cup is full of water. Is the cup half full?

Yes. Suppose you rent a car that only has half a tank. You are responsible for filling the tank to its original level. You return the car with a full tank. Have you failed to fulfil your obligation?

'Full' does not preclude 'half full'. 'Full' *entails* 'half full'. ('Full' does preclude 'Exactly half full'.)

A full cup of water is also 3/4 full, 7/8 full, and so on, for infinitely many amounts below full. We should not *describe* the cup that way. We should make the strongest relevant remark. Anything weaker suggests, but does not entail, that the stated amount is the exact amount.

Towards the end of an overnight, trans-Atlantic flight, our Norwegian pilot awakened us with 'We almost made it.' That got my attention! I recalled that Bertrand Russell crashed in a seaplane near Trondheim. Only passengers in the rear of the plane survived. Before the flight, Russell had insisted on a seat in the smoking compartment, saying, 'If I cannot smoke, I should die.'

Our Norwegian pilot had spoken truthfully. Any flight that gets all the way gets almost all the way, three quarters of the way, and halfway.

The Scientific Drinker

My friend loves wine. His liver will not argue over taste. A physician, however, spoke up for the shy organ: 'Your liver needs a month off each year.' Being a logician, my friend chose February.

This deduction would not impress John Stuart Mill. Nor would any deduction. Mill believed that deductive arguments merely unpacked information stored in the premises. A valid deduction will always beg the question. For any doubt about the conclusion should spread back to the premises that entail it.

So why do we bother with deduction? Storage and easy access – deduction lets us pack what we learned from other sources and unpack it quickly. Deduction plays the same role as mnemonics. We can remember principles with the ditty:

Minus times Minus equals Plus
The reason for this we need not discuss.

'Mnemonic' is itself a mnemonic for the Poisson distribution formula:

$$P_m(n) = m^n e^{-m}/n!$$

In other words, 'm to the n times e to the $^{-m}$ divided by n factorial'.

Do you have trouble remembering how *mnemonics* is spelled? William D. Harvey offers a mnemonic for spelling mnemonics: 'Mnemonics neatly eliminate man's only nemesis: insufficient cerebral storage.'

Only induction *increases* knowledge beyond what is contained in premises.[21] Yet all logicians before Mill focus on deduction. Mill inaugurated inductive logic by formulating rules for finding causal relationships. The method of difference says X is the cause if the effect disappears when X is removed. If you subtract alcohol from beer, you do not get drunk. So alcohol is the cause of inebriation. Mill's method of concomitant variation infers causes from correlation. The more alcohol you drink, the drunker you get. So your inebriation is caused by alcohol. Mill's method of residues says the cause is the leftover factor. A nauseous physiologist will foresee a tidy opportunity to weigh his stomach contents. He will weigh himself before and after emesis.

Sir Walter Raleigh applied the method of residues in a bet with Queen Elizabeth. Raleigh claimed he could weigh the smoke from his tobacco pipe. The Royal Curiosity piqued, Elizabeth accepted the wager. Raleigh first weighed his tobacco. Then the gentleman smoked his pipe. Finally, Raleigh weighed the ashes that remained, calculating that the smoke equalled the difference between the burnt tobacco and the original tobacco. The Queen was a good sport. She paid Sir Walter Raleigh the wager and a compliment: 'I have seen many a man turn his gold into smoke but you are the first who has turned his smoke into gold.'

---

[21] An inductive reasoner tries to make the conclusion *probable* relative to his premises. He concedes that it is possible for his premises to be true and his conclusion false. Whereas a deductive reasoner aims for a conditional probability of 1, an inductive reasoner modestly aims for a high conditional probability.

If the Queen had consulted Robert Boyle, she would have doubted that Raleigh succeeded in weighing smoke. Boyle had burned tin and found that its weight *increased* (about 25%). So either something is added by burning tin or the bit that is subtracted has negative weight (*levity* according to some later chemists). Tobacco does weigh less after burning. But maybe something was added to the ash. Or maybe something gets added to the smoke from the air. Leonardo da Vinci recognised that smoke is complicated stuff. He distinguished between the black smoke of carbonised particles and the white 'smoke' of water particulates in suspension.

Early chemists conducted their measurements with uncovered containers. They did not realise that the method of residues requires a closed environment. Biologists relearned this lesson from Louis Pasteur.

One might hope to avoid these complications with the simplest of Mill's methods – the method of agreement. This is a search for a factor common to all causes of the effect. On Christmas Eve, 1926, sixty people showed up desperately ill at a New York hospital. The shared element was poisoned alcohol. Government chemists denatured alcohol used for industrial purposes. Bootleggers hired chemists to renature it. The denature–renature competition spiralled to new chemical subtlety. That year, the government chemists pulled ahead.

Sir Edward Victor Appleton won the Nobel Prize in 1947. At the banquet he gave a speech that reveals the method of agreement's dependency on *description* of causes:

Ladies and gentlemen, you should not ... overrate
scientific methods, as you will learn from the story of a
man who started an investigation to find out why people
get drunk. I believe this tale might interest you here in
Sweden. This man offered some of his friends one evening
a drink consisting of a certain amount of whisky and a
certain amount of soda water and in due course observed
the results. The next evening he gave the same friends
another drink, of brandy and soda water in the same
proportion as the previous night. And so it went on for two

more days, but with rum and soda water, and gin and soda water. The results were always the same.

He then applied scientific methods, used his sense of logic, and drew the only possible conclusion – that the cause of the intoxication must have been the common substance: namely the soda water!

– Ronald Clark, *Sir Edward Appleton*, 1971, pp. 146–7

The speech was far more amusing to the Scandinavian audience than Appleton expected. Did the story gain something in translation? Only later did Appleton learn that the Crown Prince drank only soda water.

Is Akrasia Crazy?

Socrates: 'No one who either knows or believes that there is another possible course of action better than the one he is following will ever continue on his present course' (Plato, *Protagoras*, 358b–c). For Socrates, actions speak louder than words. Many economists agree with Socrates. They propose rational models of addiction.

Most Greeks thought people do act incontinently. 'Akrasia' is the Greek term for acting against your better judgement: Medea kills her own children to spite her husband, the sirens tempt sailors on to the rocks with their beautiful song, Alexander's soldiers drink wine during their desert march knowing that this will only dehydrate them further. ♀ Is all akrasia due to an irresistible impulse?

A Cure for Incontinence![22]

Tired of being weak-willed? Do you want to end procrastination and backsliding? Are you envious of those paragons of self-control who always do what they consider best?

Thanks to a breakthrough in therapeutic philosophy, you too can now close the gap between what you think you ought to do and what you actually do. Just send $1,000 to the address below and you will never again succumb to temptation. This is a MONEY-BACK GUARANTEE. The first time you do something that you know to be irrational, your money will be refunded, no questions asked. Of course, you might nevertheless have some questions. How can you act incontinently when you know that the 'irrational' act will earn you a $1,000 refund? Well, that's what's revolutionary in this new cure for incontinence.

Old approaches focus on punishing the weak-willed. These follow the antiquated behaviourist principle that negative reinforcement extinguishes bad behaviour. The new humanitarian approach rewards incontinence – and lavishly at that. The key is to make the reward so strongly motivating that an otherwise irrational act becomes rational.

Some may seek a refund on the grounds that the reward for incontinence played no role in their (apparently) incontinent act; although aware of the reward, they would have performed the act anyway. These people should distinguish between actual and hypothetical incontinence. If you act in accordance with your judgement as to what is best overall, then you did nothing irrational.

True, the hypothetical incontinent act is a sign that you have a weak will. But the presence of this disposition gives you all the more reason to block its manifestation – by sending $1,000. Granted, there are people who cannot be swayed from temptation by a mere $1,000. These recalcitrant individuals are advised to send in more than $1,000. Give until it hurts.

---

[22] This originally appeared in the venerable journal *Mind*. The editor suggested that he place it in the Advertisements section. This led some colleagues to infer that I had found a loophole to 'Publish or Perish'.

Rush your cheque to:

Dr Roy Sorensen
Department of Philosophy
New York University
503 Main Building
100 Washington Square East
New York, New York 10003–6688[23]

Lewis Carroll's Pig Puzzles

'If it had grown up, it would have made a dreadfully
ugly child: but it makes rather a handsome pig.'

Alice, after releasing a pig that metamorphosed from a baby.

The pig is a favoured character in Alcuin of York's book of
puzzles – and subsequent medieval commentary. This affection for pigs has been passed down, logician to logician.
Porkophilia extends to authors who only benefited from light
attendance in logic classes. When a scheming girl tells an
uncooperative Bertie that he is a pig, he replies, 'A pig, maybe.

---

[23] Note from the United States Postal Service. Dr Sorensen has moved to
Washington University in St Louis. Please direct your $1,000 cheques to
his new location.

But a shrewd, level-headed pig'. (P. G. Wodehouse, *Code of the Woosters*).

The medieval sensibility about pigs is summarised by a little boy. After finishing a pork lunch, his family made an awkward encounter with playful piglets. The boy was delighted, 'Ah pigs, fun to pet and fun to eat!'

In Lewis Carroll's 'The Pig-Tale' (which originally appeared in *Sylvie and Bruno*), an ambitious pig laments not being able to jump. A frog offers to teach him for a fee. The contract is made. The frog demonstrates by jumping on to an old water pump. He urges the pig to 'bend your knees and take a hop'.

> Uprose that Pig, and rushed, full whack,
> Against the ruined Pump:
> Rolled over like an empty sack,
> And settled down upon his back,
> While all his bones at once went 'Crack!'
> It was a fatal jump.

This puts the frog in a dismal mood; he will never get his fee! Here is a logic puzzle by Lewis Carroll, 2 July 1893. ♡ What aeronautical conclusion about pigs can be deduced from the following premises?

- All who neither dance on tight-ropes nor eat penny-buns are old.
- Pigs that are liable to giddiness are treated with respect.
- A wise balloonist takes an umbrella with him.
- No one ought to lunch in public who looks ridiculous and eats penny-buns.
- Young creatures who go up in balloons are liable to giddiness.
- Fat creatures who look ridiculous may lunch in public, provided that they do not dance on tight-ropes.
- No wise creatures dance on tight-ropes if liable to giddiness.
- A pig looks ridiculous carrying an umbrella.
- All who do not dance on tight-ropes and who are treated with respect are fat.

Lewis Carroll dates his invention of word ladders to Christmas Day 1877: 'There is only one RULE for Word Ladders: Change ONLY one letter at a time and form a new word at each step.' Here is the sample that Carroll used to introduce the puzzle in *Vanity Fair* in March 1879. To change HEAD to TAIL:

HEAD, HEAL, TEAL, TELL, TALL, TAIL

In *Doublets*, Lewis Carroll has a word ladder in which he changes GNAT to BITE in six steps: GNAT, GOAT, BOAT, BOLT, BOLE, BILE, BITE. Fred Madden cites this word ladder to explain why *Through the Looking Glass* has a gnat in a railway carriage alongside a goat.

♡ Now try driving PIG into STY.

Lewis Carroll's most peculiar pig puzzle features four sties.

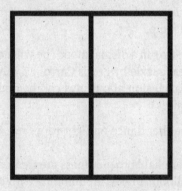

♡ Your task is to place 24 pigs in these sties so that, no matter how many times you walk around the sties, you always find that the number of pigs in each sty is closer to 10 than the number in the previous one.

A Round Trip from Small to Large

Hao Wang shrank the sorites paradox:[24]

1. One is small.
2. If n is small, then $n + 1$ is small.
3. Therefore, one octillion is small.

To emphasise how big an octillion is, Greg Ross has you imagine yourself in hell. You will be released after completing one task: 'All you have to do is type the integers, in order: ONE, TWO, and so on. The first time you strike the C key, you'll be released into paradise.' Assume it takes 10 seconds on average to correctly type each number. ♀ How long will you type before reaching the first typing of the letter C that will set you free?

♀ Now that we have scaled up to LARGE, can we use a word ladder to climb back down to SMALL?

Partway Down the Slippery Slope

Slippery slopes are so treacherous that novices are advised to avoid taking the first step. The surest way not to tumble down the mountain is to avoid gaining momentum through a first step.

But an experienced mountaineer will spot exceptional circumstances in which one can slide a few steps down. My favourite example is a foothold found in a sequence of footnotes. J. E. Littlewood had written a paper for the French journal *Comptes rendus*. A Prof. M. Riesz did the translation. To acknowledge this service, Littlewood appended three footnotes to the end of the article:

I am greatly indebted to Prof. Riesz for translating the present paper.

I am indebted to Prof. Riesz for translating the preceding footnote.

---

[24] Also known as the paradox of the heap: One grain of sand is not a heap. Adding one grain of sand to a non-heap never turns it into a heap. Therefore, a pile of a million grains of sand is not a heap.

I am indebted to Prof. Riesz for translating the preceding
footnote.

Littlewood notes that this could have gone on indefinitely,
but 'I stop legitimately at number 3: however little French I
know I am capable of copying a French sentence.'

Below are slippery-slope arguments that provide a foothold
at lower altitudes. ♀ Can you find the footholds?

One minute after noon is closer to noon than 1 p.m.
   If n minutes after noon is closer to noon than 1 p.m.,
then so is $n + 1$ minutes.
   Therefore, 59 minutes after noon is closer to noon than
1 p.m.

Any object can move at least 1 metre per second.
If an object can move at least n metres per second, then it
   can move at least $n + 1$ metres per second.
Therefore, there is no upper bound on how fast an object
   can move.

Contrapositive Thinking

Julius Caesar was an adept propagandist. He characterised
himself as the contrapositive[25] of his adversaries: 'I hold that
anyone not against me is with me; but they hold that anyone
not with them is against them.' The two propositions are logically equivalent. They are true exactly if there are no neutrals.
Yet the statements differ attitudinally towards apparent neutrals. Caesar insinuates that anyone who seems to be neutral
is really a friend. Ceasar's rivals insinuate that any apparent
neutral is really their enemy.

Contraposition is a classic formula for advertising slogans

---

[25] The contrapositive of a conditional 'If P then Q' is 'If not Q then not
P'. If contraposition is not valid, then *modus tollens* is not valid. *Modus
tollens* is valid: If P then Q, not Q, therefore, not P ... Confession I just
used contraposition to defend contraposition. To which circle of hell does
Dante assign question-beggars?

dating from George Eastman's 1913 classic 'If it isn't an Eastman, it isn't a camera.' He pioneered the contrapositive slogan as a way to protect a trademark name. When a product becomes popular, its name tends to become a generic term. Then your rivals can sell it under the well-reputed name. This was the fate of *aspirin, cellophane, escalator, dry ice,* and *thermos.*

To avoid genericide, Eastman introduced a contrapositive slogan that would become tautology if the name were generic. Hearers avoid interpreting people as making trivial remarks. They prefer to interpret the remark as a substantive remark – even if this means the substantive remark is false. So the contrapositive pressures speakers to avoid treating the trade name as generic. Notice that none of the contrapositive slogans is true – though their contrapositives are valid inferences. (If you start with a false premise, a valid inference need not yield a true conclusion.) The advertiser is hoping the slogan will make itself *less* believable.

The strategy tends to be adopted during fads. The popularity of yo-yos yo-yoes. During the 1987 yo-yo fad, Americans began to use 'duncan' indiscriminately for any yo-yo. Alarmed, the Duncan Toys Company defended their trademark name with the contrapositive slogan: 'If it isn't a Duncan, it isn't a yo-yo.'

Contrapositives themselves need brand differentiation from converses and inverses:

Plain Conditional: If p, then q.
Converse: If q, then p.
Inverse: If not p, then q.
Contrapositive: If not q, then not p.

Most teachers are content to illustrate contraposition with a single sentence. They will say that the contrapositive of 'If a giraffe has a sore throat, then he will need a big bottle of cough syrup' is 'If a giraffe does not need a big bottle of cough syrup, then he does not have a sore throat.' W. P. Cooke goes much further. He contraposed an entire song!

Here are the original lyrics of Tex Ritter's song 'Rye Whiskey':

If the ocean was whiskey and I was a duck,
I'd swim to the bottom and never come up.
But the ocean ain't whiskey and I ain't no duck,
So I'll play Jack o' Diamonds and trust to my luck.
For it's whiskey, rye whiskey, rye whiskey, I cry,
If I don't get rye whiskey, I surely will die.

Cooke presented the contrapositive lyrics in the November 1969 issue of the *American Mathematical Monthly*:

If I never reach bottom or sometimes come up,
Then the ocean ain't whiskey or I ain't a duck.
But my luck can't be trusted or the cards I'll not buck,
So the ocean is whiskey or I am a duck.
For it's whiskey, rye whiskey, rye whiskey, I cry,
If my death is uncertain then I get whiskey (rye).

Contemporary logicians analyse universal generalisations as conditionals. 'All men are mortal' means 'For all x, if x is a man then x is mortal'. So universal generalisations also have contrapositives. The contrapositive of 'All men are mortal' is 'All non-mortals are non-men'.

Contraposition has its most paradoxical effect in the Raven paradox.

1. Nicod's criterion: All universal generalisations are confirmed by positive instances. That is, 'All Fs are Gs' is confirmed by 'x is an F and a G'.
2. Contraposition: 'All Fs are Gs' is equivalent to 'All non-Gs are non-Fs'.
3. Equivalence condition: Whatever confirms a statement confirms a logically equivalent statement.
4. Therefore, a white handkerchief confirms 'All ravens are black'.

By contraposition, 'All ravens are black' is equivalent to 'All non-black things are non-ravens'. A white handkerchief is a non-black thing. So the raven generalisation predicts that it is not a raven. And it is correct! The non-black thing is a handkerchief.

Carl Hempel (1905–1997), one the most important empiricists of the twentieth century, defends the soundness of the reasoning. According to Hempel, biologists do not cite their white handkerchiefs as evidence for 'All ravens are black' because the amount of evidential support is minuscule. If I have a ticket in a million-ticket lottery and learn that your ticket is a loser, then that is a little evidence that I won. But it is too little to mention. This explains why we do not pursue indoor ornithology.

Queer Quantities

The Pythagoreans believed that the universe was governed by numbers. They recognised only the natural numbers as numbers. So everything had to be expressible in terms of relationships between these numbers. A crisis developed when they applied the Pythagorean theorem to an isoscles right triangle. For they soon realised that hypotenuse does not have a length that is expressible as a ratio between natural numbers. $\sqrt{2}$ was the original queer quantity. Pythagoreans want reality to measure up – but in the proper units!

Mrs Ellen Gould White (1827–1915), founder of the Adventist movement, had a revelation that entails irrational saints. Her discovery is rooted in three passages in Revelation (7:4, 14:1, and 14:3). These passages speak of 144,000 redeemed saints standing before God's throne. They are singing a new song, with God's name written on their foreheads. According to Revelation 7, they represent 12,000 saints from each of the 12 tribes of Israel (see also Matt. 19:28).

In a trance Mrs White saw 144,000 saints standing on a sea of glass in 'a perfect square'. Some of her followers maintained that 1,200 saints mentioned in Revelation were one side of the square. But the square root of 144,000 is not 1,200. It is the irrational number 379.47331922 …

So in addition to proving that there are saints, White has

proved that there are irrational saints. She never explicitly draws the consequence. White leaves us to do the maths: Each side of the square has 379 whole saints and one 0.47331922 ... saint. Since there are four sides, there are four of these partial saints.

There was terrestrial precedent for partial individuals in White's lifetime. American slaves counted as 2/5 of a person for calculating how many congressmen were to be allocated to each state.

In England the 1907 Deceased Wife's Sister's Marriage Act made it legal for a man to marry the sister of his deceased wife. Until 1921, however, it remained illegal for a woman to marry the brother of her deceased husband. Suppose brothers marry two sisters. One brother and his sister-in-law die. The remaining brother marries the remaining sister. This is a legal marriage for the man. However, it is not a legal marriage for the woman. So if they have a son, the child is legitimate for the father and illegitimate for the mother. Thus, their son is a half-bastard.

Paul Dirac (1902–1984) was not a half-bastard. However, he did come up with a couple of queer fish.

While a student at Cambridge, Dirac attended a mathematical congress. Participants were asked to solve an ancient English puzzle about fishermen and fish:

Three fishermen lay down to sleep, not having counted or divided their catch. They are each fair men but do not quite trust each other. The most worried fisherman wakes up. He decides to divide the pile of fish and take his share before the others awake. But the number of fish was not divisible by three. Since he could make them divisible by subtracting one fish, he throws a fish back into the water. He takes exactly a third of the remainder. His conscience was clear. He was leaving an even number of fish that could be divided in half. The fisherman departed with his share. Later, the second most anxious fisherman wakes up. In ignorance of what the first fisherman has done, he goes through the same process. He departs with his share. Still later, the third fisherman awakes in the night. In ignorance of the previous fishermen's activities, he goes through the same process. What is the minimum number of fish in the catch?

Dirac immediately answered that the fishermen had begun with –2 fish. The first fisherman threw one into the water, leaving –3. He took a third of this, leaving –2. The second and third fisherman followed suit. ♡ (Question: What was the intended, positive solution to the problem?)

The anecdote underscores Paul Dirac's emphasis on mathematical elegance rather than physical reality. This came to the fore in the discovery of the positron. In the early 1930s, Dirac was focused on an equation he had developed for explaining the electron. He noticed that the equation had two solutions just like the square root of 4. Either 2 or –2 will work from a mathematical point of view. One solution of his equation yielded the negatively charged electron. The other solution yielded an unintended particle. This 'positron' was exactly like the electron except it possessed a positive charge.

Even to Dirac, the positron seemed too strange to be taken seriously. However, a cloud chamber detector yielded a mirror image of the electron's signature. This showed the positron existed. Dirac concluded, 'The equation was smarter than I was.'

New Zealand's Arthur Prior

David Hume has persuaded almost all philosophers and scientists that one cannot validly argue from purely factual statements to evaluative ones.

But prior to Hume, ethicists did base their prescriptions on what God wills or what is natural or what is pleasurable.

In every system of morality, which I have hitherto met with, I have always remark'd, that the author proceeds for some time in the ordinary way of reasoning, and establishes the being of a God, or makes observations

concerning human affairs; when of a sudden I am
surpriz'd to find, that instead of the usual copulations of
propositions, *is*, and *is not*, I meet with no proposition
that is not connected with an *ought*, or an *ought not*.
This change is imperceptible; but is, however, of the last
consequence. For as this *ought*, or *ought not*, expresses
some new relation or affirmation, 'tis necessary that it
shou'd be observ'd and explain'd; and at the same time
that a reason should be given, for what seems altogether
inconceivable, how this new relation can be a deduction
from others, which are entirely different from it ... [I] am
persuaded, that a small attention [to this point] wou'd
subvert all the vulgar systems of morality, and let us see,
that the distinction of vice and virtue is not founded merely
on the relations of objects, nor is perceiv'd by reason.

– Hume, *Treatise of Human Nature*, §3.1.1, 'Moral
Distinctions Not Deriv'd from Reason'

Hume's point is often formulated as logical limit: there are
no valid arguments that contain solely descriptive premises
and a normative conclusion. Scientists have endorsed the
principle that they provide facts rather than values. If facts
entailed values then we could do ethics by observation and
experiment. But good and evil are not emprical properties.

The New Zealand logician A. N. Prior showed that this
cannot be strictly the case with the following specimen:

Tea-drinking is common in England.
Therefore, tea-drinking is common in England, or all New
   Zealanders ought to be shot.

The argument is sound. The first premise is true. The argument is a valid instance of the form: *P*, therefore, *P* or *Q*. The
argument is only pragmatically odd. Uttering the conclusion
makes it seem as if there is some support for the second disjunct. It is like the inference in Ross's paradox:

I ought to pay for this book.
Therefore, I ought to pay for this book or steal it.

Given the truth of 'I ought to pay for this book', the argument is sound. It is merely misleading because we generally add disjuncts only if they make the disjunction more probable. Since the tea-drinking premise is descriptive and conclusion is normative, Prior maintained that he had derived an 'ought' from an 'is'. Prior allows that others might reasonably regard disjunctions of description and normative statements to be descriptive. Instead of arguing the point, Prior just gave them a different derivation:

Tea-drinking is common in England, or all New Zealanders ought to be shot.
Tea-drinking is not common in England.
Therefore, all New Zealanders ought to be shot.

This argument has a false second premise. But it is still valid – which is all that Prior needs for a counterexample to Hume. He could have easily produced a sound argument:

Either kiwis are rare in New Zealand or mothers ought to feed their children.
Kiwis are not rare in New Zealand.
Mothers ought to feed their children.

Prior's dilemma show that Hume's thesis must be framed in terms that go outside of pure logic. To keep in the debate he must instead say that there are no *substantive*, valid derivations of an 'ought' from an 'is'.

This is more of a judgement call. Consider examples that appeal to the reliability of an expert:

Everything Alfie says is true.
Alfie says lying is wrong.
So lying is wrong.

The first premise is open to empirical refutation. So why isn't that a valid derivation? Whether these examples succeed or not, Prior performed a service by showing that Hume's thesis is not simply a point about logic.

Most Remote Capital City

💡 What capital city is most distant from any other capital city? Hint: How do you find the unique solution to a differential equation?

The Logic of 'Australia'

New Guinea is shaped like the tilde, ~ , the sign of negation:

Under this negation is Australia – providing a helpful clue to the meaning of 'Australia'. On the surface 'Australia' appears to be the *name* of the smallest continent (or the largest island). But Ludwig Wittgenstein cautioned us against our tendency to model all words on names. We must distinguish surface grammar from depth grammar.

Taking Wittgenstein's warning to heart, Mr L. Sturch plumbs the depth grammar of 'Australia'. His investigation reveals that 'Australia' is a type of negation operator applied to sentences. Thus it is a fundamental error to regard:

the question 'Is there any reason for saying that in Australia the winter is in the summer?' has the same logic as 'Is there any reason for saying that in France frogs are esteemed as a source of food?' It is a mistake to think that the name 'Australia' has the same logical grammar as 'France', 'Switzerland', 'Siberia', 'Rutlandshire', or 'North Dakota'. It is no more like such names than 'Utopia', 'Erewhon', or 'Ruritania' are. It is nonsense to say 'In Ruritania the population is increasing' unless you are playing a language-game in which it is stipulated that Ruritania is 'a real place' (to use the material mode). Now it is clear that 'Australia' is not a real place; or better, that the word 'Australia' is not a name. The words 'in Australia' are used simply to signify that the contradictory of what is stated to be the case 'in Australia' is in fact the case. Thus we say 'In Australia there are mammals that lay eggs' (meaning that there are none in reality); 'In Australia there are black swans' (meaning that all real swans are some other colour); 'In Australia people who stand upright have their heads pointing downwards' (meaning that this is self-contradictory).

Since Sturch's result is the result of a purely linguistic investigation, it cannot be a synthetic truth. Instead, it falls into the category Daniel Dennett defines in his *Philosophical Lexicon*: 'A. Priori, n. A species of undeniable truth first discovered in New Zealand.'

Predicting Your Predictor

To refute the thesis that all events are foreseeable, Michael Scriven conjures an agent 'Predictor' who has all the data, laws, and calculating capacity needed to predict the choices of others. Scriven goes on to imagine another agent, 'Avoider', whose dominant motivation is to avoid prediction. Therefore, Predictor must conceal his prediction. The catch is that Avoider has access to the same data, laws, and calculating capacity as Predictor. Thus he can duplicate Predictor's reasoning. Consequently, the predictor cannot predict Avoider. ♥ Is Scriven's refutation valid?

The Freedom of a Coin Toss

In the Coen brothers' movie *No Country for Old Men*, Anton Chigurh is a remorseless hitman. He is free from the moral inhibition against killing. Indeed, Anton revels in his capriciousness. When whimsical, Anton gives victims a chance in the form of a coin toss. If the coin is called correctly, their life will be spared. If the gamble fails, the victim has participated in their own murder. Both parties partake in this existential arbitrariness.

Anton has a moral eccentricity. Most people believe that they are obliged to keep their promises but not obliged to keep their threats. Anton rejects this asymmetry. If he makes a threat, then Anton feels obliged to execute that threat.

Anton's resolution to carry out threats is a chilling echo of Immanual Kant's resolution to carry out punishments: 'Even if a civil society resolved to dissolve itself with the consent of all its members – as might be supposed in the case of a people inhabiting an island resolving to separate and scatter themselves throughout the whole world – the last murderer lying in prison ought to be executed before the resolution was carried out.' In the *Metaphysics of Morals* Kant goes on to claim that those who shirk their duty to punish are themselves infected by the guilt.

Anton had tried to get Llewelyn Moss to give him a bag of money by telephoning a threat to kill Moss's wife. Moss had already sent his wife into hiding at her mother's. He decides to take his chances and keep the money. Anton hunts Moss down.

Anton now has the money. He has killed the man who defied his threat. Anton could safely leave with the fortune. But Anton is a man of his word.

He stalks Moss's wife. When Carla Jean returns from her mother's funeral, she discovers Anton waiting in her bedroom.

Carla Jean: You don't have to do this.

Anton [smiles]: People always say the same thing.

Carla Jean: What do they say?

Anton: They say, 'You don't have to do this.'

Carla Jean: You don't.

Anton: Okay.

[Anton flips a coin, catches it, and covers it with his hand.]

Anton: This is the best I can do. Call it.

Carla Jean: I knowed you was crazy when I saw you sitting there. I knowed exactly what was in store for me.

Anton: Call it.

Carla Jean: No. I ain't gonna call it.

Anton: Call it.

Carla Jean: The coin don't have no say. It's just you.

Anton [puzzled]: Well, I got here the same way the coin did.

Fair Tosses from an Unfair Coin

People who try to be random by flipping coins will be distressed to learn that the procedure has biases. The coin is not quite symmetrical. This yields a bias in favour of heads. The act of tossing is not quite symmetrical. This yields a bias towards the original orientation of the coin.

♀ Is there a way to get a fair toss from a biased coin?

Predicting Random Choices

You are trying to decide between free will and determinism. Conveniently, you have two friends, Freewill Frida and Determined Dennis, eager to convert you. You are welcome to visit them at any time. They live equidistant from your apartment and are connected by a subway line. Freewill Frida lives uptown. Determined Dennis lives downtown. A train leaves every 10 minutes either from your local station to Frida or to Dennis.

You decide to visit each randomly. In particular, you leave your apartment at random and board whichever train arrives first at your local station. You reckon that this will give each side an equal amount of time to make their case.

Dennis has been keeping a record of your visits. He reveals

that 90% of your visits are to him, not Frida. If your arbitrary choices were free then the number of visits should be far closer to 50%. So your 'free choices' must actually be determined. Dennis has many opportunities to re-argue this point because you continue a streak of visits to his apartment.

Finally, the streak ends. You find yourself at Frida's. How does she explain the fact that 90% of your random visits wind up at the Determinist's door?

Frida checks the train schedule. Although a train runs in either direction every 10 minutes, each uptown train to her stop is timed to arrive 1 minute after a train bound for Dennis's downtown stop. This ensures that you are likely to appear at your local station during the 9-minute interval between the departure of the train to Frida and the arrival of the train to Dennis's apartment.

Frida says the puzzle exploits our tendency to focus on our own randomness. Random agents can still be predictable if their environments are biased. You will predictably lose the lottery because your random choice fails to favour the one winning ticket among a million losers.

There could be an upscale version of the puzzle, a kind of 'pre-established harmony', in which a random agent behaves like clockwork. This is a vivid counterexample to the principle that an agent's randomness precludes the agent's predictability.

Randomness does preclude predictability relative to some search spaces. For instance, if we divide the 10-minute subway interval into equal 1-minute intervals, then there is no way to predict which interval will be picked by the random rider. Relative to that intervalled description, the subway rider is decidedly unclocklike. However, this relative unpredictability is cold comfort to those who wanted to be unpredictable relative to other sample spaces. The moral is that predictability is relative to a description. This corrects our tendency to think that randomness confers an absolute immunity to prediction.

The link between determinism and predictability has been attacked from other directions. Those who believe we are free have asserted that an agent might freely make himself predictable by, say, making appointments. Those impressed by the collectively orderly behaviour of random particles in thermodynamics have made way for sociology by inferring that the behaviour of a group can be predictable even if its members behave randomly. The novelty of the lesson drawn from the subway puzzle is that it makes the individual's particular behaviour predictable even *without* his cooperation. Moreover, the lesson is drawn in a way that brings the holistic nature of predictability plus its relativity to descriptive frameworks.

Wittgenstein on Ice

The more narrowly we examine actual language, the sharper becomes the conflict between it and our requirement. (For the crystalline purity of logic was, of course, not a *result of investigation*: it was a requirement.) The conflict becomes intolerable; the requirement is now in danger of becoming empty. – We have got on to slippery ice where there is no friction and so in a certain sense the conditions are ideal, but also, just because of that, we are unable to walk. We want to walk: so we need *friction*. Back to the rough ground!

Ludwig Wittgenstein, *Philosophical Investigations*, §107

Classic Physics Riddle: You are on a frozen lake. The ice is perfectly smooth. ♀ How can you get off the ice?

The Unbearable Lightness of Logical Conclusions

When my son Maxwell was a toddler, he did not believe he was ever an infant. This scepticism became manifest when he started identifying himself in photographs. Maxwell was accurate with photographs that were taken after age six months. But he dismissed earlier pictures as photographs of 'BABIES'.

I tried to persuade Maxwell that he was once a baby by

turning the pages of his photograph album in reverse chronological order. Since we were now beginning with the most recent photographs, Maxwell was quite confident: 'THAT'S ME!' Eventually his 'ME!'s dwindled to 'ME's, which were followed by 'Me's, then 'me's. We then reached a point when Maxwell stopped making identifications. He just smiled awkwardly, shrugged, and made this sound 'Ummm ...'

I told a friend about how Maxwell had shrugged off my photographic refutation. She agreed that my argument had true premises. She agreed that the conclusion followed from the premises. But she defended the reasonableness of Maxwell's shoulder-shrugging. She pointed out that the slippery slope could have been extended to sonograms of Maxwell. Did I think the ninth-month sonogram was of Maxwell? The eighth month? The seventh month? ... Eventually I just smiled awkwardly, shrugged, and made this sound 'Ummm ...'

Oh, there are a few people willing to go 'all the way'. Not all of them are anti-abortionists. Japanese on both sides of the abortion debate concede that they were once fertilised eggs and that it is appropriate to pray at special grave shrines for the souls of aborted fetuses. Perhaps some Japanese are willing to go back further to scattered people composed of un-united sperm and egg combinations. Rewinding further, we reach proto-sperm and proto-egg materials. And then the increasingly scattered stuff that went into all THAT. Hence, we 'discover' that each person has a kind of diffuse, backward immortality.

Maxwell's reaction to the slippery-slope argument is more sensible than this metaphysics of beginningless human beings. I say this not because there are philosophers who would agree with Maxwell's scepticism about having once been a baby. (The old Bertrand Russell questioned whether he was the same person as the young Bertrand Russell.) What makes Maxwell's shoulder-shrugging more sensible is his instinctual reluctance to follow the argument wherever it leads. Contrary to the advice of Socrates, we should treat the strangeness of our conclusions as a reason to doubt our reasoning. These doubts will lead us to reject sound arguments when their conclusions are strange but true. But we need this simple form of quality control to rationally reshape our sense of the absurd – in baby steps.

Impossible Crimes

As an articulate runaway slave, Frederick Douglass gave speeches in northern states. He introduced himself in a confessional style: 'I appear before you this evening as a thief and a robber. I stole this head, these limbs, this body from my master and ran off with them.' That would get a chuckle.

Suicide was a graver matter. Suicide was classified as murder even where slavery was regarded as an absurdity. In nineteenth-century England, anyone found guilty of deliberate self-murderer would forfeit his estate. On New Year's Eve 1819, Elton Hamond committed suicide. The 33-year-old tea dealer composed a carefully reasoned letter arguing that self-murder is impossible:

> To the charge of self-murder I plead not guilty. For there is
> no guilt in what I have done. Self-murder is a contradiction
> in terms. If the King who retires from his throne is guilty of
> high treason; if the man who takes money out of his own
> coffers and spends it is a thief; if he who burns his own
> hayrick is guilty of arson; or he who scourges himself of
> assault and battery, then he who throws up his own life
> may be guilty of murder, – if not, not.

Hamond builds methodically on his impossibility result. He also considers the possibility that his suicide be wrong on other grounds such as desertion of duty. He notes that he could have feigned mental illness but honesty compels him to forgo such subterfuge.

The jury concluded that he was insane.

Double Belief

In 'The Honour of Divine Parentage' the Irish playwright George Bernard Shaw (1856–1950) explains the origin of the Christian doctrine of the trinity. Alexander the Great claimed to be the son of Apollo (to secure supernatural authority) *and* the son of Philip (to sustain the right to succeed his father as king of Macedonia). Alexander wanted both sources of legitimacy and so insisted on both lines of descent. The Roman emperors followed Alexander's example of having both royal ancestors and divine ancestors.

According to Shaw, disciples of Jesus elaborated on the Greco-Roman model, securing the political legitimacy through the royal House of David by means of his mother's husband Joseph while simultaneously insisting on divine parentage through the Holy Ghost.

How could people back then be so illogical? Shaw thinks this capacity for irrational identity beliefs is still strong:

> Such double beliefs are entertained by the human mind
> without uneasiness or consciousness of the contradiction
> involved. Many instances might be given: a familiar one
> to my generation being that of the Tichborne claimant,
> whose attempt to pass himself off as a baronet was
> supported by an association of labourers on the ground
> that the Tichborne family, in resisting it, were trying to do
> a labourer out of his rights.

Shaw, an outspoken socialist, is referring to a butcher in Australia who claimed to be the long lost son of Lady Tichborne (lost in an 1854 shipwreck). Persuaded that her son Roger had been rescued at sea and taken to Australia, she urged his return so that he could assume his role as the Eighth Baronet. Most of the family regarded the butcher as a low-class imposter. They sought to expose him by ruses such as presenting fake relatives that he would 'recognise'. The case eventually went to court. Class ranks closed. The people of breeding opposed him, while the lower classes supported this man who shared their humble origin.

The trial was as sensational as it was lengthy. But the jury quickly convicted the butcher of perjury.

The Evil of Doing the Impossible

The difficult we do at once. The impossible takes a little longer.

Unofficial motto of the US Army Corps of Engineers

Motivational speakers agree that doing the impossible is admirable. According to them, Francis of Assisi provided a three-step approach: 'Start by doing what's necessary; then do what's possible; and suddenly you are doing the impossible.'

The first stage is certainly blameless. 'Ought' implies 'can'. If one could not have done otherwise, then the act cannot be forbidden.

The second stage is riskier. While some possible acts are permitted, others are forbidden.

The third stage is condemned by Jaakko Hintikka. Doing the impossible is terribly wrong. It is forbidden to do anything that entails the destruction of the world. Doing the impossible entails everything – including the destruction of the world. Therefore, it is forbidden to do the impossible.

What is the appropriate penalty? In 2002, the conceptual artist Jonathon Keats sponsored a petition to get Berkeley, California, to acknowledge the law of identity: Everything is identical to itself. Anyone caught being distinct from himself, within city limits, would be subject to a misdemeanour fine of up to 0.1 cent.

Why such a light penalty? Any violation of the law of identity, 'For all $x, x = x$' entails heinous crimes. I support the death penalty.

Note that I do not support the death penalty for *denying* the law of identity. The Arab commentator Avicenna (Ibn Sīnā, 980–1037) was too harsh towards those who deny the law of non-contradiction: 'As for the obstinate, he must be plunged into fire, since fire and non-fire are identical. Let him be beaten, since suffering and not suffering are the same. Let him be deprived of food and drink, since eating and drinking are identical to abstaining' (*Metaphysics*, I.8, 53.13–15). However, I do support the death penalty for those who *violate* the law of non-contradiction.

Georg Hegel believed he violated the law of non-contradiction when he walked. Crossing a room requires that you first walk halfway, then three quarters of the way, then seven eighths, and so on. But an infinite number of tasks cannot be completed in a finite amount of time. Instead of accepting Zeno's conclusion that motion is impossible, Hegel maintained that contradictions can come true. So did Karl Marx.

Did Keats have some strategic reason for attaching such a light penalty to violations of self-identity? Keats gathered only 65 signatures. He found no backers on the Berkeley City Council. Perhaps a more forceful brand of identity politics would have yielded a measure of legal protection for the principle of identity.

Identity Theft

When I began teaching logic at New York University, a purple-haired student warned me about identity theft. I was incredulous, 'That's impossible!' Sensing that I was new in town, she thickened her New York accent, 'Well I don't know where you are from, Professor, but it is possible in Manhattan.'

She was so adamant that I had a second thought: 'Well, if a thief steals my identity, then *he* will be the victim!'

Infinite Chess

Is there a number higher than infinity?
Oh yes, infinity plus shipping and handling.
Johnny Carson

♡ Can a chess game go on forever?

Consider a chessboard that is infinite in all directions. ♡ Can you checkmate a lone black king with your white king and queen?

Infinite Two-Minute Debate

The length of debate about a flight maneuver is always inversely proportional to the complexity of maneuver. Thus, if the flight maneuver is simple enough, debate approaches infinity.

Robert Livingston

A fast-talking brother and sister debate whether noon is 12:00 a.m. or 12:00 p.m. Since they are children, they agree that victory goes to whomever has the last word. (An anagram for 'negation' is: get a 'no' in.)

The fast-talking siblings are equally stubborn. When they run out of reasons, they just start gainsaying each other faster and faster: Yes, No, Yes, No, …

The pair compress their infinite debate into a period of two minutes. When n seconds remain before noon, the previous answer is contradicted after $n/2$ seconds. So the contradiction proceeds at an ever-accelerating rate:

    11:58:00 Brother: YES!
    11:59:00 Sister: NO!
    11:59:30 Brother: YES!
    11:59:45 Sister: NO!
    11:59:525 Brother: YES!

By noon, the infinite debate is over. Who won?

The victor cannot be Brother; he never said YES without his sister countering NO. Nor can Sister be the victor. She never said NO without her brother countering YES.

You cannot say: Sister. You cannot say: Brother. ♀ But mustn't it be one or the other?

Indian Debate Tournament

Those who cannot understand how to put their thoughts
on ice should not enter into the heat of debate.

Friedrich Nietzsche, *Human, All Too Human*

The tradition of debate inherited from the ancient Greeks makes it seem a Western invention. Debates outside Greek conventions tempt intervention. In the 1960s, the BBC's Michael Barratt was the moderator in a debate between spokesmen for Rhodesia's two freedom movements, Zanu and Zapu. Dissatisfied with the Africans' dialectic, Barratt interjected, 'That's all very well – but two blacks don't make a white.'

India has a tradition of debate tournaments.

Consider a tournament arranged among 29 scholars. Each debate is a one-on-one knockout match. ♀ How many debates will be needed to determine the champion?

Winning by Losing

You may already be a loser.

From a letter received by Rodney Dangerfield

There are many good losers. But who is the best loser? The question arose when a father was trying to stop his daughter from being a sore loser. Like many little girls, she found defeat so upsetting that she was reluctant to compete.

The father had long exploited his little daughter's desire to win. They competed for who could be quietest at the library, who could brush teeth longest, who could reach the bathtub first ...

The daughter complimented her father for being a very good loser. The father asked why he was such a good loser. 'Because you are fat and slow!' came her unwelcome answer.

The father decided to frame the issue to elicit a more thoughtful response: Who is better at losing – you or me? The daughter replied, 'You are the *better* loser because you have more experience at it.'

The father tweaked the question: who *won* at losing, you or me? Who was the *best* loser in the world? This put the daughter in a pensive mood. While the girl bathed, the father recalled how the Arabs speak of 'winning by losing'. For instance, they cast Gamal Abdel Nasser as the ultimate victor in his disastrous Six Day War with Israel. When Nasser resigned, the Egyptians rallied behind him. Although he had lost, Nasser had stood up to the West.

George Gamow and Marvin Stern's *Puzzle Math* has a tale of a bored Englishman in the domain of Sultan Ibn-al-Kuz. The Englishman signals two passing Bedouins who were riding by. He proposes a 'reverse race' to a distant palm tree. The man whose horse comes in last will receive a gold coin. The Bedouins are puzzled but eager for the coin. They start the race but make little progress. For each holds his horse back.

Just as they are about to give up, a dervish appears in front of them. The Bedouins jump off their horses and prostrate themselves before the dervish in the hot sand. They ask the dervish for advice about how to complete the race. The Bedouins had thought of solutions such as fixing the race or conspiring to split the money. But the dervish says that one should be honest in all dealings – even with the British. He whispers a solution into their ears. The Bedouins happily mount up and ride as quickly as they can to the palm tree. The puzzled Englishman pays the gold guinea. ♀ How did the dervish manage to resolve the Englishman's dilemma?

Five years later the daughter seemed to have forgotten all the character-building conversations about being a good loser. But then one day the father refused to give his daughter a dollar to buy candy. Thinking a minute, she cheerfully responded, 'Hey Dad, I bet you a dollar that if you give me two dollars, I'll give you three dollars.' Intrigued, he gave her two dollars. She heaved a great sigh, hung her head in defeat, and conceded, 'I lose.' She returned one dollar and then bought the candy with the remaining dollar.

Minimising Selfishness

In the 'Fool's Luck' episode of the television drama series *I, Claudius* (1976), two of the emperor's freedmen are preparing a report. Emperor Claudius favours a new port but worries about the expense. He has delegated the financial question. Narcissus tells Pallas that the estimate must wait for an engineering survey. Pallas disagrees; they should immediately report that the port would be very expensive.

> Pallas: The more expensive it is, the less likely it is it will ever be built.
>
> Narcissus: What are you suggesting? That we exaggerate the cost?
>
> Pallas: Well, my dear Narcissus, you have money in corn. I have money in corn. Lots of people have money in corn. The more corn that can be landed in winter, the lower the price will be. That worries me.
>
> Narcissus: That could be construed as a very selfish point of view.

Pallas: Is there less selfishness in wanting the price of corn to be low?

Narcissus: There are more people who want it to be low.

Pallas: Doesn't that add up to more selfishness rather than less?

Narcissus: That is sophistry. One cannot argue with you.

Pallas: Let's get the report. I'm sure the cost will take care of the philosophical considerations.

Lawrence of Arabia Collars a Leopard

♀ Why can't a leopard hide?
♀ How can a leopard change its spots?
♀ How do you collar a leopard?

In 1913, T. E. Lawrence faced the third riddle. A young leopard, a gift from a government official in Jerablus, had outgrown its collar. The leopard was an effective watchdog but had no loyalty to Lawrence.

Enticing the leopard into a box had made it even nastier. Lawrence did not want to put his hand in the box. So he stuffed the cage with canvas bags until the leopard lost freedom of movement. He then opened the top of the box, put the collar on the wedged leopard, and released the beast.

A Bridge without Pillars

Suppose I wanted to justify the choice of dimensions for a bridge which I imagine to be building, by making loading tests on the material of the bridge in my imagination. This would, of course, be to imagine what is called justifying the choice of dimensions for a bridge. But should we also call it justifying an imagined choice of dimensions?

Ludwig Wittgenstein, *Philosophical Investigations*, §267

Engineering for Astronomers: You must build a bridge over the equator. You can use scaffolding. But the final bridge must be without any pillars or other contract with the ground. That way we could give the bridge a push and it would rotate, as a moving walkway. ♀ How do you build this bridge without pillars?

Wittgenstein had been training to be an aeronautical engineer before he went into philosophy. Some of his favourite riddles were remembered from this period. One can be adapted to the equatorial bridge. ♀ Suppose the bridge is 1 foot longer than the circumference of the earth. How far would it be above the ground?

Advice from Shih Teng

There is a Chinese tale about the sage Shih Teng. A wealthy man drowned in the Wei River. The man who recovered the body demanded a ransom. The family asked Shih Teng how to respond. The sage advised waiting: 'No other family will pay for the body.'

The kidnapper became worried. He also sought counsel from Shih Teng. 'Wait,' replied the sage, 'from who else can they obtain the body?'

Each piece of advice derives plausibility by concentrating solely on the other's predicament. The failure of co-advisability alerts us to a flaw: each counsel overlooks how each party's expectations are influenced by their beliefs about the other party's expectations.

In game theory, if my perspective embeds your perspective, then you must include your own perspective in my perspective. In decision theory, there is no such feedback loop. Nature is indifferent to your decision. Shih Teng was mistaking a game-theoretic problem as a decision-theoretic problem.

To prevail in this spiral of expectations, one must exceed the altitude of the other party. This is feasible when parents are pitted against their young children. A mother can replicate her toddler's attempts to replicate her reasoning.

Out-replication is feasible against cognitively diminished adults. Panic simplifies people by making them incapable of taking one step back to take two steps forward. A drowning swimmer has an overwhelming desire to ascend. So when a drowning man scrambles on top of the lifeguard, the lifeguard *dives down* – and is quickly released.

There is a tendency to generalise to all insanity. We think that a sane perspective may encompass a sane one but not vice versa.

In *The Amazing Dr Clitterhouse* Edward G. Robinson plays a physician who studies crime. Initially, Dr Clitterhouse measures his own physiological and emotional reactions before, during, and after four jewellery heists. Through a fence, the 'Professor' gets an opportunity to increase the pool of subjects by displacing the head of a criminal band, Rocks Valentine (played by Humphrey Bogart). After collecting six weeks of data, Dr Clitterhouse announces his retirement. The whole gang wishes him well – except the bitter Rocks Valentine. Rocks investigates the mysterious Professor and discovers that he has a medical office on Park Avenue. Rocks slips into Dr Clitterhouse's splendid office and reads his incriminating manuscript *Crime and Research*. When the physician returns, Rick dictates his terms at gunpoint: instead of being published, the manuscript will be hidden in Rick's secret deposit box. Second, Clitterhouse must work for Rick. Third, Dr Clitterhouse must include his wealthy patients as victims.

Clitterhouse feigns capitulation. To escape the predicament and to test his own reaction to the ultimate crime, Clitterhouse poisons his nemesis.

When apprehended, Clitterhouse's lawyer advises that he plead insanity. Clitterhouse worries that his book *Crime and Research* would be dismissed if authored by a certified lunatic. His lawyer argues insanity anyway. Dr Clitterhouse protests. He takes the stand to prove he was perfectly logical. The jury gives the verdict of not guilty by reason of insanity. The foreman explains: 'Well, Your Honour, the prisoner's only hope lies in proving himself insane when he committed the crime. In fact, his life depends on it. But there he sits, doing his best to prove himself sane, then and now. Only an insane man would do that, so he must have been and still is insane.'

Were the jurors one step beyond Dr Clitterhouse? Some members of the audience may be put in mind of a story beloved by Redd Foxx. A motorist gets a puncture at the edge of a lunatic asylum. As he gets out to fix the flat tyre, he notices an inmate staring at him through the fence. The motorist hurries, glancing up every few seconds to make sure the lunatic does not try anything. Distracted, the motorist steps on the hubcap holding the four lug nuts – catapulting them down a storm drain. He gazes forlornly into the drain. Then the motorist begins to pace back and forth at a loss for what to do. Finally, the inmate speaks: 'Take one lug nut off each of the remaining tyres. You will then have three lug nuts for each of the four tyres.' 'Ingenious!' exclaims the motorist, 'What is someone like you doing in a mental hospital?' The patient replies: 'I am here because I am crazy, not because I am stupid.'

Thales' Shady Measurement of Pyramids

Hieronymus of Rhodes reports that Thales made a careful study of shadows, thereby devising the simplest way of measuring the height of an object.

To measure a pyramid, Thales found a spot next to the massive monument. He then marked his length on the ground (perhaps by simply laying in the sand). Once Thales' shadow had equalled his height, Thales knew that at this moment of the day, the length of each object's shadow equalled its height. Accordingly, Thales walked over to the tip of the pyramid's shadow. Marking that point, he measured the length of its shadow and thereby derived its height.

Hieronymus' story is geometrically suspicious. In *The Shadow Club*, Roberto Casati notes that a pole will cast a shadow that matches its length when the sun is at a 45-degree angle. But a squat object will not; the potential shadow is, as it were, stuck inside the object. The Egyptian pyramids are not much steeper than 45 degrees so they cast very little shadow when the sun is at 45 degrees. Possibly, Thales performed the calculation with an obelisk and the feat was retold to include a grander object.

The Cowpox Transmission Problem

In 1797 the British physician Edward Jenner showed that exposure to cowpox provides immunity to smallpox. Thus the risk of contracting a terrible disease could be eliminated by deliberate infection by a mild disease. By 1802, news of Jenner's discovery had reached the ears of King Charles IV of Spain. He wished to stop the spread of smallpox in the New World (a side effect of the Spanish conquest). However, cowpox victims recover too quickly for any carrier to travel across the ocean. ♀ How did he transport the disease?

Kant's Gloves

Immanuel Kant was impressed by the mirror image difference between a pair of 'identical' gloves. The intrinsic properties are the same. There is no difference in shape, mass, and so forth. Their internal relations are the same: there are pockets for the thumb, index finger, middle finger, ring finger, and little finger – in that order. Yet the gloves look different and behave differently. Your left glove will not fit your right hand.

Can the difference be traced to how the gloves relate to other objects? Imagine a single glove in otherwise empty space. The glove is either a right glove or a left glove. So the handedness of the glove cannot be due to its relation to another object. It must be due to how it relates to space itself. Therefore, Isaac Newton must be correct in characterising space as absolute. Gottfried Leibniz must be mistaken in construing space as abstraction from the relations between particular objects (in the same way your family tree is an abstraction from relationships with your kin).

The hand–glove relationship can also be of practical

importance. You are a Liberian surgeon in 2014. You must use sterile gloves to protect both yourself and your Ebola patients. Sadly, you have only two pairs of sterile gloves and must operate on three patients. ♀ Can you don the gloves in a way that keeps everyone safe?

An Antipodal Algorithm

Geometrical tourists visit points, lines, figures, and volumes. BBC television's Simon Reeves has a series with geometrical episodes: 'The Equator', 'The Tropic of Cancer', and 'The Tropic of Capricorn'. In *Pole to Pole*, Michael Palin travels from the North Pole to the South Pole. He circumnavigates the earth by walking around the South Pole. At the equator, he plants one foot in the Northern Hemisphere and the other in the Southern Hemisphere. Such affordances are a standard attraction for geometrical tourists.

Geometrical tourists also visit antipodes that are more accessible than the North Pole and South Pole: Madrid, Spain, and Wellington, New Zealand, Bogotá, Colombia, and Jakarta, Indonesia, and best of all, Cherbourg, France, and Antipodes Islands. These are only approximate antipodes. Geometrical tourists tend to be perfectionists. They chafe at the inexactitude. They might luckily visit precise antipodal points. But an exact match is unlikely. Even if they get lucky, they cannot tell whether it happened.

W. V. O. Quine to the rescue! In *Quiddities* he explains how an enterprising geometrical tourist can reliably visit two *precise* antipodes:

> Note to begin with that any route from New York to Los Angeles, if not excessively devious, is bound to intersect any route from Winnipeg to New Orleans. Now let someone travel from New York to Los Angeles, and also travel from roughly the antipodes of Winnipeg to roughly the antipodes of New Orleans. These two routes do not intersect – far from it; but one of them intersects a route

that is antipodal to the other. So our traveler is assured
of having touched a pair of mutually antipodal points
precisely, though he will know only approximately where.

Quine's travel plans do not suit intuitionists. They do not
accept non-constructive proofs.

Quine has given us yet another reason to accept classical logic!

The Invisibility of Function Words

> If ifs and buts were candy and nuts, we'd
> all have a merry Christmas.
>
> Don Meredith, Monday Night Football Announcer

There is a charming dialogue between Augustine (354–430)
and his son Adeodatus. (Augustine is the saint who prayed,
'Grant me chastity and continence, but not yet.') Father and
son agree that all language is for teaching and reminding. A
question reports what the speaker wants to know. An order
reports what the speaker wants done. Since a sentence pictures a fact, words are signs. Signs are names. The meaning
of a name is the bearer of that name. A mother teaches her
toddler 'moon' by pointing to the moon.

Father and son apply the principle to a line from Virgil's
Aeneid, ii.659: *Si nihil ex tanta superis placet urbe relinqui* (If
it pleases the gods that nothing be left of so great a city). *Si*
translates as *if*. What is the bearer of 'if'? Lacking an exter-
nal referent, Adeodatus suggests that *if* signifies doubt in the
speaker's mind. Augustine tentatively agrees. He urges his son
to go on to the second word *nihil* ('nothing'). Adeodatus is
forced to say *nihil* refers to *what is not*. His father objects that
to refer to *what is not* is to fail to refer. In that case *nihil* should
be meaningless. Adeodatus is stumped. They decide to skip
nihil and move on to the next word.

Although the sentence is a gauntlet of counterexamples,
father and son never surrender the principle that all words
are names. Only in the late middle ages do logicians distinguish between content words that have meaning on their own

and function words that only having meaning by virtue of how they contribute to the meaning of a whole sentence.

The medievals taught logic with puzzle sentences (*sophismata*). These flush out function words in static sentences by drawing out consequences. (Glass beads in a still pool become visible when the water is swirled.) Consider 'All men are donkeys or men and donkeys are donkeys.' A future defender of the faith could argue both sides. To prove the sentence true he would treat 'and' as the main connective: [All men are donkeys or men] AND [donkeys are donkeys]. To disprove it, the student would treat 'or' as the main connective: [All men are donkeys] OR [men and donkeys are donkeys].

The Black Death discredited the Church in the fourteenth century. To be taken seriously, intellectuals adopted the personas of outsiders. They were not fooled by the arid sophistry of the corrupt Scholastics! When these outsiders knew what to steal, they could loudly claim to find nothing of value while discreetly pouring Medieval wine into Renaissance bottles. When they did not know what to steal, they mixed metaphors and threw the baby out with the bathwater. A woman is caught in the act in a woodcut from Thomas Murner's 1512 *Narrenbeschwörung* (Appeal to Fools):

Logic only recovered from this purge in the nineteenth century. Many of the lessons had to be relearned by psychologists. Under the influence of the empiricists, they assumed that any meaningful word must be backed by an idea. That mental image must concretely picture a state of affairs.

This pictorial principle appeared confirmed by reasoning

tasks that elicit rich mental imagery. Picture the letter J and the letter D. Mentally rotate the D so that it is on top of the J. What does the figure look like?

There are more demanding problems that involve mental cuts and rotations. Does a 5-5-8 triangle exceed the area of a 5-5-6 triangle?

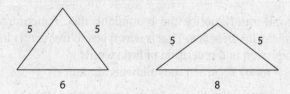

Each can be decomposed into two 3-4-5 triangles ... so they're equal.

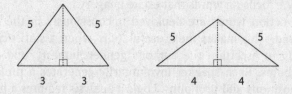

But subjects solved other puzzles without images. For instance, given that Joe is richer than Bill, and Joe is poorer than Ed, find the relation between Bill and Ed. Many subjects solved the problem by imagining a diagram with three vertical dots. The subjects were not able to cite any image, feeling, or act of will that made the top dot represent Ed rather than Bill. These imageless thoughts became a headache for the introspectionists.

After the behaviourists threw out the bathwater of introspectionism, imageless thoughts tended to be treated as non-thoughts. Psychologists only regained fourteenth-century insights after Noam Chomsky wrote a devastating book review of B. F. Skinner's *Verbal Behavior*. Chomsky treated natural languages mathematically as syntactic systems in which function words are pivotal.

Psychologists began to document the retiring nature of little words such as 'the'.

A
BIRD IN THE
THE BUSH

People rarely notice the redundant 'the'. Function words lack pictorial presence. That is why typos so frequently involve the omission and repetition of little words.

How many F's are in the following sentence?

FINISHED FILES ARE THE RESULT OF YEARS
OF SCIENTIFIC STUDY COMBINED WITH THE
EXPERIENCE OF YEARS.

Most people forget to read the OF's and report only three F's. We focus on words that excite imagery.

Function words are deployed unconsciously in the background. This makes them useful 'tells' when a statistician is trying to ascertain the author's gender, honesty, and other attributes. Each speaker involuntarily generates a profile of prepositions and pronouns. Logical analysis requires a higher profile for these terms – especially the *logical constants* 'not', 'and', 'or', 'if', 'all', 'some', and 'is'.

The Spartans made logical constants visible by isolation. King Philip of Macedonia, before his victory at Chaeronea, sent a message to the Spartans asking for their support. The Spartans sent back a one-word answer: NO.

Annoyed, Philip sent a second message warning that if he entered Laconia, then Sparta would be razed to the ground. Again, the Spartans responded with a single word: IF.

The Spartans were spotlighting doubt on the second premise of Philip's syllogism:

If Philip will enter Laconia, then Sparta will be razed.
Philip will enter Laconia.
Laconia will be razed.

This argument has the logical form later dubbed *modus ponens*. The more descriptive name is 'affirming the antecedent' (below the antecedent is labelled A and the consequent C).

IF **A**, then **C**.
A.
Therefore, **C**.

The pattern formed with this IF renders the inference valid. In other words, the truth of the premises would force the truth of the conclusion. By emphasising IF, the Spartans were restricting their doubt to the *second* premise which affirms the antecedent. And indeed Philip decided that the costs of a 'victory' over the Spartans would be too high. He left them alone.

The constants can also be made prominent by repetition and by elongating their scope. Rudyard Kipling's 'If—' begins:

If you can keep your head when all about you
Are losing theirs and blaming it on you;
If you can trust yourself when all men doubt you,
But make allowance for their doubting too:
If you can wait and not be tired by waiting,
Or, being lied about, don't deal in lies,
Or being hated don't give way to hating,
And yet don't look too good, nor talk too wise;

The sentence marches on for three more stanzas recruiting more and more *if*s. The stoical reader must have a stiff upper lip to reach the consequent: '[then] yours is the Earth and everything that's in it, And – which is more – you'll be a Man, my son!'

In his letter to the Philippians St Paul (as translated in the King James version of the Bible) highlights a logical constant with the subtler technique of conceptual repetition:

Finally, brethren, whatsoever things are true, whatsoever things are honest, whatsoever things are just, whatsoever things are pure, whatsoever things are lovely, whatsoever

things are of good report; if there be any virtue, and if
there be any praise, think on these things.

Philippians 4:8

'Whatsoever' is a generalised conditional of the form 'For
all x, if x is F, then x is G' (Whatever is an F is a G). The con-
ditionality courses underground, welling up in the last pair of
explicit *if*s.

The logical constants spell out the inheritance rules for
truth. For instance, the rule for AND says that the conjunction
is true when both conjuncts are false and is false for all other
assignments of truth-values to the conjuncts:

P	Q	P AND Q
T	T	T
T	F	F
F	T	F
F	F	F

Similar tables can be constructed for OR, NOT, IF, and IF
AND ONLY IF. The austerity of this vocabulary allows the logician to economise with a small collection of concise laws. As
the Spartan King Charilaus replied when asked why the list of
Spartan laws was so short, 'Men of few words require few laws.'

Henry Sheffer (1882–1964) was able to reduce all of the
connectives of sentence logic to a single stroke function ↑.
The dual of conjunction has no name in ordinary English (or
other natural languages). But computer scientists know it as
NAND:

P	Q	P NAND Q
T	T	F
T	F	T
F	T	T
F	F	T

Bertrand Russell immediately hailed NAND as philosophic-
ally important. It allowed him to because it showed that we

cannot trace philosophical problems about Non-Being to the peculiarities of negation.

Sheffer's function became commercially important because logic machines could be built with a single type of circuit, nowadays called a NAND gate. The right imagery is supplied from a caption in Stan Augarten's *State of the Art: A Photographic History of the Integrated Circuit*: 'Computers are composed of nothing more than logic gates stretched out to the horizon in a vast numerical irrigation system ...' (Indeed, engineers have a choice. Sheffer found a second function, NOR, that can also perform solo.)

Human beings are not engineered. They are 'kluges' – inelegant contraptions, cobbled together from what happens to be available (a famous example being the improvised carbon scrubbers on the ill-fated Apollo 13 moon mission). An engineer will take one step back to go two steps forward. But Mother Nature is near-sighted. A mutation is retained only if it provides immediate progress. So our 'design' is dominated by false summits, workarounds, and quick-and-dirty solutions. Human logicians should not try to emulate a computer that can scrimp by with a single logical connective. We should allow ourselves a comfortably large stock of keywords.

Puzzles can be organised around familiar words. Instead of meeting new faces, you then recognise shy introverts – emboldened by an environment in which they call the shots.

Necessary Waste

Responding to a budget crisis, a politician said we should eliminate wasteful spending. I agreed!

But then I had a second thought: 'Wait, he is passing off a platitude as a pearl of wisdom. Of course, we should eliminate waste! "Waste" just means what ought to be eliminated. Who could be against eliminating wasteful spending?'

Economists, that's who! Preventing waste requires effort that could be spent on other activities. Think of a shopper spending hours in a grocery store to avoid superfluous spending. She is not saving enough to justify the price-checking.

Educated by the economist's anti-perfectionism, my third thought was that the politician had made an *interesting* mistake. He was like the opponents of toxins who ban them regardless of dosage. The goal should be to find the optimal level of waste: Before I was too wasteful. Then I was not wasteful enough. Now I am wasteful just right.

My contentment with the economist's optimal trade-off did not last. Mathematicians asked: What guarantees the existence of an optimum?

They had learned a lesson in the nineteenth century. Karl Weierstrass demanded existence proofs of minima and maxima. This struck his colleagues as excessively sceptical.

Mathematical possibility is wider than physical possibility. So when geometers formalise their reasoning, they have a strengthened disposition to assume the existence of minima and maxima.

To curb this presumptiveness, Karl Weierstrass gave memorable illustrations of optimising problems with false existential presuppositions. Suppose a pilot needs to fly from a point directly *above* A to point B. Which is the shortest path?

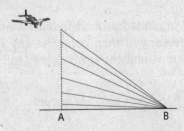

As the candidate points of descent lose altitude their paths to B shorten. But there is no shortest path.

Weierstrass's colleagues continued to conjure minima into existence. What is the minimum area for a triangle with a given perimeter? Answer: A straight line segment conceived as a triangle with zero altitude! Weierstrass frowned on such can-do sophistry. We should instead acknowledge that some problems have no solutions.

Weierstrass's ghost haunted me. I felt one century behind.

I reluctantly concluded that there is no best amount of waste. There are only less bad amounts of waste. Consequently, whatever we do about waste, it will be a little bit wrong.

Weierstrass's ghost could wander further back in history and find more eminent victims. At Oxford, Robert Grosseteste (1168–1253) distilled Aristotle's *Physics*, Book V, into the slogan 'Nature operates in the shortest way possible.' Grosseteste applied the principle in his metaphysics of light.

William of Ockham (1287–1347) continued the Oxford tradition of parsimony: 'It is futile to do with more things that which can be done with fewer.' But what if each option uses less than its predecessor but no option uses the least? A scale perfectly balanced between a pair of kilogram weights can be tipped by adding half a kilogram to one side, or a quarter of a kilogram, or an eighth of a kilogram, or …

For any choice, there is an option that gets the job done with less.

Relative futility does not entail absolute futility. The job can get done – but only if we use superfluous means. As Voltaire said in his poem 'Le Mondain' (1736): 'The superfluous is very necessary.'

The Art of Counterexample

David Hume is a great counterexample man. John Locke had based our political obligations on a social contract. Although we never explicitly consented, we tacitly consent through our continued presence in the state. This triggers Hume's sympathy with the poor:

Can we seriously say, that a poor peasant or artisan has a free choice to leave his country, when he knows no foreign language or manners, and lives, from day to day, by the small wages which he acquires? We may as well assert that a man, by remaining in a vessel, freely consents to the dominion of the master; though he was carried on board while asleep, and must leap into the ocean and perish, the moment he leaves her.

'Of the Original Contract', 1748

To Adam Smith's claim that we sympathise because it is pleasant to do so, Hume cites the infectious ennui generated by dismal personalities.

But instead of continuing with Hume's counterexamples, I want to recount how a young woman counterexampled the great counterexampler – and thereby became England's first sculptress.

David Hume served as secretary to Field Marshal Henry Seymour Conway, whose daughter Anne was a highly educated young woman Hume enjoyed the company of such women and they enjoyed his.[26] Anne was no exception.

While together on a London street, Hume and the 17-year-old Anne met a small Italian boy. The lad was carrying on his head a large tray that displayed plaster figures. Hume paused to admire his artworks. He conversed at length with the young artist. Eventually, Hume gave the child a shilling and finally dismissed him. Anne was annoyed with Hume for wasting their time with 'this poor ignorant little boy'. Hume replied that the boy was far from ignorant. She should not sneer at the figures he had modelled with such science and art: 'With all your attainments now, you cannot produce such works.'

---

[26] Hume had been in the military and thought the coarseness and degeneracy an experimental demonstration of the degree to which women are responsible for civilisation. When Jean-Jacques Rousseau broke down and wept for forgiveness in Hume's lap, the Scot was deeply moved. He confided to Mme de Boufflers with the request that she tell only the ladies in her circle. He explained that men would ridicule the incident as childish.

Rankled, Anne immediately obtained wax and modelling tools. She carved and moulded the block until she was able to present the philosopher a bust of himself.

Hume admitted, 'It is clever enough for a first attempt.' But, a bit ungratefully, he added that work in soft material is rather easy, nothing like the challenge posed to the sculptor who must take chisel to stone.

Indignation rekindled, Anne obtained a block of marble. Soon she presented Hume with a rough copy of his head in marble. Hume now admitted defeat. She had surprised him with her industry and artistic flair.

After receiving further encouragement from an expert, Horace Walpole, Anne formalised her study. Her father hired tutors in sculpture and anatomy. Anne became England's first female sculptor – under her married name, Anne Seymour Damer.

1798 caricature of Damer chiselling Apollo *a posteriori*.

Her husband turned out to be gambler. To avert ruin, she separated from him. His spiral of dissolution ended with a pistol shot to his own head.

This deepened Anne's notoriety. She focused on her career. She wore the practical clothes of a man. Her emotional attachment was to a woman. That invited gossip that they were lesbians.

The gossip intensified as she won commissions. The threat to male artists led her to be caricatured.

But Anne persevered. She created many more counterexamples to Hume about her artistic capacity. The most telling is in the Uffizi gallery of self-portraits in the Vasari Corridor. It bears an inscription: ΑΝΝΑ ΣΕΙΜΟΡΙΣ ΔΑΜΕΡ Η ΕΚ ΤΗΣ ΒΡΕΤΤΑΝΙΚΗΣ ΑΥΤΗ ΑΥΤΗΝ ΕΠΟΙΕΙ (Anne Seymour Damer from Britain, made herself).

The Philosophy of Scale Effects

Jonathan Swift's *Gulliver's Travels* contains the story of Lilliputians who live in a miniature environment. From their perspective, things look the same as from an ordinary scale. This raised the question of whether one could detect a universal change of size. In *Science and Method*, Henri Poincaré[27] writes:

Suppose that in one night all the dimensions of the

---

[27] France's Poincaré (1854–1912) is the last polymath. He made major contributions as a mathematician, physicist, logician, and philosopher of science. At 17, Poincaré's exam scores showed there was room for improvement: he passed 'letters with "good", got a "fair" for science, and a zero in mathematics. He could not even answer the correct question!'

universe became a thousand times larger. The world will remain similar to itself, if we give the word 'similitude' the meaning it has in the third book of Euclid. Only, what was formerly a metre long will now measure a kilometre, and what was a millimetre long will become a metre. The bed in which I went to sleep and my body itself will have grown in the same proportion. When I wake in the morning what will be my feeling in face of such an astonishing transformation? Well, I shall not notice anything at all. The most exact measures will be incapable of revealing anything of this tremendous change, since the yard-measures I shall use will have varied in exactly the same proportions as the objects I shall attempt to measure.

– Poincaré, *Science and Method*, 1914, p. 94

Some recoil at universal expansion on the grounds that we should prefer continuity over change. A little heard objection is parsimony. Universal expansion requires more stuff. We should prefer hypotheses postulating smaller universes.

But why stick to our presently believed size? Less is more parsimonious than more. Universal shrinkage is not as objectionable as universal growth.

No scientist draws this little conclusion. Their main efforts are to challenge Poincaré's supposition. Some delegate the issue to metaphysicians. They say that the scientist, in his role as scientist, is indifferent between empirically equivalent hypotheses.

Operationalists are more dismissive. They object that Poincaré has posed a pseudo-problem. Their idea, elaborated by the logical positivists, is that the lack of a verification procedure to test the supposition makes the supposition meaningless. Poincaré notes that operational detectability is theory-dependent. The positivists need meaningfulness to be absolute. It is also disturbing that the same logic that forbids a preference for universal change in size also forbids a preference for the universe remaining the same size.

The correct response to Poincaré is to challenge the assumption that there is no empirical difference. Even without physics, a logician can note that alternatives that do not empirically contrast *with each other* can still contrast with other hypotheses. The hypothesis that everything doubled in size last night yields different predictions than the hypothesis that only some things doubled. If only some of the objects grew larger, the scene would be a mix of objects with discordant relative sizes. You would not know whether some have grown or others have shrunk. But you would not know that not all of them doubled in size last night.

A physicist might be tempted to say that Edwin Hubble showed that Poincaré's hypothesis is verifiable. Spectroscopic analysis shows that nearly all heavenly bodies are moving away from the earth. Since this cannot be due to a repulsive force, Hubble inferred that the same sort of observation must hold universally. The best explanation of this uniformity is that space itself is expanding. Picture dots on a balloon. As the balloon inflates, each dot 'sees' all the other dots move away from it. Analogously, all the heavenly bodies are moving away from each other. The speed of flight increases with distance. The speed limit for objects does not apply to the space in which they are situated. So the universe can expand faster than the speed of light. Surprisingly, the rate of expansion is *accelerating* (counter to what the law of gravity led physicists to expect). So the universe is getting darker and darker.

Physicists smiled when S. Sambursky, in 'Static Universe and Nebular Red Shift', offered a counterexplanation: the universe and everything in it is shrinking. Their amusement was shared by laymen interested in science (*Popular Science*, November 1937, p. 29). The diminutive draws derision.

More serious interest in the possibility grew in the 1950s with Paul Dirac's speculations about 'inconstants'. These are so-called 'constants' that are actually variables which change very slowly. In Shakespeare's play, Julius Caesar says, 'I am constant as the Northern Star.' Astronomers have since discovered that the Northern Star (= the North Star = Polaris) slowly shifts position. In a similar spirit, a few physicists hypothesised that all the fundamental constants were shrinking in value – scaling us down in the process. This gave some legitimacy to science fiction movies such as *The Incredible Shrinking Man* (1957). Just as the shrinking man fears he will shrink out of existence, a micro-cosmologist might gloomily predict that the universe will shrink to nothing.

Stephen Hawking and Leonard Mlodinow note that Hubble's expanding space is not the same sort of growth as entertained by Poincaré: 'If everything were free to expand, then we, our yardsticks, our laboratories, and so on would all expand proportionately, and we would not notice the difference'. (*The Grand Design*, 2010, p. 125). They explain that, on Hubble's hypothesis, the objects do not participate in the expansion; the universe is becoming more dilute.

However, George Schlesinger would complain that Hawking and Mlodinow missed a decisive difference between linear and geometrical relationships. Doubling the radius of the earth *quadruples* its moment of inertia. Since the rate of angular rotation decreases by a factor of four, the day will be measurably longer. Mercury columns in manometers will double in height. The speed of light will also appear to increase. Although the simplest measurements are linear (measuring length with a ruler) many others are geometrical. Galileo exploited this point to explain why the largest animals are aquatic. J. B. S. Haldane (1892–1964), the courageous self-experimental biologist, generalises the constraint in his classic essay 'On Being the Right Size': 'You can drop a mouse down a thousand-yard mine shaft; and on arriving at the bottom, it gets a slight shock and walks away. A rat would probably be killed, though it can fall safely from the eleventh storey of a building; a man is killed, a horse splashes.' According to Haldane, the only trouble we would have verifying Poincaré's hypothesis of noctural expansion is that we would wake up dead.

Although Poincaré's hypothesis fails to actually raise the issue of whether size should be minimised, it remains an instructive near miss. Philosophers and physicists did *believe* Poincaré's hypothesis established empirical equivalence between hypotheses that only varied in scale. But no one seized on the opportunity to shrink the universe to a more economical size. Their actual order of preference was: No Change, Bigger, Smaller. In other words, Conservativism prevails over Gigantism, which in turn prevails over Dwarfism.

Humble Exercise

Teddy Roosevelt was a larger than life president of the United States. He pushed his weight around nationally – and internationally. Cartoonists pictured the Rough Rider as Gulliver among the Lilliputians:

Teddy tosses a spadeful of Panama dirt on the capital city of Colombia.

Roosevelt believed in vigorous physical exercise – especially outdoors. He feared being unmanned by Civilisation.

Old Four Eyes also believed in vigorous mental exercise. Contrary to stereotype, one of these exercises was to make himself insignificantly small. William Beebe recalls in *The Book of Naturalists* a ritual he participated in ('forty or fifty times in the course of years') at Roosevelt's Sagamore Hill residence:

> After an evening of talk, perhaps about the fringes of
> knowledge, or some new possibility of climbing inside
> the minds and senses of animals, we would go out on

the lawn, where we took turns at an amusing little astronomical rite. We searched until we found, with or without glasses, the faint, heavenly spot of light-mist beyond the lower left-hand corner of the Great Square of Pegasus, when one or the other of us would then recite:

That is the Spiral Galaxy of Andromeda.
It is as large as our Milky Way.
It is one of a hundred million galaxies.
It is 750,000 light-years away.
It consists of one hundred billion suns, each larger than our
    sun.

After an interval Colonel Roosevelt would grin at me and say: 'Now I think we are small enough! Let's go to bed.'

Philosophy for the Eye

Agostino Carracci (1557–1602) drew the earliest known 'droodle' (a minimally drawn figure that is posed as a visual riddle):

The solution, a blind beggar behind a street corner, depends on visual thinking – a type of mentation that has so far had marginal representation in philosophy.

The central philosophical riddles are verbal. They tap into our faculty for language. But along the periphery, there are visual riddles. They tap into our faculty for vision.

Visual riddles in mathematics have decisive, correct answers derived from well-defined operations. For instance, in the figure below how much larger is the big square?

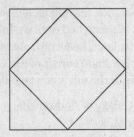

Many people answer by mentally folding the corner triangles into the inner square. Since the match is perfect, they conclude that the big square is twice as large as the little square.

Compare this with the philosophical riddle of whether we see in the dark. On the one hand, there is the truism that we need light to see. On the other hand, we use our *eyes* to learn whether it is dark (not ears, nose, tongue, or hands). We do not infer that it is dark from a mere failure to see; we equally cannot see in a dazzling light. Darkness has a characteristic way of appearing: total 'pitch blackness'.

Paradoxes overburden the audience with too many good answers. They do not rely on ambiguity, metaphor, or misdirection. So they contrast with the riddle 'How many triangles are in the figure below?'

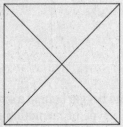

The solution is eight: four small ones and four bigger ones (composed of pairs of adjacent smaller triangles). This riddle tricks us by counting superimposed triangles as distinct triangles. Paradoxes do not rely on these shallow shenanigans. Everything is done in plain sight. The problem is that there are *too many* good answers. This is an embarrassment of riches because the answers are incompatible.

The abstractness of mathematical riddles contrasts with the visual riddles in children's books. A typical 'I-spy' riddle presents a cluttered drawer along with the instruction to find a cufflink. This is an effortful, visual search with a definite outcome.

Visual riddles in philosophy may be abstract or concrete. But they are rarely decisive. The point of the riddle is to tease out hidden conflicts. For instance, Fred Dretske is happy to use the cufflink example. But Dretske, in *Seeing and Knowing*, asks a different question: 'Did you see the cufflink when you first looked at it – or only after you recognised it as a cufflink?' On the one hand, we are inclined to accept the principle that if you look at something, then you see it. Euclid relies on this principle when mapping out the visual field. On the other hand, we are inclined to believe that seeing implies believing – or at least noticing.

To uphold the objectivity of perception, Dretske weakens the link between seeing and believing (to allow observation to surprise theory). This resolution of the dilemma depends on delicate weighing of evidence, not an 'Aha!' insight of riddles in mathematics and children's books.

The agenda for visual riddles is set by the questions our visual system evolved to answer. In daylight, 'What is that?' is nearly always answered effortlessly. Vision seems to be passive. But we are also designed to see at night. Seeing is so important that the system will not quit even when the quantity of data is meagre and the quality of data is abysmal.

The visual system is plucky. It compulsively tries to identify objects that are almost wholly occluded.

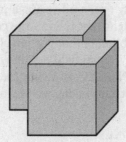

We see these partially visible objects as whole objects, not as fragments from which we must infer a whole object. The visual system does not give up even if the object is completely covered, as when we see, or 'see', a car under a tarpaulin. We strain to see objects that are filtered through mottled glass. We do not give up if the object is presented from an unrepresentative perspective. And the visual system soldiers on when the objects are only available in outline, as in the case of silhouettes.

As the dots become fewer and more distant from each other, the connecting perceiver must rely on lengthier lines of interpretation. Where does the observation end and the theory begin? To some extent, theory and observation go hand in hand, with theory extending the range of the observable.

A limit to the contribution of theory is suggested by the following droodle:

What are you seeing? A round square (side view).

This 'solution' is intended to provoke an objection: Nothing counts as a depiction of a round square because nothing counts as seeing a round square!

Just what sorts of things can be seen? Round squares are not on the list. Nor are things that are outside our light cone (given the causal theory of vision which says we see only causes of visual experience).

We see those objects and events which generate appropriate effects in our brains. But is that list complete? What about after-images? When a flashbulb goes off and washes out the photopigments in my eye, am I seeing a private visual object (the blob of white light that follows the course of my roving eye) or am I merely blind in that portion of the visual field?

Which parts of my visual field are things that I see? David Macaulay's (1978, Plate XV) drawing *Locating the Vanishing Point* portrays pedestrians taking a close look at the vanishing point.

We may wish to correct Mr Macaulay and point out that the real vanishing point of Macaulay's picture is above the depicted vanishing point. But is it really in the picture at all? When you look at real railway tracks converging to the horizon, do you see the vanishing point along with the railway tracks?

One may be inclined to say that these architectural features of the visual field are not among the things we see. They are like the boundaries of our visual field. Vision reveals its limits without portraying them directly.

But many visual boundaries are internal to the field. The visual system is designed to demarcate objects from their boundaries. This leads to C. S. Peirce's puzzle about the colour of the line dividing a black inkblot from its white background:

The boundary is visible. (It is not like the boundary of a spot of invisible ink.) But there is no more reason to say the boundary is white than to say it is black.

The linguist Ray Jackendoff's solution to the puzzle is that the boundary belongs to the figure rather than the ground. But this does not resolve boundary ownership for cases involving competition between two figures:

Is the boundary between the squares black or white? We have no more reason to answer one colour rather than the other. And the principle that nothing can be white all over and black all over excludes the possibility that the boundary is both black and white.

Discussing an example in which the squares are red and blue, Bernard Bolzano suggests that the colour is either red or blue but we cannot just tell which it is. This struck Franz Brentano as a monstrously arbitrary solution. He preferred to reject the principle of colour exclusion: 'If a red surface and a blue surface are in contact with each other, then a red and a blue line coincide' ('On What Is Continuous').

Brentano's answer can be driven to contradiction. Suppose the black square is a shadow and the white square is a beam of white light. Brentano must say that the boundary between the shadow and the beam is both light and shadow. But shadow is the *absence* of light!

One may wonder whether we can see absences. What is there to see?

Undeterred by privation, Richard Taylor gives a brutally empirical argument that we see absences. L ⊗ O K! You see an x in the left O and the absence of an x in the second O.

Taylor's critics concede that we see an absence of an x but insist that we are only *inferring* this negative thing from the positive things on the page. They think we only see negative things indirectly, in the way we see wind when it causes trees to bend and leaves to flutter.

Many genres of visual riddles are just extreme cases of classic problems for the visual system. For instance, animals must learn how to spot concealed predators and prey. Artists magnify the challenge to create the genre of 'hidden pictures'. Their growing sophistication is manifest in this 1872 Currier and Ives print 'The Puzzled Fox: Find the Horse, Lamb, Wild Boar, Men's and Women's Faces'.

Ironically, the pair of birds on the branch are passenger pigeons – a species that rapidly went extinct after the picture was made.

For a more deliberate and paradoxical depiction of an absence, find the hidden figure in 'Napoleon and Tomb at St Helena'.

What you discover is an absence!

An object's shadow provides clues about its contours, orientation, and relative depth. So it is important to assign a shadow to the correct object. This problem is made profound by overdetermining the shadow:

Is the shadow cast by the High disc or the Low disc? Since one disc is enough to block the light, either disc can be removed without affecting the appearance of the shadow beneath Low.

The object closest to the shadow is Low but it does not block the light. The High disc blocks light but a shadow cannot penetrate the opaque object Low.

The visual field is partly organised by occlusion relations. We see the relative distances of objects by noting what blocks what. (That which prevents information flow is itself a source of information.)

In front-lit circumstances, the front (opaque) object blocks the rear object. But what about when objects are back-lit? Silhouetted objects are seen by virtue of the light they block, not the light they reflect.

Suppose you are viewing a double-eclipse as in the figure below.

Travelling east is the heavenly body Far. Travelling west and nearer to you is the smaller body Near. Near is close enough to exactly compensate for its smaller size with respect to shadow formation. Near and Far look the same size from your vantage point. When Near falls exactly under the shadow of Far, it is as if one of these heavenly bodies had disappeared. Do you see Near or Far? You initially side with common sense: you see Near rather than Far: Near completely blocks your view of Far. You are seeing something. Therefore, you are seeing Near.

However, when you dwell on the idleness of Near and the fact that it is completely enveloped in the shadow of Far, your loyalty shifts to Far. It is Far that blocks the light. Near would be blocking your view of Far if it were front-lit. But in the case of back-lit circumstances (when seeing objects by seeing their silhouettes), the principles of blockage are reversed. It is Far that is blocking your view of Near!

In the eclipse puzzle, the problem is to ascertain which of two objects is being seen in silhouette. In cases of causal over-determination, we have trouble singling out the cause. Thus the causal theory of perception predicts we will have trouble deciding on what we see.

This prediction of puzzlement is further confirmed by situations in which the visual task is to tell whether one is viewing an object or a shadow. The difficulty of this task was overlooked until computer scientists tried to design artificial vision. Computers have terrible difficulty distinguish between shadows and dark objects.[28] The distinction can be more than a technical challenge for programmers: Suppose a conceptual artist suspends a solid cone beneath a lamp to cast a shadow.

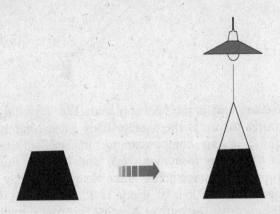

He has duplicated the shadow by moulding a brick of black clay (the truncated cone on the left). The artist has treated the brick's surface to match the shadow on the right. When the brick is slid into the exact spot of the shadow, there is no discernible difference.

---

[28] Computers may take solace in the fact that many toddlers are frightened by their shadows; just have your computer google: YouTube baby scared by shadow.

The artist has made the brick disappear! (Objects can only be seen if they interact with light, whether it be by reflection, refraction, or absorption.) The artist has also made the shadow disappear! (A shadow cannot exist wholly within an opaque object; that is why your shadow does not tunnel into the ground.)

When I enrolled in geometry I was surprised by how some C students metamorphosed into A students. I wondered whether they had an epiphany.

The real explanation is that the subject-matter changed, not the students. Geometry emphasizes visual thinking – a skill these students had not been previously asked to exercise.

I was reminded of the metamorphosis when I taught Ned Block's article:

WHY DO MIRRORS REVERSE LEFT/RIGHT BUT NOT UP/DOWN?

Some reticent students suddenly spoke up – while some of the outgoing students quietened down. Much of Block's diagram-rich article involves mental rotation to bring out the ambiguities of 'reverse', 'left', 'up', 'forward', 'clockwise', and other terminology governing the horizontal, vertical, and front–back axes. Some of my colleagues cannot understand the article while some average undergraduates find it a relaxing break from 'words, words, words'.

Most philosophers survey the world from the tower of language. Each healthy human being is a linguistic genius (though not a metalinguistic genius). Module by module, *Homo sapiens* evolved a mental architecture that has allowed us to rise on the accumulated luck and diligence of our ancestors. Up from the mud and ooze, we have accreted a nearly Olympian vantage point.

The tower of language overshadows a cluster of smaller towers. These are the towers corresponding to the sensory systems. Tallest among this group is the tower of vision, 'the master sense'.

Like the speech detection input system, the sensory systems feed output to a central system. The central system is rational and flexible. It assesses information holistically, more or less consciously, and, as a consequence, much more slowly and fallibly.

Progress in understanding the central system, the realm of consciousness, has been far surpassed by advances in understanding the machine-like operations of the modular systems. Linguistic philosophers have succeeded to the extent that they echo the research strategy of modular psychologists and psycholinguists: instead of flying into the flame of consciousness, they crawl into the dark recesses of our linguistic reflexes. What worked for the linguistic system should work for the sensory systems – especially the visual system.

I enjoy philosophy of perception because I can share so much of it with non-philosophers. Ordinary folk immediately grasp what is challenging in examples such as those presented above. They respond in a sophisticated way, drawing many of the distinctions natural to a philosopher.

This is especially true for students. Indeed, they often seem more visually sophisticated than the philosophers I revere.

The 'Flynn effect' suggests that there might be something to this impression. Since their inception, scores on IQ tests have been rising three points a decade in all industrialised nations. The gains have been greatest for tests that emphasise visual thinking such as the Raven's Progressive Matrices. These present sequences of figures that require an extrapolation to a new shape or the interpolation of a missing figure.

You do not engage in this iconic style of thinking when writing or reading or having a conversation. But you do when playing Tetris or mastering the interface of your new smartphone.

The improvements on the Raven's Progressive Matrices prompted the discoverer of the Flynn effect, the moral philosopher James Flynn, to conjecture that the massive rise in IQ is due to a more visually stimulating environment. (I have trouble surprising my students with visual illusions because they already learned most of them from the backs of cereal boxes.) Since the early twentieth century, successive generations have been exposed to a proliferation of picture advertising, light displays, cinema, television, video games, and increasingly sophisticated computer graphics. People have responded with more highly developed skills at visual analysis.

If Flynn is correct about the rise of visual thinking, then the overshadowed tower of philosophy, vision, may be quietly acquiring new stature.

Synthetic *A Priori* Lies

Although blinded at the age of 4, Ved Mehta's books are seasoned with visual descriptions. How did he do it? Here is the trick. Ved Mehta asked his interviewees to be his eyes. He incorporated their descriptions of the landscape, their abodes, and their attire. In *The Fly and Fly-Bottle* Mehta visits philosophers:

> My first call in Oxford was at the house of Richard Hare, of Balliol ... He looked like a monk, though he wasn't dressed like one; he wore a well-made dark tweed jacket and a pair of well-pressed dark-grey flannel trousers – and he had his legendary red and green tie on.
>
> – Mehta, *The Fly and Fly-Bottle*, 1963, p. 43

This passage puzzled an acquaintance who had seen Hare only dressed informally. (Hare disapproved of socks.) When she asked about the 'famous tie', Hare was also puzzled. What Hare had told Mehta was that he wore a tie that was red all over and green all over. The editor must have recognised that nothing can be red all over and green all over and so changed Mehta's text to a 'red and green tie'.

Possibly, Hare told the lie punitively. Mehta writes as if he is giving visual testimony. He is actually conspiring with interviewees, passing off their visual testimony as his own. Hare may have resented Vehta's requests to cooperate and decided to sabotage the deception.

Hare was an ethicist with a muscular superego. During World War II, he had been captured by the Japanese and forced to work as a coolie. This made him ferociously intolerant of immorality. Hare explicitly argued that moral reasons override all others. There is no compromise. There are no exceptions for the blind.

Right or wrong, Hare's lie is a fascinating specimen. 'My tie is red all over and green all over' is the negation of a synthetic *a priori* proposition.

Synthetic *a priori* statements do not owe their truth to the meanings of their words. 'Red' and 'green' are primitive terms and so lack definitions. Yet we somehow know 'Nothing is red all over and green all over' to be true without being confirmed by experience.[29]

We do need experience to trigger the development of colour concepts. Experience may also be needed to sustain the concepts. Ved Mehta did not recognise the absurdity of 'My tie is red all over and green all over.' So he may have lost the concepts after he became blind.

Or Ved Mehta still possessed the concepts but failed to exercise them. Some synthetic *a priori* propositions are not obvious. For instance, some geometrical theorems are counterintuitive and Immanuel Kant believed that all of Euclid's axioms are synthetic *a priori*.

Kant believed that people who believed beyond their evidence were guilty of self-deception. He forbade all lying but permitted telling misleading truths. This suggests that *a priori* lies might be permitted.

R. M. Hare believed his version of rule utilitarianism converged with Kant's ethics. What a bold consilience if both

---

[29] Or so say the rationalists. Empiricists deny that there are any synthetic *a priori* propositions. For empiricists believe that all substantive truths about the world are learned by experience.

ethical systems agreed on the permissibility of lying to a blind man!

Passive *A Priori* Deception

Immanuel Kant never permits lying – even to save an innocent life. Yet he sometimes permits deception, even verbal deception – as long what you assert is true. If someone infers a falsehood from a truth, then that his own fault. He had all the resources needed to avoid the mistake.[30] Indeed, Kant excoriates the hearer's error as self-deception.

Most people disagree with Kant. They think there is only a minor difference between the butcher who deceives a customer by secretly putting a thumb on the scale and a greengrocer who *actively* deceives a customer with arithmetic sophistry:

> Mrs Greengrocer: Sorry, I am out of the 12-inch circumference asparagus bundles. But you can have two 6-inch circumference bundles.
> Mr Shopper: That is the same thing so the price is the same.
> Mrs Greengrocer: No, the two small bundles together contain more than the large one.

Mr Shopper is persuaded and pays extra. ♡ Who was telling the truth?

But what about *passive a priori* deception? This occurs systematically when a new business tries to rationally outcompete an established rival. In the 1980s, the A & W restaurant chain introduced the Third Pounder. In addition to being bigger than the McDonald's Quarter Pounder, this new hamburger was preferred in taste tests. The price was the same. Yet sales were weak.

---

[30] René Descartes traces all errors to wilfulness. God gave us all the equipment needed to infer only truths from truths. But we recklessly infer more than our evidence warrants. The Manufacturer is not responsible for abuses of His product.

Interviews revealed that customers felt overcharged by the new hamburger: 'Why should I pay the same amount for a third of a pound of meat as a fourth of a pound?' Customers judged the size of the fraction by the size of the denominator. They inferred 1/4 is greater than 1/3. A & W tried to correct the fallacy. McDonald's did not. Was McDonald's omission immoral?

All of the people I have asked answered no. They say McDonald's was not obliged to join A & W in improving reasoning with fractions. Channelling Kant, they put all the blame on the customers.

Perhaps this explains why many customers do not correct cashiers when the miscalculation is in the customer's favour. Given that the customer did not court the error, he does not feel obliged to correct the cashier's mistake. It might be nice to correct the error. But the correction is above and beyond the call of duty.

Now someone asks you to specify two faces of a die. You pick 2 and 5. He hands you two dice and asks you to throw the dice. He will bet you at even odds that either the 2 or the 5 will show (perhaps both). You note that there are four other faces of a die. You calculate he has only a 2 in 6 chance of winning. You take the bet and win. He pays and offers to repeat the bet as frequently as you want.

You think the bettor is making an *a priori* error. Perhaps you are reluctant to exploit his foolishness. You explain your calculation. He is not persuaded. He presses you to continue the bets. Perhaps to teach him a lesson, you roll the dice all evening.

Unexpectedly, you lose quite a bit of money. Puzzled, you laboriously draw a chart of all 36 outcomes of two dice. You discover that 2 or 5 appear in 20 of the 36 possible outcomes. Therefore, the probability you will win is 16/36 rather than 4/6. You realise that you have been the subject of an *a priori* con. The trick was to exploit your attempt to exploit another man's fallacy.

You cannot excuse yourself on the grounds that the 20

favourable cases are scattered haphazardly. They arise systematically, appearing as a tidy grid pattern in the probability space.

	1	2	3	4	5	6
1	1,1	1,2	1,3	1,4	1,5	1,6
2	2,1	2,2	2,3	2,4	2,5	2,6
3	3,1	3,2	3,3	3,4	3,5	3,6
4	4,1	4,2	4,3	4,4	4,5	4,6
5	5,1	5,2	5,3	5,4	5,5	5,6
6	6,1	6,2	6,3	6,4	6,5	6,6

There are two favourable rows and two favourable columns of six items each. So you could have got the correct number by multiplying 4 by 6 and then subtracting the four overlap cases: $24 - 4 = 20$ favourable cases.

Do you have any basis to complain? Should the con man be blamed for the deception or should we blame you? Your harshest critics may regard the con artist as performing a public service. The presence of these tricksters would cause you to think twice about trying to exploit the fallacies of others.

Crete Revisited

The population of Crete is 108,310. Ancient legend has it that all Cretans are liars. To debunk the myth, the Cretans organise personal statements:

Cretan 1: Exactly 1 of our personal statements is false.
Cretan 2: Exactly 2 of our personal statements are false.
Cretan 3: Exactly 3 of our personal statements are false.

.

.

.

Cretan 108,309: Exactly 108,309 of our personal
    statements are false.

Cretan 108,310: Exactly 108,310 of our personal
  statements are false.

♀ Which Cretans speak the truth?

Less Lucky the Second Time?

Linus Pauling won a second Nobel Prize in 1962. With a witty
affectation of modesty, Professor Pauling insisted that his
second prize was less remarkable than his first. The chance
of winning your first Nobel Prize is one in several billion (the
population of the earth). The chance of winning a second
Nobel Prize is one in several hundred (the population who
have received at least one Nobel Prize).

A parallel argument can be made for Tsutomu Yamaguchi,
the only person documented to have survived both the Hiroshima and Nagasaki atomic bombings.

He was in Hiroshima on a business trip when it was bombed
on 6 August 1945. Injured, he spent the night in the city and
returned to his hometown of Nagasaki to convalesce. The
Americans bombed that city three days later.

Mr Yamaguchi was known as 'Lucky'. ♀ Was he as lucky the
second time?

Professor Ignorance

Most scholars try to learn as much as possible. Professor Ignorance tries to learn only as much as needed. She is a privacy
advocate. Professor Ignorance tries to solve problems with the
least knowledge possible.

Professor Ignorance earned her nickname in a single day.
Her colleagues in the Statistics Department needed to know
their average salary. But each was reluctant to disclose their
personal salary.

Professor Ignorance finessed the problem. She added her
salary to her phone number. (As we shall see, any big number
would have worked – as long as she did not reveal the number.)

Professor Ignorance wrote this sum on a slip of paper and handed it to the person on her left. That person was instructed to add his or her own salary to the number. They were then to pass a slip containing only that incremented sum to the next individual. When the circuit was completed, Professor Ignorance had a slip of paper containing a single enlarged number. From this she subtracted her phone number. The remainder was divided by the number of people in the room. Now she knew their average salary – while remaining ignorant of each specific salary.

In appreciation, three colleagues treated her to lunch. The waiter asked, 'Do you each want the buffet?'

First professor: I do not know.
Second professor: I do not know.
Third professor: I do not know.
Professor Ignorance: Yes, we each want the buffet.

The waiter asked her how she knew when no one else did. She explained: 'If the first professor did not want the buffet, he would have answered no. The same goes for each subsequent professor – except for the last professor. Since I was the last and I knew I wanted the buffet, I deduced that everybody wanted the buffet.'

She was teased for having violated everyone's privacy. Her maxim was 'Knowledge for the collective, ignorance for the individual'. Yet she had figured out everyone's state of mind. That's how she earned the nickname: Professor Ignorance.

Her specialisation is a survey technique called 'randomised response'. The method is used to sidestep bias against embarrassing answers. For instance, if a student is asked 'Have you cheated on an examination within the last year?', he will be reluctant to answer yes. The randomising solution is to have the student roll a die. If the die comes up 6, then the student is to answer yes. Otherwise, the student answers the question with simple candour. Since only the respondent knows the outcome of the die, the yes-answer does not disclose whether the student cheated. The student can hide behind the possibility that the affirmative response is from Lady Luck.

The survey results are still instructive because 1/6 of the yes-answers can be subtracted. This yields the correct percentage of students who cheated on an examination in the last year.

Professor Ignorance protects her own privacy with randomised answers. She has business cards stating that embarrassing questions will be answered randomly. The small print on the back of the card explains her procedure. A question with an embarrassing yes-answer will be answered affirmatively if the second hand of her wristwatch falls within a privately designated ten-second interval. Otherwise the question will be answered frankly.

I asked her whether this meant that she lied 1/6 of the time. She pointed to the smallest print on the business card. The sentence explained that the technique actually involves the substitution of a disjunctive question: *Is the second hand in the designated zone or if it is not in the designated zone then is the answer to the embarrassing question affirmative?*

Professor Ignorance believes that ignorance of statistics leads to needless immorality. One of her examples is the rule: 'Do not walk on the grass.' It is true that if everybody walks on the grass, then the lawn will be ruined. But the grass can tolerate a moderate amount of walking. Prohibiting everyone from walking on the lawn is wasteful. Realising this, many pedestrians become rule breakers. This erodes respect for the law. Pedestrians should instead give themselves a small chance of walking on the grass. The groundsman could post the exact chance.

I asked Professor Ignorance whether I could report her Random Ethics. She was reluctant because of her passion for privacy. One measure of her commitment is theological. Professor Ignorance is an atheist on the grounds that omniscience conflicts with omnibenevolence. If God existed, He would know too much.

Despite her convictions about privacy, Professor Ignorance also believes that morality must be public. To follow the rules, we need to know what they are. How was Professor Ignorance to protect privacy while also meeting the requirement that ethics be common knowledge?

She applied her Random Ethics. Specifically, she gave me permission to write *two* essays. One of the essays should be fiction. The other should be non-fiction. Both must end with the following disclaimer: A flip of the coin has settled whether you are reading fiction or non-fiction.

Nothing Is Written in Stone

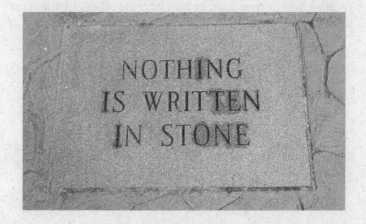

♀ Is the engraved sentence true or false?

Self-Fulfilling, Self-Defeating Prophecies

♀ Can an announcement be both self-defeating and self-fulfilling?

The Philosopher's Petition

> City councillor: 'I move, Mr Chairman, that all fire
> extinguishers be examined ten days before every fire.'

The following petition was printed in the November 1985 *Proceedings of the American Philosophical Association*: 'Proposed nominees must be asked to consent to nomination, and before giving a firm answer must be told who the other nominees are to be' (p. 278). ♀ Is the petition coherent?

Napoleon's Meta-Discovery

> We expect all things from you, General,
> except a lesson in geometry.
> Simon Laplace

Construct equilateral triangles on the sides of any triangle.

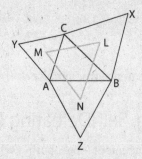

The centres of those equilateral triangles (LMN) themselves form an equilateral triangle. I learned this as 'Napoleon's theorem'. This sparked interest in the theorem.

Later I wondered whether the name of the theorem was just a way of motivating students to study the proof. Did Napoleon really discover it?

Napoleon had an avid interest in geometry. Mathematicians find it plausible that Napoleon could have worked out the proof. For, as they cruelly observe, *many* amateurs have deduced the theorem. It is the most rediscovered theorem.

Experts can see how easy the theorem is to prove. Amateurs cannot. So amateurs develop hopes of having made a discovery. The theorem is a vanity trap.

Napoleon's theorem conforms to Stigler's law of eponymy: 'No scientific discovery is named after its original discoverer.' The law has many instances in logic. Russell's paradox was discovered by Georg Cantor, Jourdain's visiting card paradox was discovered by G. G. Berry, and Moore's paradox of analysis was formulated by C. H. Langford as an objection to Moore.

And what of Stigler's law? Stigler points out that Robert Merton formulated the law before him. The general principle was formulated before Merton by Alfred North Whitehead: 'Everything of importance has been said before by somebody who did not discover it' (*The Organization of Thought, Educational and Scientific*, 1917, p. 127). Several books have provided hundreds of instances of Whitehead's thesis. This includes multiple discoveries of the fact that there are multiple discoveries.

Although Napoleon's theorem conforms to the principle, it also provides evidence against it. For it is an interesting discovery that Napoleon's theorem is the most rediscovered theorem.

Discoveries about discoveries are themselves discoveries. Since the chain extends without limit, the very process of discovery creates new facts to discover. These discoveries must be made in chronological order. So it cannot be case that everything has already been discovered before.

What should I call this discovery? Taking inspiration from Napoleon's theorem and Stigler's law of eponymy, I dub it 'Napoleon's meta-discovery'.

Handicaps on Deduction

I overlapped with Professor Timothy Williamson when he concluded his final year at the University of Edinburgh. I was surprised that he would wear a tie at work even on Sundays. No one was around. Such a professional!

After he became the Wykeham Professor of Logic at the

University of Oxford, we went out to dinner. I looked forward to the opportunity to continue a running debate we had about vagueness.

Despite this being a formal restaurant, Professor Williamson removed his tie. With relief, I removed my tie. I complimented him on the wisdom of this new informality. He asked me to explain my enthusiasm. I reported research that ties restrict blood flow to the brain. Pilots are forbidden from wearing regular ties because they reduce visual acuity. If Professor Williamson and I followed the example of the pilots, the quality of our reasoning should improve.

Hearing this, Professor Williamson put his tie back on. He clinched it extra tight, explaining, 'That is all right, I am only debating with *you*.'

The incident made me wonder whether there is a healthier form of logical handicapping. One possibility is to impose more restraints on the types of refutations one may offer. Let me illustrate with my favourite example of a logical myth. The myth is so powerful that it is endorsed by the *Oxford English Dictionary* – despite a century of debunking by logicians. The *OED* defines 'induction' as

> The process of inferring a general law or principle from the observation of particular instances (opposed to deduction)

and by symmetry defines 'deduction' as

> The process of deducing or drawing a conclusion from a principle already known or assumed; spec. in Logic, inference by reasoning from generals to particulars; opposed to induction.

You have three tasks:

First, refute the *OED* any way you wish.
Second, refute the *OED* with the following handicap; your counterexample must use a single premise – and that premise cannot differ from the conclusion.
Third, refute the *OED* without using any premises at all.

Logical Insults

There's a guy who asserted both *p* and not-*p*, and
then drew out all the consequences ...

Sidney Morgenbesser on George Santayana

According to Dick Cavett, 'There are two kinds of insult. "I
was bored by your book" is one kind. "Your book? Once I put
it down, I couldn't pick it up," is the other.' The second insult
requires the hearer to actively infer the unwelcome message.
The deeper the victim must dig, the deeper the dig.

By this measure, logicians should have the deepest insults.
And, indeed, the deepest I know of is by the logician and set
theorist Ernest Zermelo. At the time he was a privatdozent at
the University of Göttingen when Felix Klein dominated the
mathematics department. Wolfgang Pauli recalls:

> Zermelo taught a course on mathematical logic and
> stunned his students by posing the following question: 'All
> mathematicians in Göttingen belong to one of two classes.
> In the first class belong those mathematicians who do what
> Felix Klein likes, but what they dislike. In the second class
> are those mathematicians who do what they like, but what
> Felix Klein dislikes. To what class does Felix Klein belong?'
>
> – Quoted by E. L. Schucking, 'Jordan, Pauli, Politics, Brecht and a
> Variable Gravitational Constant', *Physics Today*, October 1999

None of Zermelo's students could solve the problem. ♥ Can
you?

Logical Humility

The American cowboy Will Rogers (1879–1935) got a job in
a circus demonstating his skill with a lariat. To cover failed
lassos, he developed self-deprecating humour. The crowds
enjoyed the jokes so much that he began to deliberately miss.
Eventually, the act became comedic social commentary. He
went on to act in movies and write a nationally syndicated

newspaper column (expertly packed with misspellings and malapropisms).

He adopted the persona of an affable home-spun philosopher of ignorance. 'There are three kinds of men: The ones that learn by reading. The few who learn by observation. The rest of them have to pee on the electric fence for themselves.' Although he teased the high and mighty, Rogers took pride in his universal affection for people – even vilified communists such as Leon Trotsky:

> I bet you if I had met him and had a chat with him, I would
> have found him a very interesting and human fellow, for
> I never yet met a man that I dident [*sic*] like. When you
> meet people, no matter what opinion you might have
> formed about them beforehand, why, after you meet them
> and see their angle and their personality, why, you can see
> a lot of good in all of them.
>
> – From: *Saturday Evening Post*, 6 November 1926

Rogers would shrug his shoulders, look at the floor, and scratch his head in puzzlement. He knew how to deepen the bow of humility by inference. When the 1928 presidential nominating convention could not decide on a stance towards Prohibition, Will Rogers remarked, 'I'm not a member of an organised political party. I'm a Democrat.'

The Will Rogers of mathematicians is Jerry Lloyd Bona: 'The Axiom of Choice is obviously true; the Well Ordering Principle is obviously false; and who can tell about Zorn's Lemma?'

The joke is that set theorists have different psychological reactions to the three principles even though they are mathematically equivalent. Given any one of them as a premise, there is a proof of the other two.

The axiom of choice is intuitive to contemporary set theorists. Given any collection of sets with members, there will be a set corresponding to any selection of members of that collection. In other words, we can always form a group by drafting members from other groups. There is no restriction on the recruiting method. In particular, we do not need to be able to isolate an individual with a definite description. Nor do we need to have a name. That is fortunate because there are more real numbers than names. The number of sentences in a natural language is only the low-order infinity corresponding to the natural numbers. The quantity of real numbers is at the next level of infinity. So there are infinitely many anonymous real numbers. The axiom of choice lets us skip the choosing process and just enjoy a prepackaged choice.

The 'well-ordering principle' is not controversial for natural numbers: every non-empty set of positive integers contains a least element. But it seems false as applied to the real numbers because there is not least real above, say, 0. How can *every* set admit a well-order?

Lastly, Zorn's lemma is so byzantine that most mathematicians do not have any intuition about whether it is true or false: If a partially ordered set S has the property that every chain (a totally ordered subset) has an upper bound in S, then the set S contains at least one maximal element. Bemused, they go off the deep end: ♡ 'What is brown, furry, runs to the sea, and is equivalent to the axiom of choice?'

Blasphemous Tautologies

First Maxim for Balliol Men: Even a truism may be true.

Dr Mohammed Younus Shaikh was alleged to have made the following remarks at the Capital Medical College in Islamabad on 2 October 2000: The Prophet Muhammad did not become a Muslim until the age of 40, the age at which he received the first message from God. The parents of Muhammad, the founder of Islam, were not Muslims because they died before Islam existed. Muhammad wed without an Islamic marriage contract because he was 25 and no one had yet received the message from God that inaugurated Islam. Lastly, Muhammad was unlikely to have been circumcised or to have shaved under his armpits or to have shaved his pubic hair, because those practices were unknown to his tribe.

Shaikh was found guilty and sentenced to death and a fine of 100,000 rupees. Jerome Neu summarises Western puzzlement at the charge of blasphemy in *Sticks and Stones*:

> To many that might seem not only a truthful claim (based on the practices of the Prophet's tribe), but (with regard to the first part of the claim) even a logically necessary truth, given that Muhammad is not thought to have received the revelations which became the foundation of the new religion of Islam until age 40.

A logically necessary statement carries no information since it is compatible with every way the world can be. Since there is no information, it cannot carry derogatory information.

I shared Neu's puzzlement. If a tautology is blasphemous, then a pious Muslim should deny the blasphemy. It seems more blasphemous to say that the parents of Muhammad were Muslims prior to his founding of Islam. For this implies that Muhammad did not found Islam.

Contradictions have a better prospect for being blasphemous. For they do entail defamatory statements. The conjunction 'Perzo is a paedophile and it is not the case that Perzo is a paedophile' entails Perzo is a paedophile. That is defamatory because it so specifically mentions Perzo. Put yourself in Perzo's shoes as he listens to such a contradiction.

But what about a contradiction that makes no mention of Perzo, say, 'Sitara sings and it is not the case that Sitara sings.' In classical logic, this statement entails that Perzo is a paedophile:

1. Sitara sings and it is the not case that Sitara sings.
2. Sitara sings. (From 1 by simplification.)
3. Either Sitara sings or Perzo is a paedophile. (From 2 by addition.)
4. It is not case that Sitara sings. (From 1 by simplification.)
5. Perzo is a paedophile. (From 3 and 4 by disjunctive syllogism.)

If saying something that entails defamation is itself defamation, then all contradictions are defamatory.

We are at the threshold of a new defence of the law of non-contradiction: violations defame everybody.

Instead of crossing this threshold, we should back away from the presupposition that insults are entirely semantic. Information is also carried by the fact that one uttered the sentence. If I say, 'Either Perzo is a paedophile or it is not the case that Perzo is a paedophile', I imply that the first disjunct might be true, that is, that there is evidence of Perzo being a paedophile or at least that the available evidence does not exclude it. So I can convey derogatory information by uttering the tautology. The utterance is a contingent event and unproblematically conveys information.

Section 295C of Pakistan's Penal Code warns, 'Whoever by the words, either spoken or written, or by visible representation, or by any imputation, innuendo, or insinuation, directly or indirectly, defiles the sacred name of the Holy Prophet Muhammad shall be punished with the death sentence or imprisonment for life and shall be liable to fine.' A logician might make sport of Section 295C by defiling Muhammad while honouring his *name*.

This is a diversion that can only be pursued at a distance. The legislators were aware of the cat and mouse game that is created by blasphemy bans. A blasphemer can implicate disparaging information with a truth that does not entail this information. Indeed, the blasphemer may even hide behind a tautology. So Section 295C is written broadly to forbid even indirect derogatory remarks.

The rationale for such a broad and severe prohibition is twofold. First, that there is the intrinsic wrong of blasphemy. Second, the blasphemer endangers the community since Allah collectively punishes believers (and infidels) who fail to punish blasphemers.

Dr Shaikh's defence was that the lecture never occurred. He claimed that foreign office policymakers were offended by his criticism of their abuses of power. They orchestrated a complaint signed by eleven students.

After two years in jail Dr Shaikh was released on appeal. He attempted to sue his accusers, the mullahs and the Taliban. A fatwa was issued against him. Mohammed Younus Shaikh fled the country and now resides in Switzerland.

Generality Jokes and Consistency Proofs

Not all jokes turn on ambiguity. Some turn on *generality*.[31] My oldest specimen was recorded in the fourth century in Macrobius' *Saturnalia*. A provincial comes to Rome. The citizens gawk because the newcomer bears an uncanny resemblance to Emperor Augustus. The First Citizen summons his lookalike. 'Tell me, young man, did your mother come to Rome anytime?' The emperor's double replies: 'She never has. But my father frequently was here.'

The humour comes from an alternative model that would account for their resemblance. The audience must display the same skill as exercised in riddles about kinship.

My niece got a butterfly and flower tattoo with the sweetly lettered motto 'What you give is what you get'. Her hulking brother responded with a tattoo displaying the same motto wrapped around a horned skull sporting a demonic grin. He subverted her tattoo by emphasising how reciprocity includes retribution.

Often the joke teases the audience by enticing them into thinking of a taboo solution. 'Can you name a common English word, besides sugar, in which the initial *s* is pronounced *sh*?' The riddler, with affected naivety, provides a simple, innocent solution: 'Sure.'

Often the joke involves considerable ingenuity. A man sees his mistress having lunch with his wife and remarks to his friend 'Isn't that a sight! A woman has breakfast with her lover and lunch with his wife!' His friend blanches: 'How did you know?'

---

[31] Ambiguity is the possession of multiple meanings. 'Bank' means the side of a river and means a financial institution. Generality is a single meaning that encompasses many things. 'Elephant' has a single meaning that covers both Indian elephants and African elephants. 'Pachyderm' is more general than 'elephant' but is not more ambiguous than 'elephant'.

Since truthful misleading is less blameworthy than lying, letters of recommendation contain vague claims such as: 'He doesn't care how many hours he must put in', 'There is nothing you can teach him', and 'All in all, I cannot say enough good things about this candidate or recommend him too highly.'

In generality jokes, one finds an unexpected way of satisfying a description – without any shift in meaning. These jokes employ the same skill that logicians use in consistency proofs. The simplest way to prove a set of requirements is consistent is to sketch a scenario in which all conditions are met. Will Rogers joked, 'When the Okies left Oklahoma and moved to California, they raised the average intelligence level in both states.' If someone objects that this is impossible, you can respond with a model consisting of two groups of digits:

California = 1, 2, 3, 4   Oklahoma = 5, 6, 7, 8, 9

When 5 moves west from Oklahoma to California, the mean of both populations increases.

The theorems of non-Euclidean geometry were initially derived as absurdities that followed from rejecting Euclid's fifth postulate (parallel lines never meet) while retaining his previous four axioms. In *Euclid Freed of Every Flaw*, Giovanni Girolamo Saccheri (1667–1733) tried to prove the parallel postulate by *reductio ad absurdum*. The negation of that theorem is equivalent to the statement that the sum of the internal angles of a triangle is $180°$. Saccheri first supposes that they add up to more. This leads to the conclusion that straight lines are finite – which conflicts with Euclid's second postulate that a straight line segment can be extended indefinitely. Contradiction.[32] To complete the *reductio*, Saccheri next supposes that the internal angles of a triangle sum to more than $180°$. He validly derived many bizarre consequences: triangles have a maximum finite area, there is an absolute unit of length, and so forth. He misclassifies the absurdities as contradictions and

---

[32] But not if one gives up the second postulate as well – as is done in elliptic geometry. Saccheri's project is to prove Euclid's first four postulates entail the fifth.

so believed he had completed the second half of his *reductio ad absurdum*. But these absurdities are regarded as theorems of hyperbolic geometry. For subsequent mathematicians found ways of mapping the non-Euclidean principles on to spheres. This showed that non-Euclidean geometry was consistent. Or to put the point negatively, this showed that the Euclidean axioms were not necessary truths.

To Be and Not to Be

♀ Riddle: I once had a grandfather but I never had a father. What might I be?

Lobster Logic

♀ Cross a logician with a lobster and what do you get?

The Lobster, illustrated by John Tenniel.

Lewis Carroll's poem ''Tis the Voice of the Lobster' describes a vain lobster who cannot back up his boasts:

> When the sands are all dry, he is gay as a lark,
> And will talk in contemptuous tones of the Shark;
> But, when the tide rises and sharks are around,
> His voice has a timid and tremulous sound.

Teach that weak lobster some logic and his *voice*, at least, strengthens.

The lame slave, Epictetus, scuttled about at the bottom of Roman society. An angry master had broken his leg. In lieu of physical services, the lame Epictetus tutored children. Diligent study enabled him to teach more advanced students. Eventually, Epictetus became an eminent Stoic dialectician:

> When one of his audience said, 'Convince me that logic is useful,' he said, Would you have me demonstrate it?
> 'Yes.'
> Well, then, must I not use a demonstrative argument?
> And, when the other agreed, he said, How then shall you know if I impose upon you? And when the man had no answer, he said, You see how you yourself admit that logic is necessary, if without it you are not even able to learn this much – whether it is necessary or not.
>
> – Epictetus, *Discourses*, ii.25

Epictetus is not arguing with the challenger. He is demonstrating that the challenger already agrees that argument is useful – as a test for usefulness. There is no room for argument because his 'adversary' is already persuaded.

A. J. Ayer had a very active social life, even into retirement. In 1987, the 77-year-old Ayer was at a New York party entertaining a group of fashion models. A young woman ran in screaming; her friend was under assault in a bedroom. Ayer entered to discover Naomi Campbell and Mike Tyson. When Ayer insisted on Campbell's release, Tyson was incredulous: 'Do you know who … I am? I'm the heavyweight champion of the world.' Ayer responded politely, 'And I am the former Wykeham Professor of Logic. We are both pre-eminent in our field. I suggest that we talk about this like rational men.' Campbell slipped away.

The logician W. V. Quine was frequently criticised for his close shaves with Ockham's razor. A reporter pressed him, quoting William Shakespeare's statement from Hamlet: 'There are more things in heaven and earth … than are dreamt of in your philosophy.' W. V. Quine conceded, 'Possibly, but my concern is that there not be more things in my philosophy than are in heaven and earth.'

The philosopher Peter Unger ranked himself as 'tied for last' in logic class. But he was incisive, especially when anyone failed to directly answer his questions (which were somehow both blunt and sharp). One of these questions involved the supposition that Derek Parfit was a brain in a vat. Parfit was not in the mood for fanciful cross-examination. He had just flown into New York the night before. Parfit wearily replied that he could not imagine what it would be like to be a brain in a vat. It was just too far out. Unger's riposte: You know all too well what it is like – it is exactly what is going on right now! Silence ... then a little wave of giggles rose from the back row and lapped forward. Parfit, pausing to introspect his oceanic state, conceded that Unger appeared all too correct. Parfit promised a better reply after he had a good night's sleep.

Richard Feynman enjoyed running down all intellectuals who were not physicists. In a lecture to fourth-year biology students, Feynman drew a diagram of a cat and started labelling the muscles. The students protested that they already knew the muscle groups:

> 'Oh,' I say, 'you do? Then no wonder I can catch up with you so fast after you've had four years of biology.' They had wasted all their time memorizing stuff like that, when it could be looked up in fifteen minutes.

I recently met such memorisers in a hospital emergency room. None of the staff won the Richard P. Feynman Prize for Medicine by taking out an encyclopedia. Instead of spending fifteen minutes looking up the names of the muscle groups of my broken arm, the physicians treated me straightaway.

What about mathematicians? Admittedly this takes longer than fifteen minutes: 'If all of mathematics disappeared,' reckons Feynman, 'physics would be set back by exactly one week.'

In reply, the mathematician Mark Kac[33] got more specific: 'Precisely the week in which God created the world.' Kac was alluding to Plato's saying, 'God geometrises.' Others have supplied the missing intermediate steps:

Biologists think they are Biochemists,
Biochemists think they are Physical Chemists,
Physical Chemists think they are Physicists,
Physicists think they are Gods,
And God thinks he is a Mathematician.

Of all intellectuals, Feynman preferred to target philosophers. They unite the biggest goals with the smallest achievements. After running down the philosophers in general, Feynman ran them down by speciality. He once quipped, 'Philosophy of science is about as useful to scientists as ornithology is to birds.' When this was repeated to Jonathan Schaffer, he quietly replied, 'It is likely that ornithological knowledge would be of great benefit to birds, were it possible for them to possess it.'

Logicians are sometimes on the receiving end of the snappy comeback. When Graham Priest got a tattoo, the ethicist Roger Lamb asked why. Priest, well prepared for the challenge, said it was a brute desire.

'Like eating dirt?' asked Roger.

---

[33] Kac collaborated with Feynman on a formula that links parabolic partial differential equations with stochastic processes. Kac classified Feynman as a magician rather than an ordinary genius such as Hans Bethe. Kac's 1966 article 'Can One Hear the Shape of the Drum?' concerns whether two resonators of different shapes can have exactly the same set of frequencies. If they could not, you could tell the shape of a drum from its sound tones. But it turns out the resonators can't. So the answer sounds boring. But the process of reaching the answer set off interesting research into spectral theory. The hope was to trace the spectrum back to the geometry.

The Triple Contract

Brutus composed treatises on virtue. He was also a loan shark. Debtors quipped that Brutus was a man of high principle and higher interest.

The ancients regarded all interest-based loans as loan-sharking. The Jews were willing to engage in the practice with *outsiders*. But loans within the community were to be interest-free acts of charity.

The wrongness of money-lending was not so evident to German merchants in the sixteenth century. They understood the advantage of being able to borrow for long-term projects. Ambitious businessmen supported scholarship that might circumvent usury laws.

The learned were asked: Suppose Borrower is willing to pay 5% interest for a loan from Lender and Lender is willing to loan the money at that rate. But laws against interest forbade the transaction. Is there a legal substitute for borrowing money with an interest payment?

The Dominican theologian John Eck, who debated with Martin Luther in Leipzig in 1519, hypothesised a way to contract around the usury prohibition. The first contract makes Lender and Borrower partners in a business venture. The second contract insures Lender against loss of his capital in exchange for taking a lesser percentage of the profits – perhaps 0%. A third contract guarantees that Lender receives a set rate of interest, usually 5%. Each contract is legal so the conjunction of contracts is legal. They yield the same result as the illegal 5% loan. A modern equivalent is a debenture in which a passive stockholder 'clips coupons'.

This attractive arrangement generated an investment boom in Germany. In 1555 the Jesuits withheld absolution from anyone participating in a triple contract. The Jesuits maintained that the triple contract was disguised usury. Reportedly, the Fuggers, an international banking house, subsidised Eck's defence. For Western Europe, if not Eck, this loophole became the most lucrative thought experiment in history.

Voltaire's Big Bet

What is individually permissible is collectively permissible. This principle was sorely tested by Voltaire. In 1728 Paris defaulted on its bonds. This jeopardised the ability of the government to raise money with more bonds. The finance minister addressed the problem by letting the disappointed bondholders buy lottery tickets at 1/1,000th the value of their face value. The winners would get the face value of the bond plus 500,000 livres.

The suspicious bondholders were reluctant to throw good money after bad money. They correctly perceived that the finance minister was trying to elicit yet more money from the very people the government had stiffed. 'Fool me once, shame on you. Fool me twice, shame on me.'

No one noticed that the finance minister was too clever for his own good. The value of the lottery prize greatly exceeded the combined cost of the tickets.

Well, almost no one. Two of the bondholders, Voltaire and the mathematician Charles Marie de La Condamine, organised a syndicate to buy their fellow bondholders' tickets. This would virtually guarantee a huge profit. All they had to do was keep a low profile and keep buying tickets, lottery after lottery.

Voltaire was socially adept. He was the charismatic fixer. But Voltaire was also indiscreet. Ticket holders used to write good luck phrases on the backs of their tickets. Voltaire began to write sarcastic compliments to the French finance minister. Although Voltaire signed the tickets with false names, the 'bons mots' alerted the government to the fact that the same players were winning each lottery.

In court, Voltaire and company successfully argued that their separately legal acts must be collectively legal. The court grudgingly agreed. But the government cancelled further lotteries.

Even so, the syndicate had earned between 6 and 7 million francs. Voltaire's share was half a million. That made him independently wealthy, and a royal pain, for life.

Biblical Counting

How many animals of each kind did Moses take on the ark?

Russell's Slip of the Pen

Note from Bertrand Russell Archive, dated 21 December 1904, from 12 Hermes Road, Oxford.

The third word of the next to last line should be 'true' rather than 'false'. This is the most interesting slip in the history of logic. It is a counterexample to the generalisation that every paradox starts as an idea. It illustrates the creativity of automatic behaviour.

The story begins with G. G. Berry presenting Russell with a card that resembles the current, official T-shirt of the American Philosophical Association:

Front: The sentence on the back of this shirt is false.
Back: The sentence on the front of this shirt is true.

On the one hand, if Front is true, then Back is false. But if

Back is false then Front is false. Since Front cannot be both true and false, the supposition that it is true must rejected. On the other hand, if Front is false, then it accurately denies what Back states. Since Front says nothing more than that, Front must be true. Thus the supposition that Front is false also leads to a contradiction. Either assignment of a truth-value leads to a contradiction.

Berry had split Epimenides' liar paradox, 'This sentence is false', into two, individually harmless statements. When combined, there is no consistent assignment of truth-values. Since the sentences are only paradoxical *as a pair*, any solution to the liar paradox must be holistic.

Russell was deeply immersed in the liar paradox and so understood Berry's discovery (which was subsequently miscredited to Philip Jourdain). But the great logician misrecorded the incident. Slips tend to follow the more common course of events. It is conversationally rare for 'That is false' to be met with 'That is true'. The more common response is the symmetrical 'He said, she said' exchange in which each party accuses the other of falsehood. Since automatic behaviour errs in the direction of the more frequent, Russell substituted 'false' for 'true'.

Automatic behaviour is systematic and tends to resurface after correction. And indeed, Russell repeats the slip of the pen in the 1951 edition of his autobiography. When another edition of the autobiography appeared in 1967 a reader alerted Russell. He published a correction in a letter to a newspaper:

False and true

From Earl Russell, O.M., F.R.S.

Sir,—Some readers of extracts from my autobiography have questioned—and rightly—the contradiction which I mentioned as being "essentially similar to that of Epimenides."

On a piece of paper is written: 'The statement on the other side of this paper is false.' The person turns the paper over and finds on the other side: 'The statement on the other side of this paper is false.' On turning over the paper, the recipient should read: 'The statement on the other side of this paper is true.' I regret that I made this error.

Bertrand Russell

Penrhyndeudraeth.

From the *Observer*, 12 March 1967, p. 33.

This correction was incorporated into the second printing of his 1967 edition.

However, the slip reappears in the 1971 paperback. Russell died in 1970. Consequently, the 1971 slip of the pen got the last word.

Paul Hoffman used the 1971 paperback in his intriguing biography of Paul Erdős, *The Man Who Only Loved Numbers* (pp. 113–14). A book reviewer, Cliff Landesman, complained that Hoffman fumbled the looped liar paradox. As Landesman observed, the quoted version permits us to consistently assign truth to the first sentence and false to the second sentence (and vice versa). Hoffman replied that this was the liar paradox in Bertrand Russell's autobiography.

The chagrinned reviewer asked me to clear up the confusion. I became puzzled because my edition of the autobiography was correct. I won the admiration of my university's librarian by ordering all the editions and distinct printings of the great sceptic's autobiography.

While waiting for the autobiographies, I realised that the unintended pair of sentences constitutes an inadvertent paradox. The symmetry between the sentences makes arbitrary any asymmetric assignment of truth-values. How could one of the identical twins be true and the other false?

This makes the 'no-no paradox' reminiscent of the truth-teller paradox: 'This sentence is true.' Although one can consistently assign either truth-value to the sentence, this very freedom makes either assignment arbitrary. Some have suggested that the truth-teller could be solved if there were a default truth-value, say false. But this would not solve the no-no paradox. The symmetry between the sentences provides no basis to count one as having the default truth-value.

In tracing the error back, I also discovered the reverse slip. The first edition of R. M. Sainsbury's *Paradoxes* correctly quotes the fourteenth-century Jean Buridan's 'Eighth Sophism':

> Socrates in Troy says, 'What Plato is now saying in Athens is false.' At the same time, Plato in Athens says, 'What Socrates is now saying in Troy is false.' (1988, p. 145)

However, in Sainsbury's second edition (1995, p. 145), the last occurrence of 'false' is miscorrected to 'true'.

Sainsbury's reverse slip stems from his erudition rather than the ordinary force of habit that repeatedly trips Russell. At the time Sainsbury was writing, there was far more commentary on the looped liar than on the rarely mentioned no-no paradox. The only pre-Sainsbury mentions of the no-no paradox since Buridan were by Arthur Prior (1976) and Laurence Goldstein (1992).

Sainsbury's third edition of *Paradoxes* corrects the miscorrection. I look forward to the fourth edition.

The First Female Philosopher?

A logician's wife is having a baby. The midwife immediately hands the newborn to the father. The wife asks, 'Is it a boy or a girl?' The logician studies the infant. He concludes, 'Yes.'

Who was the first female philosopher? The 'natural eunuch', Favorinus of Arelate (c. AD 80–150), may have rendered the question moot.

A hermaphrodite who leaned towards the male end of the spectrum was more likely to be granted the benefit of the doubt – and enjoy the prerogatives of manhood. Yet Favorinus did not rest on the benefit of the doubt. He courted ambivalence by speaking and dressing effeminately. This flamboyant Pyrrhonian summed up his life in three paradoxes: he was a barbarian from Gaul who spoke Greek, a eunuch accused of adultery, and a citizen who quarrelled with an emperor – and yet lived.

Favorinus' skill at balancing each argument with a counter-argument made him a popular teacher of upper-class Romans. When silenced by Emperor Hadrian in argument, Favorinus later explained that it would be foolish to criticise the logic of the master of thirty legions. When the Athenians pulled down a statue they had erected to Favorinus, Favorinus speculated that had there been a statue of Socrates, Socrates might have been spared the hemlock.

This philosopher (or was Favorinus a mere sophist or rhetorician or provocateur?) was not ready to die for his *beliefs*! Favorinus cultivated not only doubt, but also doubts about doubts, and doubts about those doubts. As Galen ruefully recounts in *The Best Education*, Favorinus first recommends that students be left to make up their own minds, then in *Plutarch* allows for the possibility of certainty, and then in *Alcibiades* argues nothing can be known. Favorinus was more of a meta-agnostic than an agnostic and more of a meta-meta-agnostic than a meta-agnostic. Favorinus can only be approached asymptotically; we get closer but never quite make contact.

As a borderline case of 'woman' or perhaps a borderline case of 'a borderline case of a "woman"', Favorinus had a predilection for embedded doubts.

To achieve *ataraxia* (tranquillity through suspended judgement) Favorinus first explored how doubts about doubts grow in the wild. He entered large issues osmotically through the pores of etymology.

Philologists tell us that readers of Ovid introduced the term 'hermaphrodite'. In *Metamorphoses*, Hermaphroditos is the son of Hermes and Aphrodite (the gods of male and female sexuality). The nymph Salmacis loved Hermaphroditos. Her prayer for union resulted in their fusion.

Since borderline status is relative to a predicate (a clear case of 'adult' can be a borderline case of 'male'), indeterminacy can be artfully reversed. In Plato's *Symposium* Aristophanes characterised hermaphroditism as a return to an original ideal state. The jealous Zeus split the two-headed, four-armed, four-footed human beings into males and females. These partially defined beings then strive for completion.

'Hermaphrodite' was introduced to cope with borderline males. Such intermediate categories only bring temporary respite from taxonomic stress. After the criteria for assignment into the *ad hoc* category conventionalise, attention turns to borderline cases in which these criteria are neither definitely satisfied nor definitely violated. For instance, there are pseudo-hermaphrodites who only possess superficial traits of the opposed gender. Since superficiality comes in degrees, there are borderline pseudo-hermaphrodites.

The cycle is familiar to lawyers. Reformers undercut litigation about borderline cases by legislating an intermediate category. However, the new category itself has vague boundaries. The lawyers exploit the fresh opportunities for litigation – precipitating a new round of legislation.

The maxim 'Hard cases make bad law' is used to justify the practice of ignoring borderline cases. By sticking to clear cases, we get simple cases.

We are doubly sure Favorinus is a borderline case of 'the first female philosopher' because of doubt about whether Favorinus is a *woman* plus doubt about whether Favorinus is a *philosopher*.

Is a Burrito a Sandwich?

You can shrug your shoulders. A judge cannot. The law requires decisive verdicts. Further, verdicts must be backed by sincere reasons. Arbitrary decisions and lies are prohibited.

In 2006 Worcester Superior Court Judge Jeffrey A. Locke had to decide whether a burrito is a sandwich. Panera Bread Company alleged that the owners of the White City Shopping Center violated their agreement to exclude all other sandwich restaurants when they permitted Qdoba Mexican Grill to sell their burritos, tacos, and quesadillas. In an eight-page decision, Judge Locke cited *Webster's Third New International Dictionary* definition of a sandwich. He explained that the difference comes down to two slices of bread versus one tortilla: 'A sandwich is not commonly understood to include burritos, tacos, and quesadillas, which are typically made with a single tortilla and stuffed with a choice filling of meat, rice, and beans.'

Linguists make fun of the judge. But what is the judge to do? He cannot join the linguists and say that there is no fact of matter.

Some legal theorists suggest that borderline cases can be handled by introducing tie-breaking rules such as 'Borderline cases are to be precisified in favour of the defence'. Others suggest adoption of the Scottish 'Not proven' as a third verdict.

Recognition of why these reforms are futile is embodied in a proposal made by the Baltimore Orioles outfielder John Lowenstein: 'They should move first base back a step to eliminate all the close plays' (Reported by the *Detroit Free Press*, 27 April 1984, at F1).

Second Place

The early bird may get the worm, but the
second mouse gets the cheese.

In the 1993 Daytona 500 stock-car race, Dale Earnhardt overtook the driver in second place. What position was he then in?

The answer is second place. Earnhardt never liked this position: 'Second place is just the first-place loser.'

In a classic Western showdown between two gunslingers, the first to shoot has the advantage – as epitomised by the epitaph: 'Here lies a man named Zeke. Second fastest draw in Cripple Creek.'

In the finale of Sergio Leone's Western *The Good, the Bad, and the Ugly,* a third gunslinger enters the conflict. Does the advantage still go to the man who shoots first?

Now second place is best. If Good shoots Bad, then while so engaged, Ugly can shoot Good thus winning the gunfight. Since no one wants to go first, the three adversaries are in a 'Mexican standoff'. (This is the harsh cousin of a Canadian standoff in which two polite Canadians each insist 'After you!')

But how is the standoff to be resolved? David Hume commonly solved problems intractable to reason by appealing to nature. So let us consult the Antarctic explorer Apsley Cherry-Garrard:

> The life of an Adelie penguin is one of the most unchristian and successful in the world. The penguin which went in for being a true believer would never stand the ghost of a chance. Watch them go to bathe. Some fifty or sixty agitated birds are gathered upon the ice-foot, peering over the edge, telling one another how nice it will be, and what a good dinner they are going to have. But this is all swank: they are really worried by a horrid suspicion that a sea-leopard is waiting to eat the first to dive. The really noble bird, according to our theories, would say, 'I will go first and if I am killed I shall at any rate have died unselfishly, sacrificing my life for my companions'; and in time all the most noble birds would be dead. What they really do is to try and persuade a companion of weaker mind to plunge: failing this, they hastily pass a conscription act and push him over. And then – bang, helter-skelter, in go all the rest.
>
> – Cherry-Garrard, *The Worst Journey in the World*, p. 360

The Drachma's Defect

Our foibles are really what make us lovable.

Goethe

Coins are unusual in that *defects* make them more valuable. Numismaticians pay extra for pennies with multiple images, nickels with broken rims, and quarters with off-centred strikes.

I value coins that are conceptually flawed. Consider the 1992 Greek 10-drachma coin honouring Democritus:

Front and back of the 1992 Greek 10-drachma coin.

Democritus taught that there is nothing but atoms and void. An atom is the smallest possible thing. So an atom lacks any proper parts. But the atom on the reverse side has electrons orbiting a nucleus!

This is the solar system atom popularised by Niels Bohr. The Bohr model of the atom is itself illogical. A positively charged nucleus corresponds to the sun and negatively charged electrons correspond to the planets. Since the electrons are accelerating (due to their circular orbits), they should lose energy and spiral into the nucleus after a few orbits. To stop this, Bohr imposed a quantisation condition: instead of losing energy continuously, the electron changes energy in discrete jumps (quanta). However, an accelerating charged particle must lose angular momentum continuously.

So why did the Bohr model continue to be popular? Because it delivered predictions that were uniquely accurate. Back in 1918, G. A. Schott explains:

> Bohr's theory of the Balmer series is based upon several novel hypotheses in greater or less contradiction with ordinary mechanics and electrodynamics ... yet the representation afforded by it of the line spectrum is so extraordinarily exact that a considerable substratum of truth can hardly be denied to it. Therefore, it is matter of great theoretical importance to examine how far really it is inconsistent with ordinary electrodynamics, and in what way it can be modified so as to remove the contradictions.

If logically equivalent statements are equidistant from the truth, then inconsistent theories should not vary in how close they are to the truth. But physicists got closer to the truth by improving on Bohr's model even when those improvements fell short of making the theory consistent.

Illogical Coin Collecting

British coins are, collectively, illogical. Euro coins progress in size with their increasing value. The British coin sizes are haphazard. The 10p coin is bigger than the 20p. The 50p combines elements of 10p and the 20p. The 2p is bigger than all the rest.

But I do not collect illogical coin *systems*. I collect illogical coins. This brings me to my favourite coin, the British £2 coin – the silver/gold two-pound coin introduced by the Royal Mint on 15 June 1998.

The design symbolises the history of British technological achievements. There are 19 gears. ♀ Why was this an unfortunate choice in the number of gears?

The Centime and the Bottle Imp

Robert Louis Stevenson's 1893 short story 'The Bottle Imp' features a creation of the devil: an indestructible bottle that contains an imp. The imp grants the bottle's owner nearly anything he wishes. The catch is that anyone who dies while still possessing the bottle goes to hell. The only way to end possession is to sell the bottle at a cheaper price to someone who is well informed about the bottle's terms of ownership.

In Stevenson's original tale, the bottle starts out at an enormous price. Eventually a boatswain agrees to buy it for the price of two centimes, a centime being the lowest unit of currency in the world. When the seller dutifully points out that the buyer is sure to go to hell, the boatswain explains that he is going to hell anyway.

But what if the devil had the foresight to require that the buyer not already be damned? If we close such loopholes, we get a 'proof' that the bottle cannot be sold for any amount of money. The bottle cannot be sold if it was bought at the lowest unit of currency, say, one centime. Thus no well-informed person will buy the bottle for two centimes. And if no one will buy at two centimes, no one will buy at three centimes. And so up to any amount of money! Yet it seems that someone would buy it for a million centimes.

In the first edition of 'The Bottle Imp', Stevenson erroneously credits the idea to B. Smith, who was actually only an actor in a play of the same name. The basic idea is in German folklore. The Brothers Grimm borrow it from a work published in 1756 and may have originated as a medieval legend. Since the plot was used in stories all over Europe, the backwards mathematical induction argument may be a thousand years old.

A Meeting of Minds

After learning that I have been married for three decades to a fellow philosophy professor, young people ask what makes for such an enduring relationship. I confess the sources of stability are difficult to discern.

A subtle pillar was exposed in an episode of *The Newlywed Game*. Couples earn points when their answers match. Agreement between spouses is all that matters. While the husbands were sequestered, their wives were asked to predict how many decades their husband would say their mothers had lived. Gloria answered, 'Ten.' When her husband Daryl returned to the set, he was asked how many decades his mother had lived. Daryl worried aloud that he did not know the length of a decade. But he soldiered on, noting that his mother just had her '44th birthday, so she'd be ... At four years a decade, she would be ten decades.'

Deadliest Gettier Case

In 1944 the United States Army wished to capture the French port city of Brest. The strategy was to draw the defenders away to each flank and then attack down the middle. A new 'sonic deception' team was deployed in a pioneering effort to use sound trucks to mislead the enemy into thinking troops were assembling for an attack. The sound trucks convinced the Germans that a tank attack was imminent. German artillery was shifted to the flank and shelling was directed towards the sound source. The new technology, designed in secret by Bell Laboratories, was working!

Then, to the horror of the American sound technicians, actual United States tanks blundered into the area targeted by the Germans.[34] The confused tank crews were decimated.

The mix-up was also fatal for a venerable definition of knowledge. Plato defined knowledge as justified true belief. Belief is not enough for knowledge because any claim to know can be refuted by showing that the claimed knowledge is false. For instance, belief that Polish calvary attacked Nazi panzer divisions is not knowledge because the Polish calvary never was deployed against tanks.

If we add the requirement that the belief must be true, there will still be counterexamples in which the truth of the belief is due to luck. To fill the gap, Plato requires that the knower also have adequate evidence. Plato's definition was accepted for over two thousand years.

The German artillery officers show that Plato's definition cannot be complete. The Germans had justified true belief that American tanks were approaching but did not know that American tanks were approaching. The Germans had reasoned from the accurate premise 'The rumbling sounds are caused by tanks' to the false intermediate step 'The rumbling sounds are *presently* being produced by nearby tanks' and then

---

[34] At the midpoint of the documentary *Ghost Army* veterans sorrowfully recall their inability to help comrades who believed that they were assisting them in a major attack.

on to a true conclusion 'There are tanks where the sounds are coming from'. The Germans had reasonably and accurately inferred the presence of American tanks. But since they had reasoned through a false step, the accuracy of their conclusion was too fortuitous to qualify as knowledge.

Philosophers were slow to recognise this phenomenon as a counterexample to Plato's definition of knowledge. Finally, in 1963 Edmund Gettier carefully describes two scenarios that appeared tailored to fellow logic instructors. Consider Smith who has ample justification for Jones owning a Ford automobile. (Smith has seen Jones driving a Ford, has been told Jones just bought a Ford, etc.) The proposition 'Jones owns a Ford' entails the weaker statement 'Either Jones owns a Ford or Brown is in Barcelona', so Smith is also justified in believing this disjunction (despite having no evidence for Brown being in Barcelona). As it turns out, Jones does not own a Ford but Brown is in Barcelona. Smith's bad luck about Jones owning a Ford has been compensated by good luck about Brown being in Barcelona. But good luck plus bad luck does not equal no luck.

In Gettier's second scenario, Smith and Jones are competing for the same job. Smith realises that Jones is the stronger candidate for the position. Smith has also counted the coins in Jones's pocket. So Smith infers that the man offered the job has ten coins in his pocket. Surprisingly, *Smith* gets the offer. Later Smith discovers that he also has ten coins in his pocket. Once again, Smith has justified true belief (that the man offered the job has ten coins in his pocket) but lacks knowledge.

The Gettier cases are difficult to teach because Smith is making aimless deductions. The normal point of adding 'or Barcelona' is that there is some separate evidence for the Barcelona alternative. For instance, you might not be sure that Brown is in Madrid but be confident that he is in one of the two biggest cities in Spain. If you learned that Brown is not in Madrid, then you would infer that he is in Barcelona. But Gettier's scenario lacks this robustness. If Smith learned that Jones does not own a Ford, he would not conclude that Jones is in Barcelona. Smith would reject 'Either Jones owns a Ford or Brown is in Barcelona'.

Gettier's job interview scenario makes Smith even more eccentric. Why is Smith counting coins of another job candidate? Why does Smith then go on to infer from *someone* with ten coins in his pocket will get the job? If he thinks Jones will get the job, why go through the indirect rigamarole of deducing that someone with ten coins in his pocket will get the job?

To make Gettier reasoning less eccentric, epistemologists turn to an example from, of all people, Lewis Carroll. He introduced the idea as a riddle, in an 1849 letter to his sister: Which is more accurate, a clock that is right once a year or one that has stopped altogether? Carroll's solution: a stopped clock because it is correct twice a day.

> You might go on to ask, 'How am I to know when eight o'clock does come? My clock will not tell me.' Be patient, reader: you know that when eight o'clock comes your clock is right; very good; then your rule is this: keep your eye fixed on your clock, and the very moment it is right it will be eight o'clock.
>
> 'But—' you say. There, that'll do, reader; the more you argue the farther you get from the point, so it will be as well to stop.'

From this sophistry, epistemologists distilled a simple case in which a man infers that the time is eight o'clock by consulting a normally reliable clock. Unluckily, the clock has stopped at eight o'clock. Luckily, the man happened to check at eight o'clock and so inferred a true conclusion. All of this reasoning is free of irrelevant digressions.

As a bonus, one can generalise to other examples. You rent a car whose fuel gauge indicates that the tank is full. You correctly infer the tank is full but later learn that the gauge was stuck. When you began the journey you did not know that the tank was full. But you did have justified true belief that the tank was full.

The virtues of Carroll's clock case may have stifled the

search for a greater variety of specimens. People still have the impression that Gettier cases are rare, marginal cases.

So it is salutary to think of natural cases that do not involve stuck measuring devices. Most people infer that there are fossil horses in the Americas because the Plains Indians had an elaborate horse culture. There are fossil horses. Indeed, equines originated in the Americas. Ancestors of European horses crossed the Bering Straits to Eurasia. But when the Eurasians crossed in the opposite direction they wiped out the large land animals in the Americas, perceiving the horse only as food rather than as a mode of transport. History would have been much different if the Indians had been the first to domesticate the horse! The Spanish reintroduced the horse in their American conquest. This invasion was halted by an Indian revolt against the Spanish in New Mexico in 1680. The Indians obtained some horses that revolutionised their ability to hunt buffalo. Horse culture spread northward across the whole Great Plains area far into Canada. By the time northern settlers encountered the Indians, the Indians looked like they always had horses.

Currently, there are systematic attempts to reintroduce species. The successes will create Gettier examples for future generations who lose knowledge of the reintroduction. Future palaeontologists are unlikely to notice any gap in the fossil record.

Gettier cases can also arise from mis-executed security measures. On 4 July 2012, the front page of the *New York Times* featured the spokesman for CERN (Conseil européenne pour la recherche nucléaire) announcing novel evidence for the Higgs boson – thereby clearing confusion from a prior 'announcement':

> On the eve of the announcement, in what was an
> embarrassing moment for the lab where the Web was
> invented, a video of Dr Incandela's making his statement
> was posted to the Internet and then quickly withdrawn. Dr
> Incandela said he had made a series of video presentations
> with alternate conclusions so that the video producers

would not know the right answer ahead of time, but the one that was right just happened to get posted.

Viewers *reasonably* inferred from the dissemination of the CERN video that it was an official announcement. They concluded that the scientists had novel evidence for the Higgs boson. This was a justified true belief – but not knowledge!

Premature Explanatory Satiation

In 'Explanation as Orgasm' Alison Gopnik assimilates the 'Aha!' of understanding to climax. Orgasm is the mark of sexual fulfilment. The Aha feeling is the mark of explanatory fulfilment. Both marks motivate actions that lead to reproductive success.

Since these marks are pleasurable, there is a temptation to furnish them even when inaccurate. An artist asks his wife, a civil engineer, 'Why are manhole covers round?' She answers, 'Because that is the shape which most economically precludes the lid from falling down the hole.' The explanation is cogent for her fellow engineers. But laymen will infer a false intermediate step: '*Only* a circle has a constant diameter.' Engineers realise that other shapes have a constant diameter. For instance, in the nineteenth century Franz Reuleaux showed that the 'triangle' at the centre of the Venn diagram has mechanical applications:

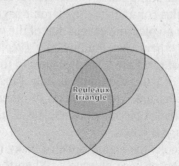

The principal reason manhole covers do not have the shape of a Reuleaux triangle is that the circular shape was easier to lathe and became the industry standard. By omitting this inelegant detail, the engineer triggers premature explanatory satiation. If she really wanted her husband to *know* why manhole covers are round, she would warn him that other figures have a constant diameter.

She did not have the heart to clutter the beautiful explanation. Just as wives wish to please their husbands, teachers wish to please their pupils – not just for the short-term delight but also for their long-term well-being. To nurture student morale, teachers sweeten lessons with the pleasures of discovery (or 'discovery').

Some of this eagerness to please may be self-interest. Students gauge how much they learn by introspection. Teachers who maximise epiphanies are perceived as effective explainers, cogent demonstrators, and artful practitioners of the Socratic method.

A teacher who courts premature explanatory satiation puts her students under the spell of an illusory insight. Instead of seeking further enlightenment, the enchanted pupils become incurious. Why inquire into what they already know?

Since there are many pleasures of learning, there are many opportunities for intellectual perversion. Should we always forgo such pleasure?

The father of utilitarianism answers no. Jeremy Bentham's hedonic calculus contradicts the Platonic sage who 'whispers in my ear that no pleasure except that of the wise is quite true and pure – all others are a shadow only' (*Republic* IX).

'Pleasures' of relief are false pleasures in the sense of being the cessation of pain. The neutral state (absence of pain) is mistaken as pleasure. The falsehood of other false pleasures derives from their objects; we are 'pleased' that p, yet unbeknownst to us, p is false.

Plato overlooks the significance of lucky inferences in his characterisation of false pleasures. When the fallacious reasoner takes pleasure in the conclusion, he takes pleasure in a truth. Yet his pleasure is invalid.

Plato should condemn some pleasures that are necessarily true and even some pleasures that are necessarily sound:

The following are primes: 3, 31, 331, 3331, 33331, 333331, 3333331.
Therefore, 33333331 is a prime.

The conclusion can be validly derived with standard techniques for establishing that a number is prime. But the premise will seduce many amateurs into employing enumerative induction: There is an ascending list of primes whose numeric representations feature a sequence of 3's that ends with 1. This run suggests that the next item in the sequence will be prime. The inference is weak because prime numbers lack the compositionality that makes for cogent inductive reasoning. The generalisation breaks down for the succeeding case: $333333331 = 17 \times 19,607,843$. These failures persist for at least the next five cases.

Plato gives partial credit. Being closer to truth is better than being distant from it. Coming close to knowledge is better than abject ignorance. Secretly incomplete explanations, the Noble Lies of pedagogy, pose a trade-off between first-order knowledge and second-order knowledge (cognition versus metacognition). For a naive audience, an oversimplified explanation provides an approximation to knowledge at the expense of the false belief that one has knowledge.

Is it better to leave the student totally ignorant and aware of his ignorance or only partially ignorant and ignorant of his ignorance? The dilemma neglects the intermediate option of prefacing the explanation with a warning that the account will be an oversimplification.

Seneca may have lacked this attractive compromise when teaching Nero. The emperor was impatient. Nero could (and eventually did) order Seneca's death. A teacher who repeatedly hedges explanations may insult her micro-Neros. Her replacement will decide to err on the side of intellectual flattery. Cynics will propose a Gresham's law of pedagogy in which bad teachers chase out good teachers.

Popularisers wish to make science intellectually enjoyable. Frequent hedging would make these authors pedants. Arguably, consumers of 'creative non-fiction' have a general awareness of the genre's penchant for oversimplifications. By continuing to read, they tacitly consent to occasional pseudo-Ahas.

Upside-Down Charity

The principle of charity says we should treat agents as rational. We use the principle to interpret artefacts. Consider an archaeologist who finds

$$XI + I = X$$

inscribed on a Roman pottery shard. One interpretation is that the inscriber stupidly believed that eleven plus one equals ten. An alternative interpretation is that the Romans had a different conception of addition – as a process that *decreases* the sum.

That is too open-minded! The archaeologist will much prefer the suggestion that he is reading $XI + I = X$ upside down. For that hypothesis makes the inscription true. And truth (or more precisely, *perceived* truth) helps the archaeologist maximise agreement with the Romans.

To his chagrin, the archaeologist also realises that he was too quick to interpret a similar inscription:

$$XI - X = I$$

Since the inscription also yields a truth when read upside down, the principle of charity does not uniquely determine the correct interpretation.

Does Charity Apply to Group Beliefs?

The principle of charity instructs us to interpret agents as rational. If groups are agents, then charity would require us to interpret them as rational. Here is a riddle that should give us pause about this extension of charity: Can a group of consistent democrats be inconsistent?

Yes. Social epistemologists have us suppose the group's beliefs are determined by majority vote. The group will believe each member of the inconsistent triad P, If P then Q, and Not-Q

	If P then Q	P	Not-Q
Member 1	Yes	Yes	No
Member 2	Yes	No	Yes
Member 3	No	Yes	Yes
Group	Yes	Yes	Yes

If the democrats are required to defer to the majority view, then they will be required to believe the impossible.

The Population of Lake Wobegan

> Welcome to *Lake Wobegon*, where all the women
> are strong, all the men are good-looking, and
> all the children are above average.
>
> Garrison Keillor

It is possible for *nearly* all children to be above average. Nearly all children are above average in how many legs they possess. The average number of legs is less than two because some children are missing a leg.[35]

Still it is impossible for *all* children to be above average

---

[35] My favourite tattoo is inscribed on the calf of a one-legged veteran: 'One foot in the grave'.

– given there are only *finitely* many of them. If there are infinitely many children then each child could be above average. For instance, each child's birth order could be above average. Each number is closer to 1 than the majority of numbers.

Conclusion: The number of children in Lake Wobegon is infinite.

Following the Argument

There are three kinds of philosophers corresponding to three kinds of motorists.

The most common kind of philosopher is driving along, sees that he is heading towards a precipice, and exclaims, 'A cliff!' He turns around.

Less common is the philosopher who sees he is approaching a precipice but keeps on going in a straight line. This kind of philosopher, exemplified by Socrates, is worth studying. He does not hide the logical consequences of his premises. Indeed, by having the courage of his convictions, he actively shows what those convictions entail.

The third type of philosopher is a driver who is motoring along safely. Off in the distance, way off the paved road, he spots a precipice. He says, 'Look, a cliff!' He turns, and drives straight off.

The Earliest Unexpected Class Inspection

Memo: From the Chairman to the new faculty

Now that you have settled in to your new post, I am required to evaluate your teaching performance. The term is well under way, so the sooner this is done, the better. If we were being scientific about sampling your teaching, the class observation would be a surprise inspection. Thus reason dictates that the visit should occur on the first day that you do not believe it will occur. But on reflection, this is an impossible demand. Could I give the inspection next

Monday? No, because you would realise that Monday is the first available unexpected day. What about the next class on Tuesday? Well the previous elimination would make Tuesday the first available unexpected day. Hence, it falls prey to the previous reasoning. And indeed, parallel reasoning would eliminate all of the remaining days. Hence, the earliest unexpected inspection is impossible. Since we hired you in a buyer's market, you have obviously noted the resemblance to the surprise examination paradox. But you may have not noticed that the elimination proceeds in the reverse direction. It is odd that such a reversal could be effected by substituting a definite description ('The event will occur on the first unexpected day') for an existential generalisation ('The event will occur on an unexpected day'). But that's logic for you. Thus I am compelled to take refuge in the philosophy department's custom of asking you to propose a day for the class visit.

A Foolproof Guessing Game

The comedy duo Bud Abbott and Lou Costello resolved disputes mathematically. Abbott would think of a number 1 to 10. If Costello guessed the number, then the controversy would be resolved in his favour. Otherwise, Abbott would prevail.

Whenever Costello guessed, Abbott would report that he had a different number in mind. Costello puzzled over his losing streak. Why does Abbott always report that Costello picked the wrong number?

Costello has an epiphany. He demands a role reversal. *Costello* will think of the number and Abbott will guess.

Abbott opposes this departure from tradition. He objects, pleads, and cajoles. Costello is adamant. Abbott reluctantly agrees to be the guesser.

With a confident smirk, Costello thinks of a number. Abbott guesses. Costello's grin flattens. He concedes that Abbott picked the number. They return to their old roles.

Since Costello will resume as guesser and Abbott will still insist on the honour system, Costello needs reforms.

To improve the chance of a correct guess, reduce the range of numbers to 1, 2, and 3. Second, Costello can ask more complex questions. He is no longer restricted to 'Is n the number you are thinking of?' Further, the range of responses will be restricted to 'yes', 'no', or 'I do not know'.

With these adjustments, even the slow-witted Costello can ask a question that will guarantee victory. ♀ What is that question?

Predicting Your Death Date

What will be the dates on your tombstone? You already know your birth date. What is your death date?

You might know the answer because you are a convict with a firm execution date. Or you might have a good estimate because you are ill and will soon die.

In the absence of such information, the best you can do is to figure out which day has the best chance of being the date on the right-hand side of the dash (–).

Each date might seem to have the same probability except that, as you age, each date gets a higher probability of being your Death Date. Very distant dates are unlikely because you will be long dead.

To focus attention, think about your Death Date at midnight, just as you trying to fall asleep, counting down your heartbeats. At 12:01 a.m., the first minute of the new day, the answer will be: TODAY.

For TOMORROW to be your Death Date, there would have to be a *conjunction* of two events: no death today and death tomorrow.

For the DAY AFTER TOMORROW to be your Death Date, there would have to be a conjunction of *three* events: no death today, no death tomorrow, and death on the day after tomorrow.

For the DAY AFTER THE DAY AFTER TOMORROW to be your Death Date, there would have to be a conjunction of *four* events: no death today, no death tomorrow, no death the day after tomorrow, and death on the day after that.

As an analogy, consider news that someone has died after playing Russian roulette. He put one bullet in a six-chambered revolver and spun the chamber each time after pulling the trigger. Which trigger pull is the most likely to have been the fatal pull?

The first! Although the probability is only 1/6, this is a higher probability than the fatal trigger pull being the second. For that would have required a miss (with a 5/6 probability) followed by a hit (with a probability of 1/6). The probability for each subsequent pull becomes less and less. (It would be very surprising if the Russian roulette player died on the hundredth pull!)

Should you live like today is the last day of your life? No, because today is almost certainly not the last day of your life. Today is only the most probable of many highly improbable death dates. Tomorrow, a new 'today' will become your most likely Death Date.

As you walk with the morning sun behind your back, your shadow is darkest in front and less dark farther from your body. For more and more ambient light penetrates the more distant portions of your shadow. Your most probable Death Date is the layer of shadow in contact with your body.

The Oldest Mosque

The Koran is traditionally dated back to the angel Gabriel's revelations to Muhammad (570–632) in 610. The rise of Islam began around the time Muslims took flight in the Hijra, moving to Medina. ♀ What is the oldest mosque?

The Referee's Dilemma

I once received a letter from a grateful author. He strongly suspected that I was the anonymous referee who provided helpful comments on his manuscript. 'If you were the referee, I thank you!'

I could not remember whether I had refereed the paper. I vaguely recognised the manuscript. But this could have been because I read it over quickly and declined to referee. Or it could have been because I did submit a referee report but not the report he found helpful.

More worrying yet was the possibility that I wrote a poor referee report. Sometimes I raise an objection that the editor obliges the author to address. The author's reply worsens the paper by knocking his analysis out of focus. Thanks to my referee work, some short, sharp papers have become long, dull ones.

Worse, I have rejected worthwhile manuscripts. Perhaps some of these authors have lost heart. If you are a victim of my poor officiating, I apologise.

So how was I to respond to the grateful author? Saying 'You are welcome' would take credit for a service I may have not performed. Asking questions to jog my memory would break confidentiality. Not answering would be rude.

All I could manage was an email message calculated to look uncalculated: 'You are possibly welcome!'

The Worst Pair of Referee Reports

The axiom of choice is well accepted among *contemporary* mathematicians. They find it natural to assume that there is always a set whose members are drawn from other non-empty sets.

But the axiom of choice used to be rejected as clearly false by some mathematicians. Jan Mycielski illustrates the division of opinion with an anecdote (*Notices of the American Mathematical Society*, 53(2): 209). Alfred Tarski had a proof that the axiom of choice is equivalent to the statement that any infinite set X has the same cardinality as the Cartesian product $X \times X$. He submitted it to *Comptes rendus de l'Académie des Sciences* (a French journal that has been published since 1666).

The referees were outstanding mathematicians, Maurice Fréchet and Henri Lebesgue.* Although Tarski's argument was valid, they agreed it was of too little interest to merit publication. Fréchet's objection was that an implication between two well-known truths is not a new result. And Lebesgue's objection? An implication between two false statements is of no interest.

Tarski never again submitted a paper to that journal. He may have been annoyed by the mathematicians' conflicting opinions about the antecedent and consequent of the conditional he had proven. But he must have also been chagrinned by their failure to acknowledge the intrinsic value of drawing a connection between apparently unrelated propositions. The logician studies the entailment relation. He connects the dots but is not interested in the dots.

Bertrand Russell used the connection theme to demarcate the boundary between pure mathematics and applied mathematics. In *Mysticism and Logic*, he notoriously asserts:

> Pure mathematics consists entirely of assertions to the effect that, if such and such a proposition is true of anything, then such and such another proposition is true of that thing. It is essential not to discuss whether the first proposition is really true, and not to mention what the anything is, of which it is supposed to be true. [...] Thus mathematics may be defined as the subject in which we never know what we are talking about, nor whether what we are saying is true. People who have been puzzled by the beginnings of mathematics will, I hope, find comfort in this definition, and will probably agree that it is accurate.

Maurice Fréchet and Henri Lebesgue are displaying a practical attitude towards logic. They are interested in using the connections to infer declarative sentences by *modus ponens* or *modus tollens*. 'If' borrows all of its interest from a potential 'is'.

If the antecedent of a conditional is obviously false, it cannot be part of a sound *modus ponens* argument. If the consequent is already well known, no argument is needed.

I had the same practical attitude towards René Descartes's *Meditations*. He presents *two* proofs of God's existence. This struck me as redundant. One proof is enough. I thought Descartes was betraying a lack of confidence in his proofs.

Yet, at the same time, I did not think that mathematicians were displaying a lack of confidence when they provided dozens of proofs of the Pythagorean theorem. I accepted those proofs as increasing understanding by drawing unexpected connections.

In philosophy, there are anti-authoritarians who bridle at a philosopher appealing to his own beliefs to support a position. The propositions under philosophical discussion are controversial and so cannot be supported by authority. All one can do is to draw connections and leave it to the hearer to figure out which way he should adjust his beliefs.

* *Lebesgue* is the correct spelling of Lebesgue's name. 'Lebesgue' is just one of those words that look misspelled, like 'misspelled'. Here is the opening of Ralph P. Boas's 'Spelling Lesson':

Weep for the mathematicians
Posterity acclaims:
Although we know their theorems
We cannot spell their names.
Forget the rules you thought you knew—
Henri Lebesgue has got no Q.

A Terrible Tautology?

In *Savage Continent: Europe in the Aftermath of World War II* Keith Lowe writes, 'One Berlin woman recorded in her diary that "all notions of ownership have been demolished. Everyone steals from everyone else, because everyone has been stolen from"' (p. 46). ♀ Is her last sentence a tautology?

Quantifier Mottos

I saw a runner streak by with the shirt slogan 'All you got is all it takes'. That is two quantifiers (a quantifier is a word that says how much). Three quantifiers figure in the design imperative of the artist Charles Eames: 'Create the best for the most for the least.' The logician W. V. Quine characterised _____ as 'what the least of us make the most of us feel the least of us make the most of'. ♀ What is it?

The Chinese Music Box

Music has no subject beyond the combinations of
notes we hear, for music speaks not only by means
of sounds, it speaks nothing but sound.
Eduard Hanslick

Formalists, such as the philosopher Roger Scruton and the composer Igor Stravinsky, follow Hanslick. They agree that (purely instrumental) music strips *all* the representational properties from sound. In contrast to portraits and landscape painting, one can understand music without understanding what it is about. Listening to music is like looking through a kaleidoscope.

These austere opponents of representationalism focus on the internal *structure* of the sounds. Their aesthetic detachment is unsurpassed. Music is closed off from the world – offering a perfect refuge.

This structural approach to musical understanding is analogous to computationalism about speech comprehension. According to the computationalist, a suitably programmed computer can understand natural language. This principle is assumed by the Turing test: a computer can think if an interrogator cannot tell, just by conversing with it by teletype, whether it is a human being or a computer.

In 'The Chinese Room' John Searle argues that Alan Turing's test is too broad:

Imagine a native English speaker who knows no Chinese locked in a room full of boxes of Chinese symbols (a data base) together with a book of instructions for manipulating the symbols (the program). Imagine that people outside the room send in other Chinese symbols which, unknown to the person in the room, are questions in Chinese (the input). And imagine that by following the instructions in the program the man in the room is able to pass out Chinese symbols which are correct answers to the questions (the output). The program enables the person in the room to pass the Turing Test for understanding Chinese but he does not understand a word of Chinese.

Since the man in the room does not understand Chinese by virtue of his capacity to appropriately manipulate symbols, neither can any computer. A computer is just a physical instantiation of a formal system – a device for changing input strings into output strings. The strings are meaningless to the computer. It is all syntax and no semantics.

Now consider a musical analogue of the Turing test: If the computer's performance in an interrogative duet is indistinguishable from that of a human musician, then the computer understands music.

The best-known example of an interrogative duet is the 'Duelling Banjos' scene in the movie *Deliverance*. A guitarist visiting the Appalachian backwoods notices a blank-faced retarded boy holding a banjo. He tests whether the boy can play the banjo by strumming some rudimentary chords on his guitar. The boy feebly replicates what was played. The guitarist tries more advanced melodies. The boy keeps up. As the tempo accelerates, the boy's play overtakes the guitarist's. 'I'm lost!' confesses the delighted guitarist. But when he extends a hand of congratulation, the boy shirks away. The idiot savant does not understand the meaning of a handshake.

A computer might also prevail over an inquisitive musician. Would that superior performance show that computer understood the music?

Searle might be tempted to answer no by adapting his linguistic thought experiment to music. Would the man in the Chinese Music Box be *merely* simulating understanding of music? The man's instruction manual resembles musical notation: *When you hear sound sequence A, B, C, respond with X, Y, Z.* As Searle emphasises in debates about the Chinese Room, the man may have memorised the manual. According to the formalist, syntactic facility is sufficient for musical understanding. The man might be missing *extra-musical* associations, such as homages to past composers (as when Charlie Parker quotes Stravinsky's *Rite of Spring* in his jazz solo on 'Repetition'). But this type of 'musical' appreciation is an accretion, not part of the music itself.

Or so says the formalist. My own opinion is that formalism is a deep insight that goes *slightly* too far, neglecting *marginal* semantic phenomena such as leitmotifs and onomatopoeia. Yet, I am almost as opposed to crediting the computer with musical understanding as language understanding. One explanation of this disproportionate reaction is that musical understanding is perceptual. A computer cannot hear a sound as a musical sound rather than a speech sound – despite the computer's sensitivity to sound waves. Possibly some of our aversion to crediting speech comprehension to computers is also due to their lack of speech perception (a delicate point that gets swamped by Searle's semantic insight).

Christmas Eve[364]

My family celebrates Christmas Eve[364]. This tradition began because my children wanted their Christmas gifts on Christmas Eve. They did not want to wait.

Their impatience concerned me. I had read research culminating in Philip Zimbardo's book *The Time Paradox*. Zimbardo teaches that there are three kinds of people. Past-oriented people make decisions by looking at precedent and are prone to nostalgia. Present-oriented people are more spontaneous and are guided by present circumstances. For instance, present-oriented children will choose one marshmallow now even though waiting ten minutes would get them two marshmallows. Future-oriented people base their decisions on costs and benefits. Future-oriented people are the kind of people who carry around postage stamps. According to Professor Zimbardo, future-oriented people rule the world.

How could I make my children defer gratification? They seemed stuck in the here and now.

The cyclical nature of Christmas suggested a loophole. I asked my children: What could be better than getting their presents on Christmas Eve? *Getting them on Christmas Eve Eve.* And what could be better than that? *Getting them on Christmas Eve Eve Eve* ... This went on and on, enabling my children to enjoy the pleasure of recursion.

When the children began to get confused by the long repetition of Eves, I was able to illustrate the advantage of superscripts. This taught my children the value of exponentiation. With this notational assist, they made it all the way to 26 December.

Thus 26 December became Christmas Eve[364]. Now my impatient children get their gifts earlier than any of their friends – even their Jewish friends who celebrate Hanukkah. But they look like children who are willing to wait the day after Christmas to get their presents.

Christmas Eve[364] holiday teaches several life lessons – while also letting parents save money by purchasing presents during the 'after Christmas sales'. But this is the season of giving. So I make this philosophical holiday a gift to you all. Merry Christmas Eve[364]!

Putting Parody into Practice

Poor Richard's Almanac is peppered with thrifty proverbs such as 'Beware of little Expenses: a small Leak will sink a great Ship' and 'A penny saved is penny earned'. Benjamin Franklin became stereotyped as a miser. Instead of resenting the imputation of parsimony, he joined in the fun. In his 1784 essay

'An Economical Project for Diminishing the Cost of Light' he calculated how many candles would be saved by having all Parisians awake at sunrise. Shifting everybody to the earlier schedule would make the most of the free sunlight. Franklin was arguing in jest. But the numbers became so compelling that he eventually supported the reform in earnest. This was the origin of daylight saving, British Summer Time, and other national measures to make the most of the sun.

In 1785, Charles-Joseph Mathon de la Cour wrote a parody of *Poor Richard's Almanac*. An even more far-sighted counterpart to Richard deposits a small amount of money to collect compound interest over several centuries. In this way, he funds public-spirited projects after his death. The author was a mathematician and had accurately expounded the miracle of compounding. Franklin's reaction was to thank him and bequeath £1,000 each to the cities of Boston and Philadelphia, with the proviso that the money gather interest for two centuries. Since Franklin died in 1790 the trusts paid out in 1990. The Philadelphia fund had accumulated $2 million (which went to scholarships for local high-school students). The Boston trust amassed almost $5 million. This established the Benjamin Franklin Institute of Technology.

Hoax Proof

The physicist Alan Sokal submitted 'Transgressing the Boundaries: Towards a Transformative Hermeneutics of Quantum Gravity' to the postmodernist editors of *Social Text* (for their 1996 'Science War' issue). Upon publication, Sokal arranged an interview with *Lingua Franca*. Sokal characterised his submission as 'a pastiche of Left-wing cant, fawning references, grandiose quotations, and outright nonsense'.

I had assumed the editors of *Social Text* were hoax-proof. Postmodernists sympathise with Jacques Derrida's 'death of the author' motif. Whereas naive readers believe that the meaning of a text is controlled by what the author intended, literary theorists believe the text can have meanings beyond those intended by the author. Consider the phenomenon of misspeaking. When a freshman says 'A library is a suppository of learning' there is a divergence between what he said and what he intended. That is why he is embarrassed.

Usually, a typo worsens a text. But occasionally there is an improvement: 'Jensen argued like a man filled with righteous indigestion' might better describe a dissatisfied restaurant patron. That reading could become canonical.

According to the postmodernists, we should treat a text as we treat Kleenex tissue. It was originally sold to remove cold cream but people began to use the tissues as disposable handkerchiefs. Air conditioners were originally dehumidifiers for printing paper. But people felt the rooms were cooler. Scotch tape was originally invented to paint cars with a sharp line. The consumer decides on the function of products.

Arguments that were intended to be specimens of poor reasoning can be valid. Even utterances that were intended to be nonsensical could be true and profound.

Given that Sokal's intentions do not control the meaning of the text, the content of a hoax is no less likely to be of merit than a seriously submitted article. Sokal's sillygisms could be sound syllogisms. The joke would be on Sokal!

The actual response of the editors of *Social Text* was an inconsistent but apt gasp of betrayal. Sokal refuted more of postmodernism than he intended!

Penny Wise

A Yorkshireman is a Scotsman with all the
generosity squeezed out of him.

British saying

An economist and two merchants are walking down the street. One of the merchants says 'Look, a twenty-pound note!' The economist replies, 'It couldn't be, someone else would have picked it up.'

The two businessmen, a Yorkshireman and a Scotsman, do

not buy this theoretical argument. They turn to the practical issue of how to divide up the £20. They agree to an auction. Each will write down a bid. The higher bid will get the £20 note but must surrender his bid to the other merchant. If there is a tie, they will split the £20.

Assume the merchants are ideal agents – but not so ideal as to have joined the economist in ignoring the £20 note.

♀ What is the best bid for the £20?

Plato's Punning Riddle

Said Plato: 'These things that we feel
Are not ontologically real,
But just the excrescence
Of numinous essence
Our senses can never reveal.'

Basil Ransome-Davies

Plato's *Republic* compares some superficial 'violations' of the law of non-contradiction to the following riddle: 'A man who was not a man saw and did not see a bird which is not a bird sitting on a branch that was not a branch and hit and did not hit it with a stone that was not a stone.'

The passage in the *Republic* V does not explicitly mention the riddle and so is a bit opaque to modern readers:

They are like the punning riddles which are asked at feasts or the children's puzzle about the eunuch aiming at the bat, with what he hit him, as they say in the puzzle, and upon what the bat was sitting. The individual objects of which I am speaking are also a riddle, and have a double sense: nor can you fix them in your mind, either as being or not-being, or both, or neither.

Elements of the answer are given in the passage. But it is not enough of a spoiler to prevent me from asking you: ♀ What is the solution to the riddle?

Chess Puzzle Puzzle

♡ Which is older, chess or the oldest chess puzzle?

The Spy's Riddle

♡ If you have it, you want to share it.
♡ If you share it, you do not have it.

Why One is the Loneliest Number

I was on acid and I looked at the trees and I realized that they
all came to points, and the little branches came to points,
and the houses came to points. I thought, 'Oh! Everything
has a point, and if it doesn't, then there's a point to it.'

Harry Nilsson

The songwriter Harry Nilsson repeatedly got a busy signal.
Being musical, he stayed on the line listening to the 'beep,
beep, beep, beep, ...' tone. The busy signal became the opening
notes of his 1969 hit song 'One (Is the Loneliest Number)' performed by Three Dog Night:

One is the loneliest number that you'll ever do
Two can be as bad as one
It's the loneliest number since the number one

The lyrics provide a self-undermining explanation of why
one is the loneliest number. How lonely could one be given
that two faithfully follows it? And what about all the other
numbers? That is an infinite amount of company!

There is also an obstacle to verification. As finite beings we
cannot inspect each member of an infinite set. In the absence
of such a survey, how can we know that none of these numbers
is lonelier than the number one?

Nilsson's 'The Most Beautiful World in the World' inspires
an explanation that avoids the above difficulties:

You're a scary old place out there, world
But I couldn't be happy without you
And I swear all my thoughts are about you
The most beautiful world in the world

Given that there is only one world, it will be the most beautiful world. Uniqueness is the royal road to superlatives.

The uniqueness of the number one is a corollary of Oskar Perron's demonstration that one is the largest natural number. He begins by defining N as the largest natural number. N^2 cannot be greater than N because N is defined as the largest number. So $N(N - 1) = N^2 - N$ cannot yield a positive number. Therefore, $N - 1$ is not positive. Accordingly, N cannot exceed 1. Yet N is at least 1. It follows that $N = 1$. In other words, 1 is the largest number.

Corollary: Given that 'number' means natural number, it follows that there are no other numbers. For any number greater than 1 would be greater than the largest number. One is the loneliest number because there are no other numbers.

Logicians believe that Perron's argument illustrates the importance of consistency proofs. Specifically, the definite description 'the largest natural number' is inconsistent. The very concept of a natural number requires that it have a successor. Each step of Perron's deduction is implied by the earlier steps. Nevertheless, the whole proof is trivial. We are merely drawing out consequences from a contradiction. Anything follows from a contradiction. Or as the Pointless Man concludes in Harry Nilsson fable *The Point!* 'A *point* in every *direction* is the same as no *point* at all.'

The Moment of Truth

The moment of truth, the sudden emergence of a new insight,
is an act of intuition. Such intuitions give the appearance
of miraculous flashes, or short-circuits of reasoning. In fact
they may be likened to an immersed chain, of which only
the beginning and the end are visible above the surface of

> consciousness. The diver vanishes at one end of the chain
> and comes up at the other end, guided by invisible links.
>
> Arthur Koestler

Declarative beliefs, such as 'Yellowstone Park sits atop a super volcano', build up a map by which we steer. They are true when they correspond to the facts. But what about conditional beliefs such as 'If the Yellowstone super volcano erupts, then the United States government will collapse'? These conditionals are rules for changing your map.

Typically, we assert conditionals for which we are ready to perform inferences such as:

Modus ponens	Modus tollens
If P then Q	If P then Q
P	Not-Q
Therefore, Q	Therefore, not-P

After all, the normal point of asserting conditionals is to prepare for a possible expansion of our knowledge. If we learn the antecedent, we will apply *modus ponens* and gain knowledge of the consequent. If we learn the negation of the consequent, we apply *modus tollens* and gain knowledge that the antecedent is false. When we lack the conditional intention to perform a valid inference, our assertion of the conditional seems like misleading advertising.

So we often face a 'moment of truth' when we either go forward with our conditionally intended inference or back down. That is, we can either stick with the conditional premise or reject it. Consistency is satisfied by either manoeuvre. So the moment of truth appears in the hourglass of practical reasoning rather than in the tide tables of theoretical logic. Logic just points out conflicts between beliefs. It does not say which beliefs to reject.

Followers of a doomsday prophet confidently assert 'If the prophet is legitimate, then tomorrow will be the end of the world.' When tomorrow passes uneventfully, some of the disappointed devotees perform *modus tollens* and abandon the prophet as illegitimate. But surprisingly many will instead reject the conditional. They will instead retract their belief in the conditional 'If the prophet is legitimate, then tomorrow will be the end of the world.' Perhaps there was a miscalculation!

My favourite example of going forward comes from chemistry. In 1835 when Auguste Comte had famously concluded 'On the subject of the stars ... we shall not at all be able to determine their chemical composition or even their density.' Soon after, Robert Bunsen and Gustav Kirchhoff were tinkering with techniques to ascertain the chemical composition of a specimen by studying the spectral properties of its flame. When a fire broke out in Mannheim across the Rhine plain, the chemists aimed their spectroscopes out the laboratory window and deduced that barium and strontium were present in the burning mass. After the incident, Bunsen and Kirchhoff took a walk in the woods. Bunsen had a thought:

> 'If we could determine the nature of substances burning in Mannheim, why should we not do the same with regard to the sun? But people would say we must have gone mad to dream such a thing.' All the world knows now what the result was, but it must have been a great moment when Kirchhoff could say, 'Bunsen, I *have* gone mad', and Bunsen, grasping what it all meant, replied, 'So have I, Kirchhoff!'
> – From: Walter Bruno Gratzer's *Eurekas and Euphorias*

If Bunsen and Kirchhoff could know the chemical constitution of the sun through analysis of sunlight, they could learn the chemical constitution of other stars by analysing starlight. And they did!

Preventing Prevarication

The author Joseph Conrad was a sea captain acquainted with the sailor's tendency to lie. In his novel *Typhoon*, the captain falls into a predicament. Two hundred members of his crew have stored several years' wages in the captain's strongbox. During a storm, the boxes were all smashed commingling all the coins. If he could trust the sailors, he could return the wages by simply asking. Each sailor had private knowledge of how many coins were in his own box which he could discreetly share with the captain. Unfortunately, the sailors are dishonest and greedy. They will exaggerate if asked how many of the coins are owed. Yet the captain is able to return the coins to their rightful owners. ♀ How?

Argument and Oscar Wilde's 'The Decay of Lying'

> The fatal errors of life are not due to man's being
> unreasonable: an unreasonable moment may be one's
> finest moment. They are due to man's being logical.
>
> Oscar Wilde, *De Profundis and Other Writings*

Oscar Wilde is routinely critical of logic. 'I can stand brute force, but brute reason is quite unbearable. There is something unfair about its use. It is *hitting below* the intellect.' Yet Wilde thinks we cannot lie with arguments.

Is it because arguments are neither true nor false? Is it because arguments are propounded rather than asserted? No, Wilde thinks a lie must be self-sufficient; it cannot appeal to anything else for support. Lies must stand on their own, as works of art.

The heroes in Wilde's dialogues honour whim. In Wilde's dialogue 'The Decay of Lying', Vivian is chided by Cyril for writing a scholarly defence of whim. Vivian is defiant: 'Who wants to be consistent? The dullard and the doctrinaire, the tedious people who carry out their principles to the bitter end of action, to the *reductio ad absurdum* of practice.'

Vivian believes that lying is the primary art form. Standing Plato on his head, Vivian further contends that objects imitate art. He argues as much in 'The Decay of Lying: A Protest'.

CYRIL: Lying! I should have thought that our politicians
kept up that habit.

VIVIAN: I assure you that they do not. They never rise beyond the level of misrepresentation, and actually condescend to prove, to discuss, to argue. How different from the temper of the true liar, with his frank, fearless statements, his superb irresponsibility, his healthy, natural disdain of proof of any kind. After all, what is a fine lie? Simply that which is its own evidence. If a man is sufficiently unimaginative to produce evidence in support of a lie, he might just as well speak the truth at once. No, the politicians won't do. Something may, perhaps, be urged on behalf of the Bar. The mantle of the Sophist has fallen on its members. Their feigned ardours and unreal rhetoric are delightful. They can make the worse appear the better cause, as though they were fresh from Leontine schools, and have been known to wrest from reluctant juries triumphant verdicts of acquittal for their clients, even when those clients, as often happens, were clearly and unmistakably innocent. But they are briefed by the prosaic, and are not ashamed to appeal to precedent. In spite of their endeavours, the truth will out. Newspapers, even, have degenerated. They may now be absolutely relied upon. One feels it as one wades through their columns. It is always the unreadable that occurs. I am afraid that there is not much to be said in favour of either the lawyer or the journalist. Besides, what I am pleading for is Lying in art. Shall I read you what I have written? It might do you a great deal of good.

Ethics of Supposition

W. K. Clifford believes that there is an ethics of belief. You are obliged to believe in accordance with your evidence. A ship-owner who lets his ship sail despite evidence that it is not sea-worthy is culpably negligent.

David Hume denies that there is an ethics of belief. Belief is involuntary. Try to believe that the number of words in this sentence is even. You cannot do it even if there is a big prize for the feat. You cannot choose what to believe.

However, Hume would agree that you can choose what you *suppose*. You can choose to make a denigrating supposition. The nineteenth-century opponent of natural selection Fleming Jenkins imagines a white sailor shipwrecked on an island of blacks. Strength of numbers will prevent this island's race from turning white – or even yellow. Jenkins's supposition can be criticised as a choice. Racist beliefs, in contrast, are merely *symptomatic* of immorality.

Richard Feynman was once picketed by feminists for a hypothetical example involving a female motorist who challenges a police officer's definition of speed. Feynman was puzzled because the woman comes off as more erudite than the police officer. But the picketers thought the supposition enforced a stereotype.

> 'Why did it have to be a woman driver?' they said. 'You are implying that all women are bad drivers.'
>
> 'But the woman makes the cop look bad,' I said. 'Why aren't you concerned about the cop?'
>
> 'That's what you expect from cops!' one of the protesters said. 'They're all pigs!'
>
> 'But you *should* be concerned,' I said. 'I forgot to say in the story that the cop was a woman!'
>
> – Feynman, *What Do You Care What Other People Think?*, 1988, p. 75

The content of belief is fixed by the evidence. But the content of a supposition can be supplemented at will. This gave Feynman a chance to stipulate himself out of a tricky problem.

Although we can choose what to suppose, the act of supposing leads to automatic reflection on the supposition. This puts us in a bind when we wish to condemn the psychological effects of a supposition:

> In 1939, Churchill began to have a nightmarish fear. As the summer progressed, Churchill became increasingly worried about the sense of defeatism and despair which he began to feel around him. At dinner on June 14, when he found himself sitting next to the American columnist

Walter Lippmann, he was shocked to learn from Lippmann that the United States ambassador, Joseph Kennedy, was telling his friends that when war came Britain, facing defeat, would negotiate with Hitler. Harold Nicolson, who was present at the dinner, recalled that the moment Churchill heard the word 'defeat' he turned to Lippmann and declared: 'No, the ambassador should not have spoken so, Mr Lippmann; he should not have said that dreadful word. Yet supposing (as I do not for one moment suppose) that Mr Kennedy were correct in his tragic utterance, then I for one would willingly lay down my life in combat, rather than, in fear of defeat, surrender to the menaces of these most sinister men. It will then be for you, for the Americans, to preserve and to maintain the great heritage of the English-speaking peoples.'

– From: Gerald Flurry's *Winston S. Churchill: The Watchman*

Churchill cannot be speaking truthfully when he says parenthetically: 'Yet supposing (as I do not for one moment suppose) that Mr Kennedy were correct ...' After all, Churchill did suppose for one moment that Kennedy was correct that Britain would negotiate with Hitler. How else was Churchill to criticise Kennedy?

This would not be the last time Churchill tried to limit what his allies suppose. At the Tehran conference in 1943, Stalin hosted a jovial dinner for Churchill, President Roosevelt, and a few further guests, including Roosevelt's son Elliott (a brigadier general in the Air Force reconnaissance division). Churchill was being teased for being too soft with the Germans. The Marshal suggested that, after the war, the German General Staff should be liquidated.

Churchill was not sure whether Stalin was joking. (The Nazis reported that the Soviets executed 15,000 Polish officers in 1940 in the forest of Katyn. The British officially accepted the Soviet lie that the Nazis had conducted the massacre.) But Churchill thought it prudent to assert, 'The British Parliament and public will never tolerate mass executions. Even if in war passion they allowed them to begin, they would turn violently against those responsible after the first butchery had taken place. The Soviets must be under no delusion on this point.' Stalin, perhaps in mischief, insisted that 50,000 must be shot. Churchill replied that he would rather be taken out to the garden and shot himself. To break the tension, President Roosevelt proposed a compromise; only 49,000 should be shot. But his son would not let the matter be dismissed as ridiculous. Elliott made a speech supporting Stalin's quota. He said that the United States Army would join him in supporting the executions. Shocked, Churchill walked off into the next room, which was in semi-darkness.

> I had not been there a minute before hands were clapped upon my shoulders from behind, and there was Stalin, with Molotov at his side, both grinning broadly, and eagerly declaring that they were only playing, and that nothing of a serious character had entered their heads.
>
> Stalin has a very captivating manner when he chooses to use it, and I never saw him do so to such an extent as at this moment. Although I was not then, and am not now, fully convinced that all was chaff and there was no serious intent lurking behind, I consented to return, and the rest of the evening passed pleasantly.
>
> – Winston Churchill, *The Hinge of Fate* (The Second World War, Vol. 4)

Churchill's caution suggests a worry about how fantasies spiral into action. In a 2011 biopic *The Iron Lady*, about another prime minister, Margaret Thatcher is given these lines:

> Watch your thoughts, for they become words.
> Watch your words, for they become actions.
> Watch your actions, for they become habits.
> Watch your habits, for they become your character.
> And watch your character, for it becomes your destiny.
> What we think, we become.
> My father always said that.

Behaviourism for Eggs

There are two cold eggs in the refrigerator, one raw, one hard-boiled. If you had a strong light source, you could check for the greater light penetration afforded by a liquid egg. Alas, you can rely only on the behaviour of the eggs. ♀ How do you tell which egg is hard-boiled without breaking an egg?

The Egg Came Before the Chicken

Vagueness theorists tend to think that evolutionary theory dissolves the riddle 'Which came first, the chicken or the egg?' After all, 'chicken' is vague. The idea is that Charles Darwin demonstrated that the chicken was preceded by borderline chickens and so it is simply indeterminate as to where the pre-chickens end and the chickens begin.

However, this line of reasoning only dissolves 'Which bird was the first chicken?' Rather than implying that the chicken-and-egg question lacks a definite answer, contemporary evolutionary theory favours the egg.

Given Mendel's theory of inheritance, the transition to chickenhood can only take place between an egg-layer and its egg. For a particular organism cannot change its species membership during its lifetime. It is genetically fixed. However, evolutionary theory assures us that organisms can fail to breed true. So although it is indeterminate as to which particular egg was the first chicken egg, we can know that whichever egg that may be, it precedes the first chicken whichever that may be. The egg's precedence is a biological rather than a logical necessity. Given Lamarck's theory of acquired traits, the chicken could have come first.

One might object that there can be no first *F* if the onset of *F*-ness is indeterminate. But consider a son who gradually grows bald in just the pattern that his father balded. The father became bald before the son even though there was no clear first stage of baldness. Here's a closer analogy. A sculptor works on a marble block only during the mornings. There is no definite first day on which the block became a statue. However, we can say:

The block first became a statue during a morning.

Indeterminate states can be determinately related. One of the virtues of the chicken-and-egg question is that it reminds us of this internal structure. The riddle also shows that there is hidden determinacy to complement the more common theme of hidden indeterminacy.

The Egg Came Before the Ellipse

After Johannes Kepler became convinced that the orbits of the planets are not circular, he concluded that the planets are not under the total control of the sun. Each planet has a degree of self-locomotion – and so must have a soul. On the basis of some preliminary curve-fitting and perhaps under the influence of creation myths in which eggs figure so prominently, Kepler conjectured that each planet's orbit has the shape of an egg.

The egg is difficult to describe mathematically because of its asymmetry; it is tapered at one end. Ellipses are tapered symmetrically at both ends. Kepler knew that Archimedes had already worked out the areas of ellipse sectors. So Kepler used an ellipse to approximate the egg.

Eventually Kepler realised that if he put the sun at one focus of the ellipse, the data fitted. The approximation to an egg fitted better than the egg itself.

Martin Gardner's Touching Problem

There are two iron bars, identical except one is magnetised. ♡ How can you tell, only by touch, which is magnetised?

Indiscernible Harm

My electricity comes from a power plant that burns coal. By leaving a light on, I cause a little more pollution. But no one will detect a difference. So if I leave the light on, there is no harm. ♀ How is my moral mathematics?

Book Review of *A Million Random Digits*

When I first encountered the Rand Corporation's *A Million Random Digits* on the library shelf, I thought it did not belong in a library. I had three protests:

1. Anyone could have written this!
2. This book is uncopyrightable!
3. This book has no information!

All three complaints met interesting ends.

Random digits look easy to produce. Readers are egged on by the Rand Corporation's introduction: 'Because of the very nature of the tables, it did not seem necessary to proofread every page of the final manuscript in order to catch random errors.'

Later I saw a statistician debunk this impression. He had half his class produce random digits by flipping a coin. The other half were instructed to fake the flips. The teacher spotted the fakes from across the room!

How did the professor achieve this long-range detection of fake randomisers? Students who faked the coin flips avoid blocks of digits. So the professor could see the absence of blocks from a distance.

Magicians exploit the aversion to blocks in mind-reading tricks. Write down a hundred fake coin tosses. Then read off the tosses one by one. The magician will predict which number is next with about 60% accuracy. He follows the simple rule of repeating failed guesses and changing successful guesses. So if he mistakenly guesses heads, he then guesses heads for the next toss. If his heads guess was correct, then he guesses tails for the next guess. This simple rule works because it avoids the blocks of digits that fake randomisers intuitively avoid. The trick is easy to program, yielding a psychic computer.

Auditors catch tax cheats by automated detection of blocklessness. To avoid arousing the computer, the creative accountant will let a random number table put the final polish on a fraudulent tax return.

Randomness is inversely related to predictability. We have trouble tracking the motion of many objects that make frequent turns. Suppose 25 ants randomly drop on a 1-metre stick. Each has a constant speed of 0.01 metres per second. Ants travel left or right, reversing directions only when they collide. ♥ What is the maximum time before all the ants fall off the stick?

The frantic motion of the ants makes the riddle seem impossible to answer. But there is a perspective on the confusing situation that allows a simple prediction. Knowledge that there is a solution makes us retract our judgement that the situation is truly chaotic.

The sequences in *A Million Random Digits* harbour no hidden order. Reading the digits on one page will not give you any basis for predicting the digits on the next page. No book is as densely packed with surprises!

My belief that anyone could have written random digits had been reversed. I now had the opposite belief: no human being could have made this up! *A Million Random Digits* definitely belonged in the non-fiction section.

But what about my belief that the book was uncopyrightable.[36] There was no creative content in *A Million Random Digits*.

This turned out to be a practical matter for Nathan Kennedy. He wanted to redistribute the tables of 100,000 Normal Deviates. To be safe, Kennedy emailed the Rand Corporation to make sure they agreed with his interpretation of copyright law. The Rand Corporation did not. Nor did the Rand Corporation give permission.

---

[36] 'Uncopyrightable' excels at blocklessness. It is the longest word that does not repeat a letter.

Kennedy had to generate 100,000 more normal deviates using the same method. Annoyed, he shames the Rand Corporation:

> Unlike the RAND Corporation, I concede that there is no creative content in these tables and therefore they are uncopyrightable. I further dedicate any copyright interest I may have in these tables to the public domain (although I do not believe that there is any copyright interest for me to relinquish). You may redistribute, modify, or use these tables for any purpose whatsoever.
>
> – http://hcoop.net/~ntk/random/

This is a marvellous example of vacuous generosity. Kennedy's largesse makes the Rand Corporation look small and petty.

Protest 3 was that, despite its heft, the book had no information. But this belief was reversed by study of how information is measured. Imagine a telephone conversation in which you are instructing a typist to print some fifty-digit sequences that only you can see:

A: 11111111111111111111111111111111111111111111111111
B: 01011010110101101011011010101101011010110101101101
C: 10001011011011000101011001110001010001001111100100

The information in sequence A can be compressed into 'Print 1 fifty times'. Sequence B can be compressed into the longer instruction 'Print 01011 ten times'. However, the information in sequence C (which was obtained from tossing a coin) cannot be compressed. Random sequences have no pattern. Since you can only list the members of the sequence, your description will be about as long as the sequence itself.

The more complex, the harder to compress. This suggests that the complexity of a sequence can be measured by the length of its shortest description. This descriptive length varies with our descriptive resources, so we need to standardise.

Happily, there is already a convention devised independently by Gregory Chaitin and A. N. Kolmogorov: the (algorithmic) complexity of a finite sequence of 0's and 1's is the length of the shortest computer program that will print out the sequence. The randomness of a sequence can be measured as a ratio of program length to string length. This ratio tends to unity for the majority of sequences. Although it is provable that most sequences are therefore random, one cannot prove that a particular sequence is random. For one cannot prove that there is no shorter program length.

The Chaitin–Kolmogorov definition of complexity resembles the definite description that drives the Berry paradox: 'the least integer not nameable in fewer than nineteen syllables'. This phrase seems to denote an integer, in particular, 111,777. Yet the Berry definite description of 111,777 is only eighteen syllables long and so is shorter than the nineteen-syllable numeric phrase that denotes 111,777. The Berry phrase denoting 111,777 cannot be shorter than the shortest phrase denoting 111,777. Hence, the Berry phrase does not exist.

In 'On the Difficulty of Computations', Gregory Chaitin develops the resemblance between his definition of 'complexity' and Berry's phrase into a proof of the following theorem: No computer can produce a sequence that is more complex than itself. The complexity of the computer equals the length of the shortest description of its operation. Code that description as a sequence, D, of 0's and 1's. If the computer could generate a more complex sequence S, then there would be a program that generates S which is shorter than the shortest program that can generate S, namely, the program coded by D. So S does not exist. It also follows that the computer's output cannot be any more random than itself.

Chaitin is well aware of the resemblance between his adaptation of Berry's paradox and adaptations of the liar paradox by Gödel and Turing. For Chaitin, Gödel's incompleteness theorem and Turing's halting problem are just two sides of the same random coin.

So how informative is *A Million Random Digits with 100,000 Normal Deviates*? Well, given its incompressibility, this is the most informative book ever published!

An Unjust but Fair Obituary

Sidney Morgenbesser would have turned in his grave if he had read the *New York Times* on 4 August 2004:

> He was once asked if it was unfair that the police hit him on the head during the riot.
>
> 'It was unfair but not unjust,' he pronounced.
>
> Why?
>
> 'It's unfair to be hit over the head, but it was not unjust since they hit everybody else over the head.'
>
> – From: 'Sidney Morgenbesser, 82, Kibitzing Philosopher, Dies'

What Morgenbesser actually said was that the blow was unjust but fair. I was told that everybody's obituary contains an injustice of this sort. If so, then the obituarists' inaccuracies are unjust but fair. Sidney was challenging John Rawls's essay 'Justice as Fairness'. If justice is fairness then fairness, such as equal treatment, should guarantee justice.

To get justice without fairness I offer up my kitchen contractor. On the first day of renovation, he received a traffic ticket for speeding. He was guilty – as was everybody else on the Long Island Expressway (when it is not in service as the world's longest car park). Shaking off his disappoinment at having won the punishment lottery, the contractor and his partner rejoined the speeders. Thirty minutes later he was pulled over again for speeding. Again, the contractor was guilty. But he resented the unfairness of having been punished twice in the same hour.

As the contractor entered my house, he knocked down a lamp. Smash! My wife and I did not know what he had gone through. We were a little puzzled at the toppler's intense silence – and the wide-eyed alarm of his partner. My wife chirped, 'Well, at least that is over with!' His partner beamed with relief, 'That's the right philosophy!'

Reflective Truth Tables

The dual of a logical connective is computed by exchanging true for false and vice versa, for every line in a truth table – including the initial columns. For instance, the dual of conjunction is disjunction:

Original			Dual		
A	H	A and H	A	H	A or H
T	T	T	~~T~~F	~~T~~F	~~T~~F
T	F	F	~~T~~F	~~F~~T	~~F~~T
F	T	F	~~F~~T	~~T~~F	~~F~~T
F	F	F	~~F~~T	~~F~~T	~~F~~T

The computation is faster if we change notation. Let conjunction be / and disjunction be \. And let true be > and false be <. The table for conjunction is then:

A	H	A/H
>	>	>
>	<	<
<	>	<
<	<	<

If you hold this new table up to the mirror, you obtain the dual of conjunction. So instead of changing twelve truth values by hand, you obtain the dual with a single operation of mirror reversal. The mirror makes some conceptual points observational. A look in the mirror reveals that the dual of negation is negation. Let's signify negation by a bar above the letter.

A	Ā
>	<
<	>

General principles of duality also take on a welcome directness. We can 'see' that the dual of any valid schema must be inconsistent because mirror reversal will change a pure > column into a pure < column.

The mirror corrects common misconceptions about duals. Students introduced to duality via a mirror are less likely to confuse duality with negation. For they realise that a single plane mirror reverses the whole field, not selected columns.

Mirror notation illustrates perspectival computation. The stereotypical form of computation involves intrinsic changes to the medium of representation: writing new symbols, erasing old symbols, turning gears, flipping switches, sliding abacus beads. Perspectival computation leaves the original inscriptions untouched. The problem solver merely alters his orientation towards the input. There is no rewriting or copying of the input inscriptions; the output inscriptions are numerically identical to the input inscriptions.

Perspectival computation is symbol manipulation without inscription manipulation. Symbols are complex objects that have manipulatable elements besides their inscriptions. Since a written symbol is an ordered pair consisting of a shape and the reader's orientation to that inscription, the symbol can be changed by changing the orientation rather than inscription. For instance, a car park attendant who rotates his ➔ sign to direct traffic left ⬅ or right ➔ is using a single inscription token to form opposite symbol types.

The motive for manipulating a symbol's orientation rather than its shape is that the shape is harder to alter. Writing a line through 1111, replacing 51 by 63, or even just appending a 0 to 4, requires physical energy, not a mere decision. Put more dramatically, the perspectival calculator sidesteps the physical constraints imposed by the manipulation of inscriptions (as in digital computing) or the manipulation of physical models (as in analogue computing). For instance, since the input symbols need not be *causally* altered, the speed of the computation is not constrained by Einstein's principle that no signal can travel faster than the speed of light.

Although there are the usual physical limits associated with *reading* the answer, the perspectival computation itself has no duration because nothing substantive is done to the data. The transformation of ➜ from part of a right-turn symbol to part of a left-turn symbol is a 'Cambridge event', like becoming an uncle. Given this non-causal aspect of perspectival computation, 'faster than light' performance is achieved even when the subcomputations are algorithmically complex, exponentially increasing, or even infinite. This raises the hope of a loophole through looming computational limits.[37]

The Bikini Palindrome

'Girl, bathing on Bikini, eyeing boy, finds boy eyeing bikini on bathing girl.' J. A. Lindon's palindrome epitomises Thomas Nagel's principle of iteration in 'Sexual Perversion'. Picture Romeo and Juliet at a pick-up bar. The walls are lined with mirrors. Juliet notices that Romeo is eyeing her. She is aroused by his interest. Romeo notices her meta-arousal. He is aroused by the fact his arousal arouses Juliet. Juliet picks up on this. Meta-arousal sets up meta-meta-arousal and so on.

Romeo and Juliet embed each other's perspectives. They resemble facing mirrors, endlessly reflecting each other's reflections. The pair sweep back and forth across Lindon's palindrome, adding layer upon layer of desire.

Perverted sex lacks this iterated arousal. There is just one-way desire for solitary sexual practices, object-oriented sex, sex with unresponsive partners, and unconsensual sex.

Even as a first pass, Nagel's iteration requirement seems too tidy to separate healthy sex from perverted sex. Perversion appears hopelessly amorphous. Yet Nagel's principle performs surprising well.

There is an intriguing structural similarity with language. Hearers need iterated mental states to understand speakers. To get my son to take a laundry basket into his inner sanctum,

---

[37] I elaborate the hope in: 'Mirror Notation: Symbol Manipulation without Inscription Manipulation', *Journal for Philosophical Logic*, 28 (April 1999): 141–64.

I leave the basket propped against the door. He will infer that I want him to put the basket back in his room. The inference will be based on him recognising that I intended this and to act by recognising this intention. This mutual embedding of mental states has the same iterated structure as iterated arousal.

What is cause and what is effect still needs be sorted. But the connection with language makes the aptness of the Bikini palindrome is more than a pure accident.

Family Resemblance for Primates

While at the Grande Galerie de l'Évolution, I was surprised by a poster, entitled 'Primate Traits', that seemed to have been ghostwritten by Ludwig Wittgenstein:

> Take a close look at these few primates. Can you tell what they have in common morphologically? Difficult? That's because there is no specific feature common to all primates, but rather characteristics that are shared by most: forward-facing eyes, prehensile hands and feet with five nail-bearing fingers and toes, and a brain that is large in proportion to their body.

In Plato's dialogues, Socrates presupposes that there is something common and peculiar to all uses of 'virtue', 'knowledge', 'pious', and so forth. The definition specifies this essence. Socrates would require 'What is a primate?' to be answered with an essential feature of primates.

This definitional model works well in geometry: A triangle is an enclosed three-sided figure. The Greeks also wanted definitions for legal purposes: Embezzlement is 'the fraudulent conversion of the property of another by one who is already in lawful possession of it'. The Greeks wanted to be ruled by laws rather than men. Definitions give fair notice of what is prohibited.

Despite the precedents of law and geometry, Wittgenstein suggests that many important terms (*art, consciousness, knowledge, number, religion*) lack a core explanatory feature. They instead get their unity from overlapping features between each pair of cases.

Renford Bambrough provides a formal model of family resemblance. Let *e d c b a* be five objects and *A B C D E* are five properties:

$$e \quad d \quad c \quad b \quad a$$
$$ABCD \quad ABCE \quad ABDE \quad ACDE \quad BCDE$$

Each object shares 75% of its properties with each other object but no property is common between all the objects.

This model gives us a stable pattern of resemblance. Any pair is guaranteed to have many common features. The order of selection is irrelevant.

Slippery-slope concepts lack the unity of family resemblance. Items arranged at the extremes, here *a* and *e*, have no common elements:

$$e \quad d \quad c \quad b \quad a$$
$$ABCD \quad BCDE \quad CDEF \quad DEFG \quad EFGH$$

These chains permit the transmutations associated with Lewis Carroll's word ladders:

APE, APT, OPT, OAT, MAT, MAN.

The chain can also be forged with rough synonyms. In 1967 Dmitri Borgmann thesaurused from UGLY to BEAUTIFUL:

UGLY — OFFENSIVE
OFFENSIVE — INSULTING
INSULTING — INSOLENT
INSOLENT — PROUD
PROUD — LORDLY
LORDLY — STATELY
STATELY — GRAND
GRAND — GORGEOUS
GORGEOUS — BEAUTIFUL

With a slippery slope, the order of comparison is critical for sustaining an ample stock of features that are common to the pair.

To stop the descent, we draw a line, cutting off some item in the spectrum as an outlier. But now we are vulnerable to ordering effects. When people hear the list (skyscraper, cathedral, temple, prayer), prayer is chosen as the outlier. When they hear the reverse order, skyscraper is the outlier. Family resemblance terms are free of this arbitrariness.

Some objected that logic guarantees that there is always something common and peculiar. In Bambrough's model, each object satisfies the following disjunction:

Object o has features $ABCD$ or $ABCE$ or $ABDE$ or $ACDE$ or $BCDE$.

A little logic can shorten this to: Object o has either (A and B) or (A and C) or (B and C). Wittgenstein characterises this response as more clever than wise: 'One might as well say: "Something runs through the whole thread – namely the continuous overlapping of those fibres"' (*Philosophical Investigations*, §67). More specifically, Wittgenstein objects that family resemblance terms are open-ended. We could add novel items.

Is 'family resemblance' a family resemblance term? Ironically not. There actually is a common property to members of a family that resemble each other, namely, descent from common parents.

Minimal Resemblance

Resemblance increases with the number of shared properties. Identity provides maximal resemblance. Judged resemblance may differ: Charlie Chaplin is said to have entered a Charlie Chaplin lookalike contest – only to finish third.

This result would not surprise psychologists who study caricatures. People are more easily recognised from slightly caricatured photographs than realistic photographs. This is just a special instance of a generalisation that holds for all animals. When trained to distinguish between a rewarded and an unrewarded stimulus, an extreme version of the rewarded stimulus will get a stronger response than the rewarded stimulus itself. This embarrasses behaviourists. A stimulus that has never been rewarded gets a stronger response than a response that has been richly rewarded!

Biologists have a natural explanation. What counts as a reward depends on the animal's innate preferences and sense of similarity. That innate mental architecture is shaped by evolution. Human beings are designed to desire sweetness because that is a sign of ripe fruit. Confectioners have designed candy that is sweeter than ripe fruit. So we prefer candy to ripe fruit.

My question concerns objective resemblance rather than judged resemblance. How can we *minimise* resemblance without making the objects completely distinct? Suppose you have four objects that must have three of six properties. Each property must be shared between two objects but no two objects can have more than one property in common. ♀ How can the objects be assigned properties to achieve this minimal resemblance?

Brother-in-Law Resemblance

♀ In 1889, Senator John William Harreld married his widow's sister. How did he do it?

As a boy, I spent more time imagining the fish I would catch than actually catching fish. What was down there? I pictured the skate as gliding on the sea floor like a roller skate. I pictured the sole as being as flat as the sole of my shoe. As it turns out, 'skate' the skating shoe is etymologically unrelated to 'skate' the fish. But when I caught skates and soles, they looked like skates and soles.

The fish and footwear had what Mark Twain described as a 'brother-in-law resemblance':

> Once a similarity is suggested, we elaborate and
> exaggerate the resemblances. It's like a cloud which
> resembles a horse after some one has pointed out the

resemblance. You perceive it, then, though I have often seen a cloud that didn't. Clouds often have nothing more than a brother-in-law resemblance. I wouldn't say this to everybody, but I believe it to be true, nevertheless. For I myself have seen clouds which looked like a brother-in-law, whereas I knew very well they didn't. Nearly all such are hallucinations, in my opinion.

– Twain, *No. 44, The Mysterious Stranger*

Mark Twain met his future brother-in-law, Charles Langdon, on a steamship tour of Europe and the Holy Land in 1867. Langdon showed Twain a photograph of his sister Olivia. Twain fell in love at first sight.

Imaginative elaboration of resemblances creates an impression that sex with a brother-in-law is incest. The incest taboo is on a hair trigger. Just a minor resemblance, such as being raised in the same household, can open the door to disgust. Once this emotion is out, it is difficult to reason it back in.

But we try. Reason will list the practical advantages of marrying brothers-in-law. An especially strong case can be made for widows. The Bible speaks up early. Genesis 38:8 actually requires a brother-in-law to marry his sister-in-law:

> And Judah said unto Onan, Go in unto thy brother's wife, and marry her, and raise up seed to thy brother.

Deuteronomy 25:5 generalises the imperative to marry widowed sisters-in-law:

> If brethren dwell together, and one of them die, and have no child, the wife of the dead shall not marry without unto a stranger: her husband's brother shall go in unto her, and take her to him to wife, and perform the duty of an husband's brother unto her.

'If anyone can show just cause why this couple cannot lawfully be married, then let them speak now or forever hold their peace.' Leviticus 20:21 shouts from the pews:

> And if a man shall take his brother's wife, it is an unclean

thing: he hath uncovered his brother's nakedness; they shall be childless.

Where there is inconsistency, there is a market for intervention by an Authority. When Catherine of Aragon was left a widow, her brother-in-law secured a papal waiver to marry her. When Catherine failed to produce a viable son King Henry VIII inferred the Pope had erred. God must not regard the pair as married. The Pope should acknowledge the error through an annulment.

This led to a hard line against brother-in-law marriage in the United Kingdom. The prohibition was based on a doctrine of Anglican Canon Law whereby those who were connected by marriage were regarded as being related to each other.

The Deceased Wife's Sister's Marriage Act 1907 (7 Edw. 7 c.47) partly reversed this by permitting a *man* to marry his dead brother's wife. The retraction of the prohibition was grudging; it did not retract the prohibition for the widow. Not until 1921 was retraction made symmetrical. Half-marriages became full marriages.

Brother-in-law resemblance is also at work in our mixed attitudes towards *argumentum ad hominem*. The label goes back to Aristotle's discussion of arguments that use your adversary's concessions as premises. For instance, Catherine of Aragon and Henry VIII debated whether they were married. If Catherine were right, about Henry VIII being her husband, he was entitled to inherit her property. When she died, he argued that, by her own premises, he was entitled to her property. He did not think his inheritance depended on sharing her premises.

Later *argumentum ad hominem* came to be used for arguments that attack the person rather than his thesis. In principle, characteristics of the person might be relevant to the cogency of the argument. But typically the personal attack is intended to exploit the cognitive dissonance of approving an argument while disapproving of the arguer. Try to recall a good argument constructed by someone you loathe. The quickest way for a Catholic to prevent Henry VIII from arguing persuasively would be to make the audience hate him.

Arthur Schopenhauer suggested that the arguments which exploit cognitive dissonance be termed *argumentum ad personam*. The historian Gabriel Nuchelmans agrees: 'Modern attempts to account for the nature of a single *argumentum ad hominem* are like efforts to construct one semantic spectrum for two homonymous words.'

Tolstoy's Syllogism

Why do you find *your* death more difficult to imagine than the death of other people? In Chapter VI of *The Death of Ivan Ilyich* Leo Tolstoy traces the asymmetry to the rich detail of your self-concept:

> The syllogism he had learnt from Kiesewetter's *Logic*:
> 'Caius is a man, men are mortal, therefore Caius is mortal,'
> had always seemed to him correct as applied to Caius,
> but certainly not as applied to himself. That Caius – man
> in the abstract – was mortal, was perfectly correct, but he
> was not Caius, not an abstract man, but a creature quite,
> quite separate from all others. He had been little Vanya,
> with a mamma and a papa, with Mitya and Volodya,
> with the toys, a coachman and a nurse, afterwards with
> Katenka and with all the joys, griefs, and delights of
> childhood, boyhood, and youth. What did Caius know of
> the smell of that striped leather ball Vanya had been so
> fond of? Had Caius kissed his mother's hand like that, and
> did the silk of her dress rustle so for Caius? Had he rioted
> like that at school when the pastry was bad? Had Caius
> been in love like that? Could Caius preside at a session
> as he did? 'Caius really was mortal, and it was right for
> him to die; but for me, little Vanya, Ivan Ilyich, with all
> my thoughts and emotions, it's altogether a different
> matter. It cannot be that I ought to die. That would be too
> terrible.'

Ivan, from a first person perspective, cannot identify with the x in 'For all x, if x is a man, then x is mortal'. Only an abstract individual can fit into the two-dimensional coffin marked by x. Or so says Tolstoy.

Most philosophers are more influenced by an opposite idea. According to Immanuel Kant, the I is 'the poorest of all representations' (*Critique of Pure Reason*, B408). Even a man with total amnesia can awake in the dark with the thought: I have a headache. His I-concept continues to function because the agent does not need to associate any distinctive descriptive content with I.

Sadly, Kant became an illustration of this phenomenon. In old age, Kant showed signs of Alzheimer's disease. He still made correct use of the first person indexical. We know this because Kant compensated for failing memory by keeping a notebook.

At first, Kant could compensate for his waning memory. But as the disease affected his reasoning, embarrassing fallacies creep in. One of Kant's pages records his resolve to forget a dim-witted servant, Martin Lampe, who had been exploiting his master's growing confusion: 'the name Lampe must now be completely forgotten'. Nevertheless, Kant still competently uses the I-concept. Even patients in the late stage of the disease deploy the concept appropriately.

The I-concept works like the variable x. The variable directly refers to objects rather than using a description. Because the concept possesses no properties, it can survive dramatic changes. I can imagine swapping bodies with a prince. I can imagine me, the prince, turning into a frog. I can imagine me, the frog, having my body destroyed – yet persisting without a body. I adopt the perspective of an abstract point, surveying the pond below.

What can be imagined is presumptively possible. So the variable x behind the I, suggests a realm to which science is blind. I donate my body to science but not my soul.

Are ideas generated by the I-concept genuine possibilities or pseudo-possibilities? The psychologist need not settle that question. He only wishes to explain why we recoil at the syllogism in Kiesewetter's *Logic*.

Woody Allen's Death Wish

In Woody Allen's play *Death*, Kleinman says, 'It's not that I'm afraid to die, I just don't want to be there when it happens.' Will Kleinman get what he wants?

Definitely, according to Epicurus (341–270 BC). Death is the end of your existence. So when your death comes to exist, you will not exist. The timing is perfect!

Ludwig Wittgenstein casts the point geometrically: 'Death is not an event in life: we do not live to experience death ... Our life has no end in just the way in which our visual field has no limits' (*Tractatus*, §6.4311).

Why worry about your death? It will not happen in your lifetime!

To this consolation, the Epicureans add 'the mirror of time'. Being non-existent after your death cannot be bad. For being non-existent prior to your life was not bad. The states of non-existence are symmetrical.

Scattered throughout the Roman Empire are Epicurean gravestones that read *Non fui, fui, non sum, non curo* (I was not; I was; I am not; I do not care). There is timeless consolation in some necessary truths.

Checkmate in Aleph-Nought

In the distance you see the border of a chess field.

Two old men are playing with heavy outdoor pieces. All you see are a white king harried by a black king and queen. The queen is difficult to budge. You offer to help move the black queen.

White [grumpily]: No kibbitzing!
Black [weary but relieved]: No need! I have almost chased white king to the final row.
You: I was only trying to prevent a hernia. Can you tell me how far the chess field extends?
White: … infinitely far …
You: How could you know?
White: We have been down the entire length, finishing this game of chess.
You: But you must have begun somewhere!
White: No, we have always been playing.
Black: You are in luck, we are about to finish.

Indeed, Black has a king and queen that is chasing the white king along last row. Finally, Black checkmates White.

Black [scolding]: See? I told you it was checkmate in aleph-nought!

A Memory Lapse

When I joined the philosophy department at Washington University in St Louis, I was pleased to see a room with the plaque:

Rudner Memorial Lounge:
In memory of RICHARD RUDNER distinguished philosopher, colleague, and friend.

However, when I asked about Rudner, no one could remember him. In the 'The Scientist *Qua* Scientist Makes Value Judgments' Rudner noted that scientists have acceptance rules: believe the hypothesis if and only if it has a probability above a threshold, say 0.95 or perhaps 0.99. The threshold for belief varies in accordance with how bad an error would be. That is a value judgement.

The stakes are sometimes of existential proportion. When

developing nuclear energy, some physicists worried that there was a slight chance of a runaway chain reaction. Each split atom splits a neighbour atom until no atoms remain to be split. The physicists calculated that the scenario had a probability of less than four in a billion. They felt that was low enough to dismiss the possibility.

Maybe they were right. But that is a value judgement.

How probable must Rudner's thesis be for scientists to accept it? Well, how bad would it be to be mistaken about whether value judgements are a core responsibility of scientists?

Or to forget Richard Rudner and his thesis?

The Penultimate State

On an election bus tour, a presidential candidate promises to visit all 48 contiguous states starting from her home state of Illinois. Her campaign can fund only a single visit to each state. However, the candidate can visit the states in whatever order she wishes. 💡 If the politician keeps her promise, which state will be next to last?

Fame as the Forgotten Philosopher: Meditations on the Headstone of Adam Ferguson

Scotland has atmospheric graveyards. The weathered grave markers are large enough to bear instructive inscriptions. I was introduced to my favourite epitaph by a fellow philosopher. We were on a stroll through the Cathedral graveyard adjoining St Andrews University. She drew my attention to the following words:

> Here rest the mortal remains of Adam Ferguson LLD,
> Professor of moral philosophy in the University of
> Edinburgh. He was born at Logieward in the county of
> Perth on the 20th June 1723 and died in this city of St
> Andrews on the 22nd day of February 1816. He employed
> the interval betwixt his childhood and his grave with
> unostentatious and steady perseverance in acquiring and
> in diffusing knowledge and in the practice of public and of
> domestic virtue. To his venerated memory this monument
> is erected by his children, that they may record his piety
> to God and benevolence to man, and commemorate
> the eloquence and energy with which he inculcated the
> precepts of morality and prepared the youthful mind for
> virtuous actions. But a more imperishable memorial to
> his genius exists in his philosophical and historical works,
> where classic elegance, strength of reasoning and clearness
> of detail secured the applause of the age in which he
> lived, and will long continue to deserve the gratitude and
> command the admiration of posterity.

My colleague and I exchanged blank looks. We did not recall Adam Ferguson. Our failure to remember Ferguson seemed to demonstrate how an epitaph can age into a self-refuting statement.

This glacial pragmatic paradox struck my fellow philosopher as poignant. Her embarrassment for Ferguson threatened to generalise. Would our scholarship be equally ground down by the mass of history? I noted that the inscription only said that Adam Ferguson's scholarship *deserved* to be long remembered. Perhaps Ferguson had been spared by this subtle qualification.

On reflection, this was little comfort. Which is worse? To have one's works forgotten because they were not worth remembering or to have them unfairly neglected?

When I returned to the David Hume Tower at the University of Edinburgh (where I was lecturing for a term), I passed the Adam Ferguson Building. To my professional embarrassment, I learned that he was a prominent figure in the Scottish Enlightenment. Although Professor Ferguson did not have the enormous intellectual legacy of his friends David Hume and Adam Smith, his reputation survives in political philosophy. He is remembered most as the intellectual historian who wrote *Essay on the History of Civil Society*. Although Hume could not shake his low opinion of the book, he was 'agreeably disappointed' when it quickly became a literary success. Hume praised Ferguson as a 'Man of Sense, Knowledge, Taste, Elegance, & Morals'. There is good evidence that Hume resigned the Keepership of the Advocates' Library so that Adam Ferguson could be his successor in that post.

Right up to his death, Hume kept up a pet debate: If Adam Ferguson, John Pringle, and David Hume were princes of adjacent states, how would they rule their kingdoms? Although Ferguson was a clergyman, he had martial virtues. This emerged while he was Chaplain to the Black Watch (Royal Highland Regiment). Sir Walter Scott tells a story in which Ferguson exceeded his commission at the Battle of Fontenoy. Instead of staying at the rear as his commission required, Adam Ferguson led the column brandishing a broadsword. When ordered to the rear, Ferguson retorted 'Damn my commission' and tossed it towards the Colonel. John Pringle also had a soldierly aspect. So Hume had grounds for claiming that Prince Adam and Prince John would cultivate the arts of war. Hume said he would cultivate the arts of peace. To protect his kingdom, Prince David would give one of them a subsidy to fall upon the other. After Prince Adam and Prince John were exhausted by a long war, Prince David would end up as master of all three kingdoms.

Posterity has treated Adam Ferguson rather decently. True, he may not be remembered by some philosophers strolling by his grave. True, students at Edinburgh may fail to remember that Ferguson Hall was named after a former professor of unusual wisdom and public spirit. But two hundred years after his death, appreciative scholars write articles about Adam Ferguson and note that his labours extended beyond theory and into practical matters. So I must awkwardly concede that, in truth, few scholars are remembered as well as Adam Ferguson. My apologies.

My pity has collapsed into self-pity. I wonder whether people will read *my* essays and books two centuries from now. At my age, Ferguson was warm friends with the best philosopher and the best economist of his time and was contributing to a cultural transformation. He had just published his most celebrated tome and had already written *A Sermon Preached in the Ersh Language*, *The Morality of Stage Plays Seriously Considered*, and *Analysis of Pneumatics and Moral Philosophy*. I am optimistic about how much sand remains in my hourglass. But I am not likely to have as much as Adam Ferguson. He lived a healthy, active life until a week before his death at age 93.

Scholars take solace in the fact that their works are preserved in libraries. But an observation by an English contemporary of Ferguson, Samuel Johnson, demonstrates that mere preservation has the fragrance of formaldehyde and chalk dust:

> No place affords a more striking conviction of the vanity of human hopes, than a public library; for who can see the wall crowded on every side by mighty volumes, the works of laborious meditation and accurate enquiry, now scarcely known but by the catalogue, and preserved only to increase the pomp of learning, without considering how many hours have been wasted in vain endeavours, how often imagination has anticipated the praises of futurity, how many statues have risen to the eye of vanity,

how many ideal converts have elevated zeal, how often
wit has exulted in the eternal infamy of his antagonists,
and ambition delighted in the gradual advances of
her authority, the immutability of his decrees, and the
perpetuity of her power?

– Johnson, The Rambler, No. 106 (23 March 1751), p. 167

Scholars want to be read and thought about. Most will settle into unread oblivion. Will I join this silent majority?

It is more likely that one belongs to the majority than to the minority. The larger the majority, the higher the probability. Since the population has been growing exponentially and the living's ability to recall the dead is fairly fixed, the forgotten will be increasingly well represented in the future. The darkness of the past grows geometrically. Hope of escaping this icy shadow diminishes proportionately.

Nevertheless, I plan to come in from the cold. Misplaced pity for Adam Ferguson can be turned into a gambit for lasting recognition. The enterprise springs from *my* epitaph:

Here lies Roy Sorensen whose paradoxes will make him
long remembered.

If I am long remembered for my paradoxes, then the epitaph is true. Well and good. If, as actuarial reasoning predicts, I am not long remembered, then my epitaph seems grimly self-refuting.

You may wonder what is the point of courting the fate that I had mourned for Ferguson in the Cathedral graveyard. The answer lies in the resemblance my epitaph bears to the mythical Phoenix. My epitaph will rise from its ashes. To see how, suppose a philosopher, say the great-great-great-granddaughter of my kind friend, discovers the epitaph but does not remember me. She concludes that the epitaph is false. Indeed, it is made false by her very failure to remember me. She is moved by the pathetic self-refuting nature of my epitaph. My kind friend's great-great-great-granddaughter will mention the poignant epitaph to great-great-great-grandchildren of others.

These future epigraph readers will draw the lesson that commemorations should be cautiously composed. Better to play it safe like Abraham Lincoln. His famous 'Gettysburg Address' has a self-effacing line: 'The world will little note nor long remember what we say here, but it can never forget what they did here.'

The Gettysburg Address continues to be read by millions. By withstanding the test of time, Lincoln refuted himself in a flattering direction.

So isn't it best to hedge one's bet and predict that one will be forgotten? John Keats deepened his fame as a poet by insisting that his Italian tomb be pessimistically engraved with the words, 'Here lies One whose Name was writ in Water.'

Censorious souls will hold up my optimistic epitaph as a lesson to all who predict posthumous recognition. Perhaps, I will gain notoriety, even celebrity as the forgotten philosopher who received slow, quiet poetic justice.

Eventually someone with a temperament like mine will notice that no one can *remember* that Roy Sorensen is forgotten. For if someone did remember that Roy Sorensen is forgotten, then Roy Sorensen would *be* forgotten. After all, memory implies truth. Anyone who is forgotten is not remembered. I cannot be both remembered and not remembered. My words rebound off this contradiction and echo gratifyingly far into the future by *reductio ad absurdum*.

The self-defeating appearance of my epitaph is itself self-defeating. My epitaph becomes a self-fulfilling prophecy by a kind of double-negation.

This Phoenix phenomenon is not foolproof. Glory seekers are sometimes confronted by censors. In 355 BC Herostratus confessed on the rack that he burned down the Temple of Diana at Ephesus to spread his name. The Ephesians decreed that his memory be abolished.

Obviously, this censorship failed. The historian Theopompus frustrated the Ephesian decree by mentioning Herostratus. But I should not take comfort in examples of thwarted censorship. Acts of failed suppression form a biased sample which leads us to underestimate diligent censors.

Happily my epitaph is not an act of arson. Censors do not deign to suppress harmless pedantry. The real threat to my scheme is permanent indifference. If my epitaph is not sufficiently circulated, it is not apt to achieve its psychological effect.

My friends have consoled me with the observation that a paradox can exist without being recognised. Nelson Goodman's grue paradox was a paradox before he discovered it and will remain a paradox after it is forgotten. The epitaph paradox is an abstract object that will forever hold a rightful place in the Platonic heavens.

Well, that is some consolation. However, it is a bit too reminiscent of Samuel Johnson's dusty libraries. Writers have generally been moved by a legacy in which their creations really persist in the minds of future people. The Roman poet Horace compared this mental legacy favourably with that offered by mere metal and stone:

> More durable than bronze, higher than Pharaoh's
> Pyramids is the monument I have made,
> A shape that angry wind or hungry rain
> Cannot demolish, nor the innumerable
> Ranks of the years that march in centuries.
> I shall not wholly die: some part of me
> Will cheat the goddess of death, for while High Priest
> And Vestal shall climb our Capitol in a hush,
> My reputation shall keep green and growing.

Well that is a bit over the top, Horace. You are wholly dead. And I will join you. What you have actually achieved is a rare relationship with thousands of years of fellow human beings. There is no need to fortify that valuable connection with an allusion to immortality.

And you did take a risk, Horace. Had your poetry been less esteemed, you would have been remembered for your vanity rather than your poetry. It is important to be remembered in the right way. Yes, my epitaph may seem to present a similar risk. But its immodesty is integral to its purpose as a paradox. Anyone who thinks through the epitaph paradox will realise that I died with my boots on.

Of course, there is much to do in the interim. I've got to spread the word. More specifically, I must make sure that my epitaph is repeated widely and in a variety of resilient forms. Notice how my epitaph eases the labour of obituarists. They need not labour to find some quaint anecdote to put a human face on my death. Their profession encourages a philosophical bent and so I expect that they will welcome my death. Thus my eager obituarists will help me meet future historians halfway.

My epitaph brings me peace of mind. When on a stroll in 1874, Lewis Carroll thought of a single verse: 'For the Snark *was* a Boojum, you see.' Although Carroll attached no meaning to the line, he was inspired to work forward, or rather, backward, until he had an epic poem that ended with exactly that verse. This is natural for a logician like Lewis Carroll. Conclusions are most easily proved by specifying them in advance and working back towards the premises. Admittedly, Carroll's *The Hunting of the Snark* is nonsense. Since I am not a nihilist, I want my last words to function more like a literal conclusion. By specifying my epitaph in advance, I can work out my life backwards from death. I thereby busy myself with the premises and lemmas from which the whole process draws validity.

♀♀♀ The Answers ♀♀♀

Introduction

Answer 1: Sand.

Answer 2: Take a small number of grains of sand from his universal collection. Ask him to recount. If his new number plus the number of grains you subtracted equals the original amount, then that is evidence he counted correctly. His repeated success at trials such as this would build your confidence he is right about the number of grains.

Answer 3: To recall Henri Poirot's sidekick Captain Hastings: 'I know it's a rather odd question, but a rather odd person would like to know.' We are assuming there are only finitely many atoms. We are assuming each individual is identical to a combination of atoms, any combination. It follows that there are exactly as many individuals as there are combinations of atoms. If there are n atoms, there are $2^n - 1$ combinations of individuals. No matter which number we choose for n, the number $2^n - 1$ is odd. Therefore, you are in an odd universe!

Your presence precludes the possibility that the universe has 0 atoms. 0 is an even number. (An even number divides by 2 without remainder: 0 divided by 2 equals 0 without remainder.) So unless something else logically precludes the empty universe, the universe would be even. Such a preclusion would refute a presupposition of 'Why is there something rather than nothing?'

Notice that the $2^n - 1$ formula still works for the case of 0 atoms. $2^0 = 1$. Indeed, $0^0 = 1$. Exponentiation is not repeated multiplication. Exponents measure how much a number has been scaled up. If you fail to scale up, exponent 0, you get the same size of number.

Answer 4: 'Numerous' is a property of the class rather than its members. The class of men over five feet tall is numerous, not members of the class. Thomas Aquinas illustrates the difference with 'alone':

Man alone is rational.
Socrates is a man.
Socrates alone is rational.

'Man' is used in the first premise to designate the class. The class of human beings is alone in having rational members. So 'alone' is modifying the class rather than its members.

Bertrand Russell argues that 'exists' works like 'numerous'. 'Men exist' says that class of men has at least one member. According to Russell, 'exists' cannot apply to members of that class. When we say 'Socrates exists' we really mean 'The class of men defended in detail by both Plato and Xenophon has at least one member.'

Answer 5: The roof will be patched tomorrow.

Hidden Messages in Songs

The hidden consequence is 'I am my baby'.

A Blessed Book Curse

Answer 1: The proof proceeds by the pigeonhole principle: If more than n pigeons must occupy n holes, then at least two pigeons must share a hole. Let the holes equal possible word lengths up to the word length of the longest book. Since there are more books than words, there are more books (pigeons) than word lengths (pigeonholes). So at least two books must be placed in the same word length 'hole'.

Answer 2: The second proof also relies on the pigeonhole principle. Given the prohibition of books with the same number of words, the only way to have more books than the maximum number of words is to have a book with 0 words. The wordless book is about nothing.

Listen for a Counterexample

Silence.

Hearing silence is successful perception of an absence of sound. It is not a failure to hear sound. A deaf man cannot hear silence.

Is hearing silence just a matter of *inferring* an absence of sound from one's failure to hear? No, a wounded soldier who wonders whether he has gone deaf can hear silence while being neutral about whether he is hearing silence. He hopes he is hearing silence but neither believes nor disbelieves that he is hearing silence.

Schopenhauer's Intelligence Test

The cracking of whips [is] a truly infernal thing when it is done in the narrow resounding streets of a town. I denounce it as making a peaceful life impossible; it puts an end to all quiet thought. That this cracking of whips should be allowed at all seems to me to show in the clearest way how senseless and thoughtless is the nature of mankind. No one with anything like an idea in his head can avoid a feeling of actual pain at this sudden, sharp crack, which paralyses the brain, rends the thread of reflection, and murders thought.

Schopenhauer is astute in singling out the crack of the whip as a special case. For the sound is a sonic boom – the first produced by human beings. The whip was the first artefact to break the sound barrier.

The timing of the boom puzzles physicists. For the sonic boom occurs when the tip of the whip is travelling at *twice* the speed of sound. Why not earlier when the tip first broke the sound barrier? The latest calculations suggest that the tip does not make the noise. Instead, the crack issues from a loop travelling along the whip.

A Matter of Life and Death

Maybe you would like to confer with your colleagues at the Harvard Medical School. In 1982 Amos Tversky told half the physicians that the one-month survival rate for surgery was 90%. Given this assumption, 84% recommended surgery over radiation. Tversky told the other half that there was a 10% mortality rate in the first month. Only 50% of these physicians recommended surgery.

But wait! The two statements are logically equivalent. One is optimistically framed in terms of 'survival'. The other is pessimistically framed in terms of 'mortality'.

When I 'corrected' the statistics I presented to you, I merely replaced a positively framed statement for a negatively framed equivalent. So I did not change the information available to you. So if you are a perfect reasoner, you should not change your mind.

But if you are not a perfect reasoner, you might have learned something about yourself that would make you less confident in your first recommendation.

The Identity of Indiscernibles

Max Black imagines a universe containing nothing but two exactly resembling spheres. Given such complete symmetry, the two spheres would be indiscernible.

Although the vast majority of philosophers agree with Black's conclusion that there can be perfect twins, there is fascinating controversy over whether his counterexample is decisive. For instance, Ian Hacking says the situation could be reinterpreted as one sphere in a non-Euclidean space. What Black narrates as a journey from one sphere to a distinct sphere, Hacking redescribes as a journey around space back to the very same sphere!

Indiscernible Pills

Add a second pill from the A bottle. Cut each of the four pills in half: ⵔⵔⵔⵔ. Take the left halves of each pill. That will be equivalent to taking 1 A pill and 1 B pill. Tomorrow, consume the remaining halves. Return to your normal regime.

One rule of thumb for solving problems is to increase the similarity between where you are and where you want to be. That is how you climb a hill or erase a blackboard. There are exceptions. When you misbutton a shirt, you are just one button shy of a fully buttoned shirt. Yet your only recourse is to completely unbutton the shirt and do it all over again. The problem for the indiscernible pills is that you have lost track of the identity of the pills. So the impulse is to reidentify. But the solution is to put another pill into the mix.

Telling a Clover from a Plover

Although you strain to tell the difference, a bee can. This and related problems were solved by the physicist and inventor Robert W. Wood in *How to Tell the Birds from the Flowers* (1907):

The Clover.   The Plover.

The Plover and the Clover can be told
          apart with ease,
By paying close attention to the
          habits of the Bees,
For ento-molo-gists aver, the Bee
          can be in Clover,
While ety-molo-gists concur, there
          is no B in Plover.
—2—

From: *A Revised Manual of Flornithology for Beginners* by Robert Williams Wood.

This book, along with *Animal Analogues* (1908) was a satire of anthropomorphic nature descriptions (part of the 'nature-fakers controversy').

Wood also debunked N-rays. Prosper-René Blondlot claimed N-rays to be a form of radiation similar to X-rays. Since only French physicists could detect the new phenomenon, *Nature* dispatched Woods to tour Blondlot's laboratory. Wood slyly removed an essential prism from the N-ray apparatus during a demonstration. The French continued to observe N-rays.

According to Walter Bruno Gratzer, in *Eurekas and Euphorias*, Wood 'would alarm the citizens of Baltimore by spitting into puddles on wet days, while surreptitiously dropping in a lump of metallic sodium, which would explode in a jet of yellow flame'.

The Emotional Range of Logicians

By the birth of Eva a few minutes after Erika. Elisabeth Kübler-Ross was one member of a set of identical triplets.

Assassination Proof

Nero's successor. The next emperor was Galba. But Seneca was not claiming that Galba could not be killed. Galba only avoided Nero's intention to kill him by good fortune. Seneca was making a logical point: 'However many you put to death, you will never kill your successor.' Seneca was correct. Before Nero was succeeded, however, he succeeded in arranging Seneca's death.

How to Succeed your Successor

Benjamin Harrison is the only other president in US history to have succeeded his successor. The puzzle seems to require knowledge of the US presidents, but the question provides enough information for the answer. Benjamin Harrison succeeded his successor because his successor was Grover Cleveland. Harrison was elected after Cleveland's first term. Although Harrison was only elected to one term, he succeeded his successor.

Not All Logicians Are Saints

Answer 1: Leave the wolf with the cabbage. After dropping off the goat, go back and fetch either one, say the wolf. Drop the wolf off on the bank and row the goat back. Now transport the cabbage over because it will be safe with the wolf. Take another empty boat ride, and then return with the goat.

Answer 2: To solve the three-cannibal problem, you need to first take all the cannibals to the opposite side of the river – the exact opposite of the desired state. One must override the rule of thumb: Make the initial state more and more like the goal state.

Lewis Carroll's Peek at Meno's Slave Boy

The solution pops out when you look at the diagram in Benjamin Jowett's (1865) translation of *Meno* (84b–d).

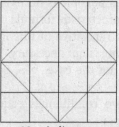

Meno's diagram.

The tilted square is exactly half the size of the big square. The simplest way to halve a square is to mentally fold the four corners to the centre. Since the match is perfect, the tilted square is half the size of the big square.

Carroll's riddle reverses the question Socrates poses to the slave boy: How can a square be doubled in size?

The boy says he does not know. But after Socrates guides his reflection in dialogue, the lad discovers how to double a square. Since Meno knows that the slave boy learned no geometry in this life, Socrates infers that the anonymous boy acquired the knowledge prior to birth. Socrates merely helped the boy to *recall* the answer. Geometry cannot be *taught* because everybody already knows it!

The Elderly Scientist

The elderly scientist is certainly correct. The reason is that any assertion of an impossibility is equivalent to a statement of possibility. 'It is impossible that p' is equivalent to 'It is possible that it is impossible that p': $\sim\Diamond p \leftrightarrow \Diamond\sim\Diamond p$. So Clarke would have to assign a low probability to the impossibility statement and a high probability to the possibility statement. It would be impossible for Clarke's two probability assignments to be both correct.

Proof of the biconditional: $\sim\Diamond p \leftrightarrow \Diamond\sim\Diamond p$. The left-to-right direction, $\sim\Diamond p \rightarrow \Diamond\sim\Diamond p$, follows from the principle that whatever is actual is possible.

The right-to-left side, $\Diamond\sim\Diamond p \rightarrow \sim\Diamond p$, follows from the principle that whatever is possible is necessarily possible: $\Diamond p \rightarrow \Box\Diamond p$. (This is the characteristic formula of the popular modal system S5.) The contrapositive of this formula is $\sim\Box\Diamond p \rightarrow \sim\Diamond p$. To say something is not necessary, $\sim\Box$, is equivalent to saying it is possibly not the case, $\Diamond\sim$. So the contrapositive can be rewritten as $\Diamond\sim\Diamond p \rightarrow \sim\Diamond p$.

Conjoining the two conditionals establishes the equivalence $\sim\Diamond p \leftrightarrow \Diamond\sim\Diamond p$.

Emily Dickinson's Hummingbird

The hummingbird egg can be placed safely in a corner. The bowling ball is too big to make contact with the tiny egg.

Telepathy for the Absent-Minded

I ensured the absence of your triplet by removing all the triplets and then substituting triplets that were each only a single letter off from the originals.

You saw the absence of your triplet. What you overlooked were five other absent triplets. So I conjured the absence of your triplet by conjuring the absence of all the triplets (and then masking their absence by substituting lookalike triplets). Seeing the absence of a triplet is not the failure to see the triplet. You failed to see the other triplets but did not see their absences.

Order of Absence versus Absence of Order

You should not spin the chamber. The key fact is that the bullets are in *adjacent* chambers. So although the random spin involves an absence of order, it preserves an order of absence.

Each row of the table below represents the six possible states of the revolver prior to your adversary's turn.

1	Bullet	Bullet				
2		Bullet	Bullet			
3			Bullet	Bullet		
4				Bullet	Bullet	
5					Bullet	Bullet
6	Bullet					Bullet

Since the gun did not fire, you can eliminate cases 1 and 6. That leaves the middle four cases. If you do not spin, the revolver advances to the next chamber. Case 2 is the only lethal possibility. Hence, by not spinning, your probability of getting shot is 1/4. If you spin, you reset the probability of death back to 2/6.

Neglect of the Absent

Nothing remains after you remove twenty letters from TNWOENTYTLHEITNTEGRS because there are only twenty letters. And the word NOTHING remains after subtracting the letters in the two words TWENTY LETTERS.

I really wanted you to get this riddle right!

Child Proof

Answer 1: You are all done! Equal slices of the sphere conserve surface area, so the children are already sure to have the same amount of crust. Well, anyway if you have ideal bread such as my wife bakes. 'If thou tastest a crust of bread, thou tastest all the stars and all the heavens' (Robert Browning).

Answer 2: The pool is 100 metres in diameter. According to Thales' theorem, whenever a right-angled triangle is inscribed in a circle, its hypotenuse is the diameter of that circle.

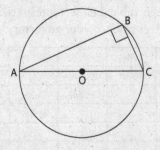

Legend has it that the first philosopher offered an ox to Apollo in thanks for the revelation. Yes, this is the Thales who kicked off metaphysics by arguing all is water.

Answer 3: Yes. Number the coins 1–9. Begin by weighing 1, 2, and 3 against 4, 5, and 6. If they don't balance, then the counterfeit coin is in the lighter group. If they do balance, then it's among the three unweighed coins.

Having narrowed the field to three suspect coins, you can apply the same principle in the second weighing. Put one coin in each tray; if they don't balance, the lighter coin is counterfeit, and if they do, the third suspect must be light.

There is a pleasing release in the switch from *a posteriori* to *a priori* reasoning. The pleasure is international. J. E. Littlewood observes that a similar puzzle wasted 10,000 scientist-hours of work during World War II. 'There was a proposal to drop it over Germany.'

Wittgenstein's Parallelograms

Yes, admits Ludwig Wittgenstein. But he thinks a young child would regard your proof as sophistical: a rectangle can be made of two parallelograms and two triangles. Proof:

A child would find it difficult to hit on the composition of a rectangle with these parts, and would be surprised by the fact that two sides of the parallelograms make a straight line, when the parallelograms are, after all, askew. It might strike him as if the rectangle came out of these figures by something like magic. True, he has to admit that they do form a rectangle, but it is by a trick, by a distorted arrangement, in an unnatural way.

I can imagine the child, after having put the two parallelograms together in this way, not believing his eyes when he sees that they fit like that. 'They don't look as if they fitted together like that.' And I could imagine its being said: It's only through some hocus-pocus that it looks to us as if

they yielded the rectangle – in reality they have changed
their nature, they aren't the parallelograms any more.

– Wigenstein, *Remarks on the Foundations of Mathematics* I, §50.

The Most Fairly Distributed Good

'Of all things, good sense is the most fairly distributed: everyone thinks he is so well supplied with it that even those who
are the hardest to satisfy in every other respect never desire
more of it than they already have' (René Descartes, *Discourse
on Method*).

What the Dishwasher Missed

Use two decks of cards, His and Hers. She secretly chooses
a subset of her deck that has the same number of red and
black cards. I do the same with my deck. We then pool these
two subsets and shuffle. A joker is placed, face down, on the
remainder of the unchosen cards. The joker becomes a hidden
boundary after we place our mixed deck on top. Now neither
of us can predict when the deck will run out.

Developmental Self-Defeat

Kodi discovered that if you sharpen a pencil inscribed with
TOO COOL TO DO DRUGS, it eventually reads COOL TO
DO DRUGS. Sharpen it some more and it reads DO DRUGS.
Sharpen it a little more and it reads DRUGS.

Random Quiz

Tomorrow (Tuesday).

For the next test to be on Wednesday, there would have
to be a *conjunction* of two events: no test on Tuesday (a 5/6
chance of that) *and* a test on Wednesday (a 1/6 chance). The
probability for each subsequent day becomes less and less. (It

would be very surprising if the next quiz day were a hundred days from now!) The question is not whether a 6 will be rolled on any given day, but when the *next* 6 will be rolled. Which day is the next quiz day depends partly on what happens meanwhile, as well as depending partly on the roll of the die on that day.

Enforcing Gresham's Law

Examine a quarter from the bucket mislabelled 'Mixed'. If the quarter is silver, then that came from the true silver bucket. So put the Silver label on it. The bucket labelled 'Non-silver' is mislabelled, so it must be the mixed bucket. Put the remaining label on the remaining bucket.

If the inspected quarter is not silver, then perform the same set of operations except change 'Silver' to 'Non-silver'.

Laziest *Reductio*

Yes. Svetoslav Savchev provides the following proof in *Mathematical Miniatures* (2003): For the sake of contradiction, assume Black has a strategy that's guaranteed to win. An ideal White opponent would realise this and just move his knight forward and then back to its original position. This would make White equivalent to Black. Both sides would have sure wins. But that is a contradiction. So White can at least draw.

Imaginary Travel Companions

Answer 1: The probability is 1/2. I have my imaginary friend walk from the opposite direction towards the five-sided building. We have the same chance of seeing three sides rather than two sides of the five-sided Pentagon.

Answer 2: The probability is 1. Imagine that on the way up, my imaginary friend was climbing down. He would have to meet me somewhere on the path.

The Twin Cities Race

The twins will finish first. Solo's argument would be sound if each twin stood by the unicycle and waited for her sister to show. But she walked after dismounting. This added distance increased their rate of progress to Saint Paul.

Deducing Names

Answer 1: 'Theognis' is the fifth daughter's name. Theognis' father was Diodorus Cronus.

Answer 2: The nursing instructor's former student was the husband of the surgeon. Since the husband was her former nursing student, the instructor remembered his name. Since the boy's name matched his father's, she deduced that the boy was Jake *Junior*.

Answer 3: Andrew, as mentioned in the first line of the riddle: And Drew His Name.

Answer 4: 'Kurt Gödel'. Note the self-reference in 'the name of the husband of Kurt Gödel's wife'.

Answer 5: Your name. You are the pilot.

The Prison-House of Language

Easy! Walk out of a door or climb through a window. There are no doors or windows, so nothing blocks you.

The riddle makes a fitting caricature of Ludwig Wittgenstein's metaphilosophy. He pictures the philosopher as having constructed a false prison out of verbal confusions. There are no philosophical problems, just pseudo-problems.

Linguistically, the riddle exploits an interesting ambiguity in 'door' and 'window'. Each word means the opening or means the thing that fills the opening. Since openings are absences, radically disparate 'things' are meant by the same word.

Bilingual Humour

Answer 1: An American.

Answer 2: Because one egg is un oeuf (enough)!

Capital Pronunciation

One such language is English. Here is a demonstration, 'Job's Job', by an unknown poet:

In August, an august patriarch
Was reading an ad in Reading, Mass.
Long-suffering Job secured a job
To polish piles of Polish brass.

I suspect the poet is from North America because his second example, 'Herb's Herbs', does not work with the British pronunciation of 'herb':

An herb store owner, name of Herb,
Moved to a rainier Mount Rainier.
It would have been so nice in Nice,
And even tangier in Tangier.

Logically Perfect Language

Writing automatically disambiguates, destroying the riddle: 'what' is a four-letter word, 'for' a three-letter word, 'which' has five letters, 'yet' is still spelled with three letters, while 'it' has only two and 'rarely' has six and 'never' is spelled with five.

The period shows that sentence is a declarative sentence rather than a question. Written English forces quotation marks that clarify whether a word is being mentioned rather than used. Commas indicate word groupings.

Punctuation marks have been introduced piecemeal over centuries. Plato preferred oral philosophy over written philosophy. One reason is that the written Greek of his era lacks modern punctuation such as separating words with spaces. Itmusthavebeendifficulttoread

Putting Out Your Second Eye

Answer 1: Only one number fits, 43. He was 43 in the year 43^2 = 1849. So he was born in 1849 – 43 = 1806. Martin Gardner points out that 'Augustus De Morgan' is an anagram of 'O Gus, tug a mean surd!'

Answer 2: If you were born in 1980, you will be 45 years old in 2025. That is the square of 45. If you were born in 2070 then you will be 46 in 2116, the centennial of this book's publication. Oh, and a little praise from the grave: My compliments on your scholarship in locating this old puzzle book!

The Eighteenth Camel

The younger judge would rule that the father's will is ill-defined: half plus a third plus a ninth is less than one. (This explains how the eighteenth camel wanders in and out of the old judge's equation.) A valid inheritance must yield a complete distribution of the legacy. The sons are left to fight for their shares in probate court.

Who is the better judge? The old judge uses a fallacious calculation to create a division that is accepted as fair by all the befuddled disputants. The sons conclude they were justly treated and so withdraw in peace.

The second judge would not rely on human foibles. He would expose the mathematical flaw in the father's will. This leaves the inheritance to continued litigation.

One day, the young judge hears of the eighteenth camel. After work, the young judge visits the old judge in his tranquil garden. The young judge patiently demonstrates the fallacy to the old man. The old judge turns to enjoy the sunset and adapts a Jewish proverb about truth and peace: 'Where there is validity, there is no peace. Where there is peace, there is no validity.'

Shifty O's

Answer 1: Potatoes. (Pot 8 o's)

Answer 2: Abbott kicks Costello in the behind and Costello bellows 'Oh!'

Anything Is Possible?

No. If anything is possible, then it is possible to prove that something is impossible. And if it is possible to prove that something is impossible, then necessarily, something is impossible.

This argument also refutes, 'You can prove anything with statistics.' (Mark Twain attributed this statement to Benjamin Disraeli.)

Unscathed is Marcus Aurelius' warning: 'Because a thing seems difficult for you, do not think it impossible for anyone to accomplish.' Generals base their defences on a barrier that seems impregnable such as desert, swamp, or powerful buffer state. The defender's inability to imagine a breach could be due to a lack of ingenuity. The less ingenious thinker cannot expose this deficit. He can only compensate by doubling up on barriers or recruiting more imaginative thinkers.

Is the falsehood of 'anything is possible' entirely bad news? No, there are comforting impossibilities: your testosterone-charged toddler cannot kill himself by holding his breath.

In principle, a toddler could gain comfort from knowing that he cannot be sucked down the bathtub drain. But speaking from experience, do not conduct a geometrical demonstration by putting his hand on the smaller drain hole.

Is Akrasia Crazy?

In his 1956 essay 'A Plea for Excuses', J. L. Austin presented a highly influential counterexample:

> I am very partial to ice cream, and a bombe is served divided into segments corresponding one to one with the persons at High Table: I am tempted to help myself to two segments and do so, thus succumbing to temptation and even conceivably (but why necessarily?) going against my principles. But do I lose control of myself? Do I raven, do I snatch the morsels from the dish and wolf them down, impervious to the consternation of my colleagues? Not a bit of it. We often succumb to temptation with calm and even with finesse.

Lewis Carroll's Pig Puzzles

Answer 1: No wise young pigs go up in balloons.

Answer 2: PIG, BIG, BAG, BAY, SAY, STY.

Answer 3:

6	8
0	10

This arrangement satisfies Carroll's requirements. Begin the circuit at the northwest sty. Walking to the northeast sty, you find 8 is closer to 10 than 6. Down to the southeast sty, you find 10 is closer to 10 than 8. Down to the southwest sty, you find nothing is closer to 10 than 10 itself. And back up to the northwest sty, you find 6 is closer to 10 than 0.

A Round Trip from Small to Large

Three hundred quintillion years will elapse before you type ONE OCTILLION. Now that we have scaled up to LARGE, can we use a word ladder to climb back down to SMALL? Yes, but as word ladders go, it is a long way to the bottom:

LARGE
SARGE
SERGE
VERGE
VERSE
TERSE
TENSE
TEASE
CEASE
CHASE
CHOSE
CHORE
SHORE
SHARE
SHALE
SHALL
SMALL

Partway Down the Slippery Slope

Answer 1: The 1 p.m. slippery slope has a false step at $n = 29$.

Answer 2: The second premise of the acceleration slippery slope is intuitive. If an object is moving at a certain rate, you can also give it a further push and make it move faster. By repeated pushes, you can accelerate it to any speed.

Albert Einstein showed that the second premise fails when $n = 299{,}792{,}458$ (the speed of light in a vacuum). He established the counterexample by embedding a speed limit in the best theory of acceleration.

Queer Quantities

Answer: 25 fish. The first fisherman took one away and divided by 3: 24/3 = 8. That left 24 − 8 = 16. He expected this even number of fish to be divided the next morning between the two other fishermen. The second fisherman came and threw away one fish to get a nicely divisible 15: 15/3 = 5. That left 15 − 5 = 10. He expected that 10 to be evenly divided by the two remaining fishermen. The third and final fisherman throws one fish away to get 9: 9/3 = 3. So he took 3. He left 6 fish. Sadly, those fish will go unclaimed.

The solution is fair but stinks.

Most Remote Capital City

Answer to the hint riddle: Unique up on it.

Answer to the riddle: There is no capital city that is most distant from any other capital city. The record books say that it is a tie between Canberra, Australia, and Wellington, New Zealand. They are 2,318 kilometres from each other. But as Bertrand Russell emphasises in his theory of definite descriptions, 'the' entails uniqueness. 'Wellington is the most southernmost capital city' is true because you can emphasise THE to confirm the uniqueness. Neither Canberra nor Wellington pass the emphasis test for being THE most remote capital city.

The uniqueness of 'the' is savoured by the narrator of Mark Twain's *A Connecticut Yankee in King Arthur's Court*:

> This title fell casually from the lips of a blacksmith,
> one day, in a village, was caught up as a happy thought
> and tossed from mouth to mouth with a laugh and an
> affirmative vote; in ten days it had swept the kingdom, and
> was to become as familiar as the king's name. I was never
> known by any other designation afterward, whether in
> the nation's talk or in grave debate upon matters of state
> at the council-board of the sovereign. This title, translated

into modern speech, would be THE BOSS. Elected by the nation. That suited me. And it was a pretty high title. There were very few THE's, and I was one of them. If you spoke of the duke, or the earl, or the bishop, how could anybody tell which one you meant? But if you spoke of The King or The Queen or The Boss, it was different.

Predicting Your Predictor

Answer: No, Scriven assumes that Predictor and Avoider can simultaneously have all the needed data, laws, and calculating capacity. David Lewis and Jane Richardson correctly object:

> The amount of calculation required to let the predictor finish his prediction depends on the amount of calculation done by the avoider, and the amount required to let the avoider finish duplicating the predictor's calculation depends on the amount done by the predictor. Scriven takes for granted that the requirement-functions are compatible: i.e., that there is some pair of amounts of calculation available to the predictor and the avoider such that each has enough to finish, given the amount the other has.

> In other words, Scriven equivocates on 'Both Predictor and Avoider have enough time to finish their calculations.' Reading the sentence one way yields a truth: against any given avoider, Predictor can finish, and against any given predictor, Avoider can finish. However, the compatibility premise requires the false reading in which Predictor and Avoider can finish against each other.

Fair Tosses from an Unfair Coin

Yes, you can make the biases cancel out by flipping the coin twice. John von Neumann provides an algorithm in: 'Various Techniques Used in Connection with Random Digits' (1951):

1. Flip twice.
2. If both tosses are the same (heads–heads or tails–tails), repeat step 1.
3. If the tosses come up heads–tails, count the toss as heads. If the tosses come up tails–heads, count it as tails.

Wittgenstein on Ice

Blow.

Infinite Chess

Answer 1: Some mathematicians have attempted to calculate the maximal length by exploiting draw rules. The stalemate rule is a mandatory draw; you have a right and duty to declare a draw. It is like the right to vote in Australia; you have a legal duty to vote. But other draw rules are like voting in the United States. You have a right to vote but no legal duty to vote. The fifty-move draw rule entitles either player to declare a draw. But one is not required to stand on that right. The same goes for the perpetual check rule and rule about repeating the same position three times.

Answer 2: No, the checkmate requires an edge. The example illustrates the importance of the shape of the chessboard.

Infinite Two-Minute Debate

Answer: No, it need not be either. My instructions only specify what happens at moments prior to noon, not noon itself. Since the description of the debate only covers times within the sequence, nothing is implied about a number outside the sequence. The debate isn't even a draw! The appearance of contradiction is a mirage generated by the incompleteness of my supposition.

Indian Debate Tournament

Answer: This can be settled with a big chart. But the simple solution is to focus on losing rather than winning. Each match must create one loser. So $29 - 1 = 28$ debates must take place.

Winning by Losing

Answer: The dervish's advice was to exchange horses. Since the prize goes to the man whose horse reaches the palm tree first, each Bedouin will now have a motive to hurry his competitor's horse to the finish line.

Lawrence of Arabia Collars a Leopard

Why can't a leopard hide? Because it is always spotted.

How can a leopard change its spots? By moving to another place.

How do you collar a leopard? *Very carefully*, ran an answer popular in Lawrence's era.

A Bridge without Pillars

Answer 1: First build the bridge with pillars. Then remove the pillars. There is no more reason for it to fall in one place rather than another. So the bridge is suspended by the principle of indifference.

Indifference may seem too feeble. But think of how you answer 'Why doesn't the earth fall?' You echo Anaximander's (610–546 BC) answer that there is no more reason for the earth to fall in one direction rather than another.

Astronomers used the bridge around the earth thought experiment to explain the stability of Saturn's rings. It also explained how the rings could rotate.

This did not answer how the rings got up there in the first place. But it did suggest that the real difficulty was getting the structure up. Once up, there is no need for a sustaining cause.

Answer 2: Almost two inches! The circumference is $2\pi r$. Let r_e be the radius of the earth. Let r_b be the radius of the bridge. The circumference of the bridge equals the circumference of the earth plus 12 inches: $2\pi r_b = 2\pi r_e + 12$ inches. The right-hand side equals $2\pi(r_e + 12/2\pi)$. Divide both sides by 2π. That yields $r_b = r_e + 12/2\pi$. Therefore, the difference in radii is $r_b - r_e = 12/2\pi = 1.9$ inches.

The Cowpox Transmission Problem

The king arranged a transmission chain comprised of 22 orphan boys. After the first two boys were inoculated with cowpox, the 22 boys were sailed towards the colonies. Skin from their arms would exude fluid that would infect the next pair of boys. (Notice the prudent redundancy; slippery-slope arguments tend to fail because a chain is *weaker* than its weakest link.) The scheme worked. In ten years, cowpox was spread to the whole Spanish empire – yielding resistance to the much worse disease of smallpox.

What became of the orphans? They were rewarded for their service by being adopted into colonial families.

Kant's Gloves

Kant said that a left-hand glove will not fit a right hand. But this holds because he idealised the glove as a rigid body. A left-handed plastic glove is not frozen stiff. It can be pulled inside out, yielding a shape that fits a right hand. You can exploit this flexibility to get extra use of gloves.

Put on *both* pairs of gloves. Perform the first surgery. Remove the outer pair of gloves. Store them. Perform the second surgery. Turn the stored pair of gloves inside out. Slip them on over the sullied second pair. This manoeuvre puts the two non-sterile sides in contact while keeping your hands in their sterile state. This also makes the remaining sterile side (formerly the inside) of the first pair of gloves available for use in the third operation.

Passive *A Priori* Deception

Both the customer and greengrocer speak falsely. Mr Shopper begins with a spontaneous fallacy of treating a geometrical relation as a linear relation. A circle with half the diameter has only a quarter of the area. The two small bundles have only half the quantity of asparagus contained in the large bundle. Half price would have been fair. Not satisfied, the Mrs Greengrocer extracts more money from the fallacious customer by claiming that the two bundles have more asparagus.

The moral question is how far Mrs Greengrocer may go. If she merely accepted Mr Shopper's conclusion that the price should be the same, then she is engaged in passive *a priori* deception. She refrains from correcting his miscalculation. However, when Mrs Greengrocer claims there is more asparagus, she is involved in *active a priori* deception.

True, Mr Shopper still has all the resources needed to catch the falsehood. So there is a question about whether Kant has any moral objection to Mrs Greengrocer.

Crete Revisited

Cretan 108,309 speaks the truth. Each of the personal statements is incompatible with every other statement. So there is exactly one true statement. That is what 108,309 says. So it is false that all Cretans are liars.

Less Lucky the Second Time?

Answer: Yes, Mr Yamaguchi was equally lucky. The same goes for Linus Pauling.

Nobel Prizes are chosen independently of past awards. That would make the events independent, ensuring that Pauling's inference is fallacious. When we work through the feigned error, Pauling's achievement is underscored rather than diminished.

Even if the prize selection is not as independent as the guidelines state, it is certainly fallacious to say that Pauling's chance of winning was one in several hundred. That would hold only if the Nobel committee had earlier resolved to award the 1962 prize only to a previous winner.

As for Tsutomu Yamaguchi, we have trouble discerning whether his nickname was in scare quotes: Was Mr Yamaguchi called 'Lucky' ironically? On the one hand, he is lucky for surviving two atomic bombings. On the other hand, he is unlucky for being involved in *two* atomic bombings. Was Lucky well-named or ill-named?

We can be more confident in the independence of the two events. His chance of surviving the second blast was not much better than his chance of surviving the first. So he was equally lucky.

Nothing Is Written in Stone

False. For something is written in stone. Indeed, that very sentence 'Nothing is written in stone' is written in stone. The inscription is self-refuting.

As a seeker of truth, I searched for an engraving of the following sentence:

'Nothing' is written in stone.

This sentence says that that the word 'nothing' is written in stone. If written in stone, this sentence would be self-fulfilling rather than self-refuting. The riddle nicely illustrates the distinction between using a word and mentioning it. It also shows that a self-refuting statement can look self-fulfilling. A pedestrian can be sure that the sentence is either self-refuting or self-fulfilling – without knowing which.

Self-Fulfilling, Self-Defeating Prophecies

Yes, because a single utterance can constitute distinct speech acts. The different speech acts are graded by different criteria. Predictions are judged solely by accuracy. Warnings are judged by both accuracy and helpfulness. So a warning can be both self-defeating by the criterion of helpfulness and self-fulfilling by the criterion of accuracy.

Consider a weatherman who warns, 'The midnight tsunami will cause fatalities along the shore.' Because of the warning, spectacle-seekers make a special trip to witness the wave. Some drown. The weatherman's announcement succeeds as a prediction by backfiring as a warning.

The Philosopher's Petition

Yes, but just barely! Opponents of the motion objected that the proposal was contradictory: if one nominee knows the identities of all other nominees, then the remaining nominees could not know the identity of all other nominees. Keeping one nominee informed conflicts with keeping other nominees informed. There is a failure of co-knowability.

Actually, the petition to give each nominee foreknowledge of all other nominees is not quite contradictory. The petition merely implies that there are no nominees and no proposed nominees.

A metaphysical anarchist, who thinks all administrative roles are fictions, could consistently endorse the petition. Except he would have to worry about the existence of petitions!

Handicaps on Deduction

Solution to the First Task: Since the first task lacks any restriction, you are free to look up counterexamples. For instance, the library at Oxford University will have logic textbooks containing examples of deductions that reason from generalisations to other generalisations:

All lexicographers are human beings.
All human beings are mammals.
Therefore, all lexicographers are mammals.

They will also have deductions that reason from particular statements to other particular statements:

Samuel Johnson is a lexicographer.
Samuel Johnson has a nose.

Therefore, Samuel Johnson's nose is the nose of a lexicographer.

Solution to the Second Task: Any deduction of the form '*P*, therefore, *P*' will be a counterexample to the principle 'All deductions reason from universal to particular and all inductions reason from particular to general'. There can be no difference in generality between the premise and conclusion. However, one may complain that the *OED* really concerns cogent arguments. Many believe that a circular argument can never rationally persuade anyone. Indeed, some insist that '*P*, therefore, *P*' isn't even an argument. It is reassertion.

Against all this consider:

> Some deductive arguments do not reason from general to
> particular.
> Therefore, some deductive arguments do not reason from
> general to particular.

Since there is no difference in the generality of the premise and the conclusion, the deduction exemplifies the very property it claims to be instantiated. So the argument is rationally persuasive despite being an instance of the form '*P*, therefore, *P*'.

Third Handicap: Now refute the generality myth without using any premises at all.

Taking the second solution to heart, consider the premiseless argument:

> Therefore, either all deductive arguments reason from
> general to particular or it is not the case that all deductive
> arguments reason from general to particular.

Any argument that has a theorem of logic as its conclusion is a valid argument. Since the deduction has no premises, it cannot be reasoning from a general premise to a particular conclusion. Since it is a counterexample to the first disjunct of the conclusion and an example of the second disjunct, the argument is more informative than the tautological form of the conclusion suggests.

Logical Insults

Pauli continues the story: 'Zermelo then crowed in his high-pitched voice, "But, *meine Herren*, it's very simple. Felix Klein isn't a mathematician."' Pauli adds a footnote to the anecdote, 'Zermelo was not offered a professorship at Göttingen.' At the risk of revealing myself to be even more pedantic than early twentieth-century German professors, I will further explain the joke. Zermelo reads 'dislike' as 'does not like', that is, an absence of liking which does not require antipathy, as in my dislike of knuckle cracking. Zermelo also assumes that if Felix Klein is a mathematician, then he is a mathematician at Göttingen. The argument proceeds by a destructive dilemma:

If Felix Klein is a mathematician, then he is in one of two classes:

Those mathematicians who do what Felix Klein likes, but what they dislike.

Those mathematicians who do what they like, but what Felix Klein dislikes.

If Felix Klein is in class 1, then Felix Klein does what he both likes and dislikes: Contradiction.

If Felix Klein is in class 2, then Felix Klein does what he both dislikes and likes: Contradiction.

Therefore, Felix Klein is not a mathematician.

Logical Humility

Answer: Zorn's lemming.

To Be and Not to Be

A bee.

Explanation: male honeybees are produced by sexual abstinence. To make worker bees, the queen stores sperm from a mating and applies it to her eggs. To make male bees, she refrains from fertilising the eggs. The drone is her clone. For honeybees, gender is a superficial trait. The same goes for angelfish; they change gender in response to social and environmental changes. Honeybees still have an orderly family tree. The lineage still obeys the Fibonacci sequence: 0, 1, 1, 2, 3, 5, 8, 13, 21, 34, 55, 89, 144, …

	parents	g-parents	gg-parents	ggg-parents	gggg-parents
male bee	1	2	3	5	8
female bee	2	3	5	8	13

Lobster Logic

A snappy comeback.

Biblical Counting

Most people answer 'Two'. However, they actually believe that *Noah* took on the ark two animals of each kind. Those under the spell of the Moses illusion are asserting what they do not believe. Why aren't they lying?

Illogical Coin Collecting

The gears cannot turn. Even if they were sized properly, an odd number of gears meshing around a circle cannot turn. The problem is that each gear turns its neighbour in the opposite direction.

The gridlock is easier to visualise with fewer gears. Consider the gears aligned as in the figure below. Superficially, they appear ready to all turn. But if you focus, you can appreciate that the gears are actually jammed.

Now focus your mind's eye on a scenario involving four interlocked gears. The four-gear assembly can turn.

The principle is that an even number of interlocked gears can turn but an odd number cannot. The number of teeth and their size do not matter. This principle dictates gridlock for the nineteen-gear circuit that is depicted on the £2 coin.

A Foolproof Guessing Game

The foolproof question is: 'Either I have the number 1 in mind or I have the number 2 in mind. Are you thinking of a bigger number than me?' If Abbott answers yes, then he must be thinking of 3. If he says no, then he is thinking of 1. If Abbott says, 'I do not know', then he is thinking of 2.

The Oldest Mosque

When I was in Istanbul, I was told that Hagia Sophia is the oldest mosque. This initially struck me as impossible. How can a mosque be older than Islam?

But the age of a thing can be greater than the period for which its description became applicable. The moon had orbited counterclockwise around the earth for billions of years before there were clocks. The Hagia Sophia mosque was built in 548 even though the term 'mosque' could not accurately describe any building in 548. (Islam only dates back 610.) The Hagia Sophia mosque was built as a Byzantine church and was converted to a mosque in 1453. Lists of old mosques are generally restricted to buildings that were founded as mosques. Hence their dates are after 610.

A Terrible Tautology?

No. The sentence somehow sounds tautological while actually careening towards the abyss of contradiction.

If everyone has been stolen from, then there might be as few as two thieves responsible for all the thefts. There cannot be a single thief because a thief cannot steal from himself. The impossibility of self-theft also makes it impossible for everyone to steal from everyone. Given that the conclusion is a contradiction and the premise is consistent, the inference is invalid.

However, the sentence before that, 'all notions of ownership have been demolished', puts the train off the rails before it falls into contradiction. For if there is no notion of ownership, there is no possibility of theft. No one can be stolen from. An argument must have a meaningful premise and conclusion. So the earlier sentence aborts the inference.

The diary entry is a masterpiece of logical violence. I wonder how much was premeditated by the Berlin woman.

Quantifier Mottos

Life.

Penny Wise

If you bid a penny, then your partner might bid 2 pennies. You would then get only 2 pennies. If you bid £19.99 then you will almost certainly win the auction but will only net 1 penny.

Scotsman's Solution: Much wiser is to bid £10. That will guarantee at least £10 in profit. If you bid higher then you will have to pay your bid. You may get the £20 but will have less than £10 in net profit.

Yorkshireman's Solution: Despite the virtues of the Scotsman's solution, £10 is not the best bet. For a bid of £9.99 also guarantees £10. That nets an extra penny!

Plato's Punning Riddle

The solution is: 'A half-blind eunuch threw a pumice stone at a bat perched on a reed, inflicting a glancing blow.'

Chess Puzzle Puzzle

The oldest chess puzzle is older than chess. Before chess, there was a similar game with different pieces. In Shatranj there are elephants instead of bishops and advisers instead of queens. These pieces move differently. However, the rooks, knights, and kings move the same as modern chess. One surviving Shatranj puzzle happens to exclude the pieces that differ from chess. This Shatranj puzzle became the first chess puzzle or at least a chess puzzle older than chess. It dates from AD 840. White is to mate in three moves.

Our present chess problems could survive the demise of chess!

The Spy's Riddle

It is a secret.

Preventing Prevarication

The captain asked each sailor to state how many coins he owned. He warned the crew that if the sum did not match the actual number of coins, he would throw all of the coins overboard.

Behaviourism for Eggs

By their behaviour. The first amazing difference is that a boiled egg will spin like a top. Keith Moffat of Cambridge University explains that there is a gyroscopic effect arising from friction between the egg and the tabletop. The egg raises its centre of gravity by exchanging some kinetic energy for potential energy. Moffat rhapsodises:

Place a hard-boiled egg on a table,
And spin it as fast as you're able;
It will stand on one end

With vectorial blend
Of precession and spin that's quite stable.

In contrast, a raw egg cannot elevate its centre of gravity because its more liquid interior lags behind the shell. But the raw egg has the last laugh when you interrupt the spin. The stilled raw egg begins to move on its own. There is a wobble because of residual internal turbulence. The boiled egg just sits there.

Martin Gardner's Touching Problem

Touch one bar to the other to form a T. If the bars stick, the crossbar is unmagnetised. If not, then the crossbar is the magnet.

Indiscernible Harm

Professor Jonathan Glover would flunk me. Glover advocates the Principle of Divisibility: 'In cases where harm is a matter of degree, sub-threshold actions are wrong to the extent that they cause harm, and where a hundred acts like mine are necessary to cause a detectable difference I have caused one hundredth of that detectable harm.' If we assign 0 harm to sub-threshold acts, we become vulnerable to grouping effects:

> Suppose a village contains 100 unarmed tribesmen. As they eat their lunch 100 hungry armed bandits descend on the village and each bandit at gunpoint takes one tribesman's lunch and eats it. The bandits then go off, each one having done a discriminable amount of harm to a single tribesman. Next week, the bandits are tempted to do the same thing again, but are troubled by new-found doubts about the morality of such a raid. Their doubts are put to rest by one of their number who does not believe in the principle of divisibility. They then raid the village, tie up the tribesmen, and look at their lunch. As expected,

each bowl of food contains 100 baked beans. The pleasure derived from one baked bean is below the discrimination threshold. Instead of each bandit eating a single plateful as last week, each takes one bean from each plate. They leave after eating all the beans, pleased to have done no harm, as each has done no more than sub-threshold harm to each person. Those who reject the principle of divisibility have to agree.

> – From: 'It Makes no Difference Whether or Not I Do It,' *Proceedings of the Aristotelian Society*, Supplementary Volume, 1975.

What goes for insignificant harms goes for insignificant benefits. Here is the closing sentence of George Eliot's *Middlemarch*:

> But the effect of her being on those around her was incalculably diffusive: for the growing good of the world is partly dependent on unhistoric acts; and that things are not so ill with you and me as they might have been is half owing to the number who lived faithfully a hidden life, and rest in unvisited tombs.

Book Review of *A Million Random Digits*

The commotion of the ants may lead you to wonder whether the ants will stay on indefinitely. You tidy up by assigning each ant its own colour. You then stipulate that the colliding ants exchange their colours. No longer do you see the ants collide. Instead you see a continuous, fixed direction of movement of 25 colour-coded ants. The furthest any ant could have been placed from the end of the 1-metre stick is 1 metre. Within 100 seconds each 'ant' moving uniformly at 0.01 metres per second will have fallen off the stick. Therefore, our longest wait for the stick to become ant free is 100 seconds.

In a letter from Paris, dated May 1900, Oscar Wilde writes, 'People who count their chickens before they are hatched act very wisely, because chickens run about so absurdly that it is impossible to count them accurately.'

Minimal Resemblance

This could be solved by combinatorics. But there is a shorter geometric solution:

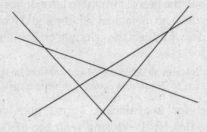

Let each line be the object and its properties be represented by intersections.

Brother-in-Law Resemblance

John William Harreld married Laura Ward on 20 October 1889. After she died, he married her sister Thurlow Ward. When John died in 1950, Thurlow became his widow. So back in 1889, John William Harreld married his widow's sister.

In 1889 no one knew that John Harreld would marry Thurlow. So no one would describe Thurlow as John Harreld's widow. (It would be like Johnny Carson introducing his bride Joanne Copeland as his future ex-wife – true but a bit of a self-fulfilling prophecy.)

The riddle is difficult because we avoid anachronistic descriptions. To explain the agent's actions we rely on the method of empathy. We step into the agent's shoes and try to understand his deeds from his time and place. It would have been difficult for John Harreld to *intentionally* marry his widow's sister.

But not impossible: A man is in love with a young woman who is estranged from her wealthy sister. How can he transfer the fortune? Since he foresees the wealthy woman will soon die and he will die soon after her, he marries the older woman.

He asks the younger sister to wait. The older sister dies. He marries the younger sister. Then he dies. The young woman winds up with the fortune.

Any children he sires with the young sister will remember their father as Uncle Dad.

The Penultimate State

New Hampshire. This is the only state that gives access to Maine, so it must be saved for *next to last*.

Acknowledgements

Three entries are reincarnations from the culture section of the *Independent on Sunday*: 'Do butterflies dream?', 22 November, 1998, p. 3; 'Towards a fairer share of dish-washing', 6 July, 1999, p. 7; and 'The unbearable lightness of logical conclusions', 24 January, 1999, p. 3. Another three originated in *Mind*: 'The Egg Came Before the Chicken', 101/403 (July 1992) 541–2; 'A cure for incontinence!' 106/424 (October 1997) 743; and 'A Plenum of Palindromes for Lewis Carroll' 109 Supplement (January 2000): 17–20.

'The Earliest Unexpected Inspection' began as a departmental memo to a junior colleague and rose through the ranks to appear in *Analysis* 53/4 (October 1993) 252. 'Fame as the Forgotten Philosopher' was published in *Philosophy* 77 (2002): 109–114. 'Philosophy for the Eye' first appeared in *The Philosopher's Magazine* 42, 3 (2008): 31–9. And 'The Chinese Music Box' is an English translation of *Das Chinesische Musikzimmer*, which appeared in *Deutsche Zeitschrift für Philosophie*: (2011) 59/1: 61–3.

Other entries are cannibals. 'Book Review of *A Million Random Digits*' partakes from 'Yablo's Paradox and Kindred Infinite Liars', *Mind*, 107/425 (January 1998): 137–55. 'The First Female Philosopher?' incorporates a section of 'Borderline Hermaphrodites', *Mind*, 119 (2010): 393–408. 'Reflective Truth Tables' consumes opening material from 'Mirror Notation: Symbol Manipulation without Inscription Manipulation'(*Journal for Philosophical Logic*) 28 (April 1999): 141–64. 'Philosophy of Scale Effects' digests some paragraphs from 'Parsimony for Empty Space' (*Australasian Journal of Philosophy* 92/2 (2014): 215–30). 'Necessary Waste' recycles some paragraphs from 'Simpler without a Simplest', *Analysis*, 71/2 (2011): 260–264. Finally, 'Premature Explanatory Satiation', 'Knowing the Area of a Parallelogram' and 'Fugu for Two' are fillets from 'Fugu for Logicians' *Philosophy and Phenomenological Research* 91/3 (2014).

I thank the editors of the above newspapers, magazines, and journals for permission to include the above articles and parts of articles.

I am also grateful to C. Felipe Romero and Maxwell Sorensen for reading and commenting on earlier drafts. Most of all, I thank John Davey for proposing the voyage, communicating mid course corrections, and guiding me to port with his editorial tugboat.